THE TOXIC SHIP

WEYERHAEUSER ENVIRONMENTAL BOOKS | *Paul S. Sutter, Editor*

Weyerhaeuser Environmental Books explore human relationships with natural environments in all their variety and complexity. They seek to cast new light on the ways that natural systems affect human communities, the ways that people affect the environments of which they are a part, and the ways that different cultural conceptions of nature profoundly shape our sense of the world around us. A complete list of the books in the series appears at the end of this book.

Simone M. Müller

THE TOXIC SHIP

The Voyage
of the *Khian Sea*
and the Global
Waste Trade

UNIVERSITY OF WASHINGTON PRESS | SEATTLE

The Toxic Ship is published with the assistance of a grant from the Weyerhaeuser Environmental Books Endowment, established by the Weyerhaeuser Company Foundation, members of the Weyerhaeuser family, and Janet and Jack Creighton.

UNIVERSITY OF WASHINGTON PRESS   *uwapress.uw.edu*

LIBRARY OF CONGRESS CATALOGING-IN-PUBLICATION DATA
Names: Müller, Simone M., author.
Title: The toxic ship : the voyage of the *Khian Sea* and the global waste trade / Simone M. Müller.
Description: Seattle : University of Washington Press, [2023] | Series: Weyerhaeuser environmental books | Includes bibliographical references and index.
Identifiers: LCCN 2023012306 | ISBN 9780295751818 (hardcover) | ISBN 9780295751832 (paperback) | ISBN 9780295751825 (ebook)
Subjects: LCSH: Khian Sea (Ship) | Refuse and refuse disposal—United States. | Refuse and refuse disposal—Location. | Waste disposal in the ocean.
Classification: LCC HD4483.M85 2023 | DDC 363.72/850973—dc23/eng/20230327
LC record available at https://lccn.loc.gov/2023012306

♾ This paper meets the requirements of ANSI/NISO Z39.48-1992 (Permanence of Paper).

To a storyteller, a dreamer, a kindred soul, and two joyful spirits

Contents

PAUL S. SUTTER

Foreword | *Globalizing Environmental Justice*

On March 22, 1987, a barge called the *Mobro 4000* left Long Island City, Queens, loaded with tons of residential and commercial waste from New York City and its suburbs, where landfill space was nearing capacity. It was headed for Morehead City, North Carolina, where a company planned to harvest methane from the decomposing trash, but environmental officials there, having heard a rumor that the *Mobro* contained hospital waste, refused to let it dock. The *Mobro* then made unsuccessful attempts to dump its cargo in other Southern states, meeting similar resistance at every stop. After two well-publicized months at sea, the "barge to nowhere" returned to its city of origin. An inspection by the US Environmental Protection Agency (EPA) found no hospital waste aboard the *Mobro*, and a New York State judge declared its cargo nonhazardous, but it would still take another month before the peripatetic waste was offloaded and fed into a Brooklyn incinerator, and its ash returned to a landfill in Islip, New York, where much of the waste had originated. As the historian Martin Melosi has noted in *Fresh Kills: A History of Consuming and Discarding in New York City*, the "journey of the 'gar-barge' inspired a media frenzy, and the *Mobro* quickly became a symbol of the emerging garbage crisis in the United States."

The extensive media coverage of the *Mobro* focused on obvious lessons from the barge's fruitless search for a suitable dumping ground. The first was precisely the crisis developing as skyrocketing volumes of municipal solid waste coincided with the tightening of environmental regulations, such as prohibitions on ocean dumping and stricter requirements for landfilling. Indeed, some have seen the *Mobro* as a catalyst for a shift to recycling and composting as strategies for reducing the waste stream. Another lesson was that exurban communities were increasingly unwilling to accept the overflowing wastes of America's cities and their suburbs. Partly this attitude was a product of NIMBYism, of communities flexing their political muscle to shunt unwanted waste elsewhere. But the *Mobro* controversy also came just a couple of years after the birth of the environmental justice movement in Warren County, North Carolina, where residents and their supporters protested the siting of a toxic waste landfill in the community, and just a few years before the pioneering environmental justice scholar Robert Bullard pointed to the systemic injustices of "dumping in Dixie," or the targeting of poor communities in the US South for waste disposal. The journey of the *Mobro 4000* thus symbolized a multifaceted reckoning with the political, social, and environmental implications of our national wastefulness and its unevenly distributed burdens.

A few other lessons of the *Mobro*'s wanderings have been less well recognized. The US waste stream was not only increasing in volume but also becoming more toxic, and a critical part of the growing reluctance of communities to accept waste and waste facilities was a fear of the potentially hazardous nature of such wastes. Moreover, as the *Mobro*'s story suggested, toxicity and uncertainty were linked: whether waste was hazardous and who got to decide were deeply contested questions. A final lesson was that the politics of dumping were increasingly global. In fact, after the *Mobro* had failed to find a dumping ground in the US South, it had turned, unsuccessfully, to places such as Mexico and Belize. While recycling may have diverted some of the nation's wastes from its landfills, the growing difficulty of dumping within the United States led to longer ocean journeys.

The journey of the *Khian Sea* exemplified the hazardous travels increasingly made by US wastes to the global South. As Simone M. Müller shows in *The Toxic Ship,* her riveting round-the-world narrative of the *Khian Sea*'s shape-shifting cruise, the US garbage crisis of the 1980s had transnational dimensions, and the *Khian Sea* and kindred ships played a key role in globalizing the environmental justice movement and spurring the creation of an international regulatory framework for defining and managing the trade in hazardous wastes. Compared to the *Mobro*, the *Khian Sea* was of decidedly greater global importance. As Müller rightly puts it, "The *Khian Sea* developed a power to shape global environmental history that went far beyond the mere facts of its voyage."

The mere facts of its voyage were and are compelling. Müller's story begins in Philadelphia, and with a foundational irony: it was a city with a large African American population, led by an African American mayor and struggling with its own version of the garbage crisis, that launched the vessel that helped to globalize environmental injustice. Almost by definition, cities like Philadelphia lacked sufficient space to dispose of their wastes. When Congress banned ocean dumping as of 1980, and surrounding communities and states balked at taking Philadelphia's waste, the city relied increasingly on incineration. While Philadelphia's incinerators placed their own unjust pollution burdens on some city residents, they reduced the city's formidable waste stream to a concentrated residue. But the resulting ash still had to go somewhere. Predictably, city leaders initially sought landfill space in the US South, but when that effort failed, they looked overseas. A poor and financially troubled city, ravaged by the urban crisis, thus foisted its wastes on marginalized communities in other nations. As the *Khian Sea* left Philadelphia in September 1986, loaded with fifteen thousand tons of incinerator ash, the environmental injustices that had come to mark Philadelphia spilled over into the larger world.

Philadelphia's garbage imperialism initially targeted the nations of the Greater Caribbean. As Müller demonstrates, what was waste to Philadelphians was imaginatively transformed into a resource in order to persuade developing nations to accept it. As the *Khian Sea* approached the Bahamas, its first stop, the incinerator ash became "fill," potentially useful to a nation that was modernizing its infrastructure and extending its land area. But the Bahamas would not let the *Khian Sea* dump its ash there without a permit, and so the ship and its owners turned successively to Costa Rica, Honduras, Panama, and the Dominican Republic. None of these options worked out either, often because of local residents' objections. In December 1987, the *Khian Sea* arrived at the Haitian city of Gonaïves, and the Haitian government—this time working with the claim that Philadelphia's ash would be useful as "top soil fertilizer"—accepted it. But after a portion of the ash had been unloaded, fears of contamination, local protest, and political instability led the government to reverse course. They asked that the *Khian Sea* reload the ash it had already offloaded, but the ship left Haiti without doing so, though still carrying a significant portion of its cargo. And as it left the Western Hemisphere's poorest nation, Philadelphia's incinerator ash underwent yet another transformation: it became toxic waste.

As the *Khian Sea* sailed on—back to Philadelphia, on to West Africa, through the Suez Canal, and eventually to Asia—it came to symbolize the fraught international trade in hazardous materials in the same way that the *Mobro* had symbolized the garbage crisis in the United States. *The Toxic Ship* exposes the fundamental injustices in a global trade in which hazardous materials moved toward poorer and less powerful nations. But whether the ash constituted toxic waste was an unresolved question. Müller walks us through the epistemological complexities of this question with clarity and assurance, demonstrating the contested nature of the science for determining toxicity, the distrust that receiving nations came to have for the US science that insisted such wastes were safe, the perceived harms of exposure to such wastes, and the differential capacities of various nations to assess and regulate toxicity. Müller also explores the fraught question of sovereignty in relation to global efforts to regulate or ban the trade in hazardous wastes. Would such regulations protect less powerful nations with limited scientific and regulatory capacities, or would they inhibit the ability of sovereign nations to enter into trade agreements of their own accord?

The journey of the *Khian Sea* not only embodied the globalization of the hazardous waste trade; it also precipitated a global environmental justice movement. This movement initially manifested itself as NIMBYism on a transnational scale, with nascent resistance movements opposing the dumping of such wastes within their territories. But resistance soon came to center on the principle of global environmental justice. International environmental NGOs such as Greenpeace got involved, hunting the renegade *Khian Sea* and similar ships, allying with developing nations, and pushing for the global regulation of such trade. Indeed, in its search for the *Khian Sea*, Greenpeace USA transformed a national toxics campaign into its Global Toxics Trade Campaign. More importantly, growing alliances among the nations of the global South drove international diplomacy on the regulation of hazardous waste trading. As Müller shows, African nations organized under the auspices of the United Nations Environmental Programme and the Organisation of African Unity to present a united front against "colonialist garbage." In doing so, they added an explicitly anticolonial logic to environmental justice efforts that had been focused on race and class. Latin American and Caribbean nations soon followed suit, and the result was a series of diplomatic agreements—including the Basel Convention of 1989 and the Bamako Convention of 1991—that created the first international frameworks to regulate the transport of hazardous wastes. As *The Toxic Ship* demonstrates so vividly, the fraught travels of the *Khian Sea* produced a compelling international movement that brought justice concerns into maturing conversations about protecting the global environment.

The *Khian Sea*—rechristened the *Pelicano*—ended its epic journey in Singapore in November 1988. When it docked, its holds were mysteriously empty. I will not reveal what became of the incinerator ash that the *Khian Sea* had carried for most of her long oceanic exile; you will have to read this book to find out. The story of the ash that was offloaded at Gonaïves had a more satisfying resolution. In 2000, it was reloaded aboard another cargo ship and returned to the United

States, where it was eventually laid to rest in a Pennsylvania landfill, back where it belonged. As with the *Mobro*, at least some of the *Khian Sea*'s contents had come full circle. Before these cremated remains of Philadelphia's trash received their last rites, the EPA tested the ash and determined that it was nontoxic. But we ought not to read that determination as the definitive word on the threat posed by Philadelphia's incinerator ash. As Simone M. Müller brilliantly shows, the toxicity of the *Khian Sea*'s cargo was a moving target, protean to the end.

Acknowledgments

Books like *The Toxic Ship* are accumulations of time, of material, and of resources. They represent compilations of thoughts, of arguments, and of scholarship. They never exist solely in and by themselves but embody ongoing conversations frozen at a particular point when a combination of scholarly achievement, resource-based necessities, and contractual deadlines compel the author to conclude the exercise of filling pages with words. They are also an embodiment of love, of kindness, and of personal debt. As I try to untangle these myriad relationships, some may remain buried in the footnotes or obscured in my memory. I hope for the forgiveness of those not specifically mentioned here.

The Toxic Ship and its story are part of the Emmy-Noether research group Hazardous Travels, Ghost Acres and the Global Waste Economy, funded by the German Research Foundation (DFG) and hosted by the Rachel Carson Center for Environment and Society (RCC) at the Ludwig-Maximilians-Universität Munich (LMU). Both institutions have created an institutional and financial framework that nourished not only my own scholarly growth and research but also this book. Team #HazTrav—that is Ayushi Dhawan, Jonas Stuck, and Maximilian Feichtner—each working on their own Hazardous Travels dissertation projects on India, Germany, and Ecuador, alongside our excellent research assistants Wangling Hu and Christina Lennartz—have provided true team spirit and an intellectual safe space in which we could grow and think together. When Regina Bichler joined #HazTrav as an associate, with her Japanese perspective on zero-waste cities, she perfectly complemented our global perspective on environmental issues.

Entire songbooks have already been composed by other alumni in praise of the hospitality and support that the Rachel Carson Center offers. I can only join in with my tune and point out how exceptionally privileged I felt to work for years at a place where almost all of my professional role models and academic sources of inspiration would at some point occupy one of the fellows' offices just down the hall from mine. What I would otherwise have had to learn from their books I could discuss with them in person. Here I offer a big thank-you to Anne Rademacher, Martin Melosi, Rob Gioielli, Joana Gaspar de Freitas, James Beattie, Libby Robin, Nicole Graham, Ruth Morgan, Christian Lahnstein, Sophia Kalanzakos, Jim Webb, David Biggs, Franziska Torma, Zhen (Jane) Wang, and Paul Sutter. Particular thanks go out to Maria Valeria Beros, Vipul Singh, and Emily Brownell for serving as official partners to Hazardous Travels and helping make this research project a truly global endeavor. Finally, the Rachel Carson Center would not have been such a productive and enriching work space without the support of its staff, foremost Arielle Helmick, Lena Engel, Kim Coulter, Katie Ritson, Carmen Dines, Sophia Hörl, and Ruhi Deol. A number of brilliant RCC interns, among them Anja Rieser, Jonathan Palmblad, and Ivan Vilovic, have supported my research, helping me think through the Basel Convention and its global reach. And as always, I thank the RCC's directors, Christof Mauch and Helmuth Trischler, who have unconditionally supported my research from the very beginning, listened patiently to its numerous iterations, and generously provided me with every possible kind of support.

In our studies of discards and the global waste economy, team #HazTrav and I have fully embraced the interdisciplinary and transdisciplinary environmental humanities perspective. Waste became not only an object, but our subject of study, and the materiality of toxicants cowrote its own stories. My understanding of the premises of global environmental justice has been strongly colored by collaboration with Antonia Alampi and Caroline Ektander—intellectuals, artists and curators. As this group grew into the Toxic Commons network, it brought the wonderful Angeliki Balayannis into my world (thank you, Thom Davies, for the introduction), and I feel exceedingly thankful that LMU's Center for Advanced Studies (CAS) has allowed the two of us to think together in the pages of joint writing projects. For years the CAS has been a scholarly retreat and a source of strength. I hope Annette Meyer, Lena Bouman, Julia Schreiner, and Susanne Schaffrath hear on a daily basis how valuable their support is, particularly to female scholars entering the world of academia. Last but not least, I want to mention the Center for Interdisciplinary Research at the University of Bielefeld (ZiF), where I found another interdisciplinary home as a fellow and speaker of the Young ZiF. Being allowed to think without the constraints of disciplinary borders or the pressures of yet another grant proposal truly illustrates the meaning of academic freedom. A big thank you to my fellow ZiF fellows, ZiF managing director Britta Padberg, and Young ZiF coordinator Marc Schalenberg.

Philadelphia is fundamental to the story of the *Khian Sea*. A fellowship at the Science History Institute (formerly the Chemical Heritage Foundation) and the University of Pennsylvania allowed me to get to know the city and to trace contacts who still remember the *Khian Sea*. Living in South Philadelphia, cycling past Dow Headquarters on my way to and from the office, and visiting Longwood Gardens, the John Heinz National Wildlife Refuge, and Valley Forge National Historical Park on the weekends brought the *Khian Sea*'s history alive to me in a way that a study solely of my sources could have never done. Being present there, together with my family, allowed me to experience the tensions between city and county, between white privilege and those struggling, and between the chemical industry, deindustrialization, and environmental amenities. The streets of Philadelphia taught me how a story of the international waste trade is rarely black and white but highly complex, and never just "out there" on some anonymous global scale, but intricately linked to a particular place, like Philadelphia. Thank you to Carin Berkowitz and Ashley Augustyniak for guiding me through research collections and city geographies, and to Lucas Mueller for questioning my distinction between planet and globe. Bethany Wiggin, Lisa Ruth Rand, and Julia Gunn were valuable contacts to help me see beyond Center City, and John Pettit of Temple University's Special Collections boosted my confidence in the story, helping me access rich collections and sharing my enthusiasm. The work of Diane Sicotte has been my personal guidebook to the history of environmental justice in Philadelphia. From Philadelphia my network of people with personal connections to the *Khian Sea* grew, and I am very thankful that they shared their stories, their memories, and also their materials with me. Without Jim Vallette, in particular, I would have abandoned the *Khian Sea*'s story as too opaque.

Colleagues and friends from around the world have helped by listening to numerous, and what may have felt to them endless, iterations of the ship's voyage. Yet they have generously given shelter to first arguments and concepts and read drafts that eventually became *The Toxic Ship*. May-Brith Ohman Nielsen provided key guidance and many a stay (virtually and in person) in Norway that helped me along at crucial points. Tora Rundhovde and Victoria Østerberg translated Norwegian accounts for me so that I could get the *Bark*'s story straight, and Claudio de Majo opened the world of Italian environmentalism to me in the context of the *Karin B*. The Deadly Dreams Network, with Judith Rainhorn and Bettina Wahrig, among others, provided early feedback, and Iris Borowy's constructive criticism led me to see beyond the victims/perpetrators binary. Heidi Tworek and Richard John have supported this book endeavor with their constant friendship and their keen interest in my new environmental topic.

Books need homes—ideally homes where they are cared for, tended to, and cherished as they make their way from manuscript to publication and then onward into the homes of readers. They need homes where a team of people takes an interest in bringing out the best in an accumulation of texts and visuals and in sharing their enthusiasm about the story with a larger readership. *The Toxic Ship* could not have found a better home than the Weyerhaeuser series at the University of Washington Press. Paul Sutter, Andrew Berzanskis, Mike Baccam, and Caroline Hall have provided unmatched support in the production process, as have Joeth Zucco and Molly Wolbright. Ben Pease strengthened this book's visual representation as he transformed my scribbles into perfect maps. Erika Bűky, with her sharp eye for detail and a strong sense for language and logic, has treated this text with great care and respect. For once I lack words to describe just how much I enjoyed working together with the team from Washington University Press, how much I learned from them, and how grateful I am for the way they cared about my ship's story. Thanks also to Greenpeace Archives, the Rubenstein Archive at the Duke University Libraries, and the Associated Press Archives for helping me with digitizing the images in this book.

My initial interest in waste as an object of historical inquiry has no academic origin story. It grew from a conversation during a summer walk around Krumme Lanke, a lake on the outskirts of Berlin, with my close friend Eva Hartmann, about her work as an environmental officer at a large-scale engineering company. Her input, as well as that of Marion Bauer, Katrin Wenzel, Christina Kunkel, and my brothers, Christopher and Thomas Müller, have grounded this work in a world beyond the ivory tower. Their curiosity and loving support kept me attached even when I felt I was disengaging from the topic of global waste. Similarly, the fact that I could finish this book, with both my parents dying and in the midst of a pandemic that obstructed archival access and turned academic parenting into an Olympic discipline, is due to the loving support, kindness, and joy that I received from my family—Christopher, Jonna, and Bruno. Their support for my endeavors means more to me than I can express on this page.

THE TOXIC SHIP

US Waste in an Unequal World

This vessel was subject to daily harassment in the form of the news media or overflying helicopters about the uncertainty of entering the Port of Philadelphia, and possible danger to the vessel and to the crew if they did enter the Port of Philadelphia. They saw on television the complete torching of Paolino's which they realized that they were going to come back to. . . . They were completely isolated and embargoed in their present position. They were not able to discharge the cargo, nor were they able to leave. And their harassment was daily and very severe.

WILLIAM P. REILLY | vice president of Coastal Carriers, on the state of the *Khian Sea* and its crew, March 1988

Often the rotor blades were audible before the helicopter became visible. The weather had been mediocre since the ship had anchored at Big Stone Beach. Two small inlets, defining the lower end of Delaware Bay, sheltered it from the waves and winds of the Atlantic. Looking out to sea—one of their pastimes since they had been grounded—the crew could observe waves with crests just about to break and a sea garnished with foam.[1] When they heard the sound of swirling air cut by metallic blades, it usually meant that members of the US Coast Guard were approaching by boat. At the beginning of the ship's nearly three-month stay, the coast guard had come frequently to check on what they called inoperable equipment and outdated charts, two almost laughable details given the dilapidated freighter's signs of wear and rust. The ship's papers were not in order either. Its stay at sea had outlasted its insurance coverage and other certificates. Technically it was a renegade ship, since Liberia was withholding its flag until the ship's papers were renewed.[2]

Sometimes, the coast guard had been accompanied by guys in white hazmat suits, who had crawled all over the ship's cargo with their gloves, their test tubes,

1

and their clipboards. Captain Arturo Fuentes Garcia was not sure what exactly these people were doing, but he knew it had to do with his cargo and would determine whether the ship could proceed up the Delaware. He also knew that their activities were of great interest to the journalists circling above in the helicopter, like vultures waiting for the lions to finish their meal.[3]

When Fuentes had taken over as captain of the freighter *Khian Sea*, he had expected nothing out of the ordinary. It became the voyage of a lifetime. Fuentes, a native of Honduras, learned about the job in November 1987, when the *Khian Sea* had already been roaming the greater Caribbean for over a year. The ship had left Philadelphia in September 1986, carrying about fifteen thousand tons of incinerator ash destined for the Bahamas. The ship was owned by Lily Navigation, Inc., and chartered by the Amalgamated Shipping Corporation, both registered in the Bahamas. The latter had a contract with the Philadelphia waste-hauling company Paolino & Sons. Paolino, in turn, had a multimillion-dollar contract with the city of Philadelphia for the disposal of up to two hundred thousand tons of incinerator ash for fiscal year 1986–87. To add to this complex arrangement of international stakeholders, the ship was sailing under the Liberian flag (at least until its papers expired). For Fuentes, these different involvements mattered little. His main contact partners were two Americans, John Patrick Dowd and William P. Reilly, president and vice president of the Annapolis-based company Coastal Carriers, which was the US representative of Amalgamated.[4]

Mostly it was Reilly who told Fuentes where to take the ship. After the original plan to unload it in the Bahamas had fallen through, Fuentes was directed to sail to the port of Gonaïves in politically fractured Haiti, where Coastal Carriers had secured a landing for the ship's cargo as topsoil fertilizer. Years later, when he testified to an attorney with the US Department of Justice's Environmental Crimes Section about what happened next, Fuentes would say the ship had "bad mojo."[5] In the middle of unloading, Haitian soldiers had ordered them at gunpoint to stop. Under cover of darkness, Fuentes set sail to take the *Khian Sea* back to Philadelphia, abandoning part of its cargo at Sedren Wharf in Gonaïves, but US officials ordered them to anchor in lower Delaware Bay and confined the crew to the ship.[6]

With morale low and nerves strained, Captain Fuentes then committed his first major crime by disobeying direct orders from the US Coast Guard and taking the *Khian Sea* back out to sea. In news interviews and later court testimony, Reilly and Dowd from Coastal Carriers made it sound as if they had been blindsided by Fuentes's move, but that was questionable. Fuentes next took the ship across the Atlantic to West Africa, the Mediterranean, and Eastern Europe, through the Suez Canal, and across the Indian Ocean to Southeast Asia, always on the lookout for a new site to unload the cargo. Meanwhile, an international network of environmentalists, US officials, and the media hunted the renegade ship. They managed to see through its attempts at disguise, such as changing the ship's name from the *Khian Sea* to the *Felicia*, the *Pelicano*, and finally the *San Antonio*. It was a game of cat and mouse that, most of the time, Fuentes lost.[7]

Fuentes's problem was the cargo and its purpose: mounds of black incinerator ash, interspersed with bits of half-burnt paper and pieces of metal. It represented the remnants of Philadelphia's waste, material that US traders had repeatedly tried to sell as fill material for land reclamation, fertilizer, or building material. The issue was not the cargo's texture or its musty smell, but minute particles of heavy metals and dioxins in material intended for use in sensitive ecosystems and relatively unprotected production contexts in countries of the global South.[8] No matter what those people in the white hazmat suits had found out from testing the ash, the label *déchet toxique*—the Haitian term for toxic waste—had stuck to the ship throughout its journey of more than two years. Always sailing on the verge of illegality, Fuentes eventually broke more laws, marine and otherwise, by dumping the cargo in the Atlantic and Indian Oceans.[9]

By following the journeys of the *Khian Sea* and other waste-carrying ships from the United States, this book scrutinizes the globalization of hazardous waste, environmental justice, and environmental governance in the latter half of the twentieth century.[10] Starting in Philadelphia, the story takes in Panama, the Bahamas, Haiti, Honduras, Sierra Leone, Guinea, Nigeria, Italy, Norway, Yugoslavia, Switzerland, the Philippines, and Singapore. *The Toxic Ship* opens by reviewing the emergence of environmentalism in the industrial world in the 1960s, a trend that was followed almost immediately by the creation of the first waste-trading schemes with countries of the global South. The story centers on the 1980s, the height of this unequal trade, before considering instruments of global environmental governance implemented in the 1990s, such as the UN's Basel Convention (passed in 1989 and implemented in 1992), and the Organisation of African Unity's Bamako Convention (passed in 1991 and implemented in 1998). *The Toxic Ship* ends in the early 2000s, when the partial cargo of incinerator ash that the *Khian Sea* had abandoned in Haiti was returned to the United States.

The international trade in hazardous substances is a broad term for a trading network that moves items ranging from hazardous waste to banned pesticides and nonmarketed consumer products. It has received considerable attention from environmental, health, and human rights activists, investigative journalists, administrators, policymakers, and scholars.[11] Most activist literature examines the trade through a normative lens and the framework of global environmental justice and environmental racism.[12] From this viewpoint, the *Khian Sea* is the flagship of the evils of the global waste economy. It and other ships like it represent all that is ethically despicable, and yet the *Khian Sea*'s activities were mostly legal, part of a multimillion-ton and multimillion-dollar trade in hazardous waste between countries of the global North and those of the global South, marked by substantial differences in political stability, economic opportunities, and environmental and health and safety regulations.

Many academic studies of the global waste economy are undertaken from the macro level of policy and legal analysis, with a focus on the Basel Convention on the Control of Transboundary Movements of Hazardous Wastes and Their Disposal and its deficiencies.[13] Scholars examine the failures of the Basel Convention to provide an international governance system for a *planetary* waste problem. Allowing for transnational "recycling" operations, often conducted without necessary equipment and under weaker health and safety regulations in the importing countries of the global South, the Basel Convention created a massive governance loophole that allowed the continuation of the trade. This loophole, in turn, has opened up discussions on the moral limits of markets.[14] Other scholars have used the history of the global waste economy to examine the unequal distribution of environmental burdens based on criteria such as race, class, gender, and disability.[15]

The Toxic Ship goes beyond the environmental justice framework and the narrow focus on the Basel Convention to chronicle the growth of a global trading system that brought the forces of economic growth and environmental protection into an entanglement that often represented a stark dilemma.[16] What led a city like Philadelphia, with a large African American population, to export hazardous waste to Panama, the Bahamas, or Haiti, and what induced local agents to import it (legally) for use in sensitive ecosystems? How did the actors involved in the global waste economy endure the conflicting pressures born from the fact that hazardous waste would not go away, but had to be disposed of somewhere? *The Toxic Ship* scrutinizes the tensions inherent to a world where, since at least the mid-twentieth century, we have been facing the issue of growing amounts of hazardous waste combined with finite planetary disposal spaces and acute, and increasing, social and economic inequality.[17] The book examines the structures and dynamics underpinning a global system that appeared to be based simultaneously on toxic colonialism and voluntary exchange, yet which was ultimately premised on different valuations of human life.[18]

Waste and Its Challenges for Data and Methodology

Waste is one of the most complex and contested objects of historical inquiry. It is not only matter "out of place," as proposed by the anthropologist Mary Douglas, but also "a concept out of order," as emphasized by the historian Zsuzsa Gille. Within social systems, waste represents the inappropriate or the rejected. It is what people, institutions, or businesses want to discard. Individuals, societies, and industries have different criteria for determining what items constitute waste and when, where, and how they dispose of them. As such, concepts of waste reveal multiple dichotomies, those "between past and present, public and private, value and its opposite," as Gille writes, but also between high and low income levels, between more and less rigorous environmental protection, and between countries in the global North and the global South. Waste has an agenda, and waste exerts power. Processes of waste production, management, and recultura- tion (in the sense of recycling or upcycling) almost always align with patterns of racial and social stratification. Waste is contentious and controversial. It always needs a place to be put.[19]

Waste emerged as a larger environmental problem in the industrial coun- tries in the twentieth century. Until the nineteenth century, the items people discarded had been mostly organic: ashes, food waste, animal carcasses, and excrement. Other forms of solid waste, such as cracked ceramics, glass shards, tattered clothes, broken furniture, and pieces of metal, were limited in quantity, and most of these objects were repaired or reused.[20] With industrialization and the dawn of mass consumption in the 1920s, merchandising made consumer goods available wherever a vastly expanding railroad network could carry them. Packaged goods rapidly replaced the items available in bulk at the local grocery store. The electrification of the home, and with it the advent of new appliances— the refrigerator, the TV, the electric light bulb, and the microwave—radically altered consumption practices and waste generation. By the late 1960s, people in the industrialized countries produced about one kilogram of garbage each day, including paper products, packaging, bottles, cans, food scraps, and increasing amounts of plastics. Consumers tossed these remnants of daily consumption into trash cans. Diesel-powered trucks would collect and compress the waste and deliver it to sanitary landfills or waste incinerators. Recycling of aluminum, glass, and paper waste was systematized but remained a contested practice in societies that had learned to consume rather than reuse.[21] The United States became a global leader in waste production. The country's generation of municipal solid waste increased from 88.1 million tons in 1960 to 267.8 million tons in 2017.[22]

A key moment for the narrative of this book came in the 1970s and 1980s, when industrial countries introduced the highly contested category of hazardous waste. Such waste existed long before it was defined as such, going back to mining, smelting, dyeing, and tanning during the early modern era.[23] But the chemical industrial revolution and the introduction of synthetic chemicals after World War II saw the explosion of wastes that posed what the US Environmental Protection Agency (EPA) would later characterize as a "substantial threat to both human health and the environment."[24] Petroleum-based chemical engineering allowed the manufacture of a host of new materials with applications ranging from dyes and plasticizers to medicinal chemicals, pesticides, and paints. Each of these products constituted a new source of hazardous waste.[25] And even the disposal of regular waste through incineration created the new, possibly toxic waste product of incinerator ash.

The toxicity of these substances often resulted from the very characteristics for which industry had developed them. Halogenated hydrocarbons, such as the pesticide DDT, can disrupt naturally occurring chemical reactions. Other synthetic hydrocarbons containing chlorine and bromine were favored by the chemical industry because of their persistence. Likewise, plastics were engineered to be durable, strong, lightweight, water-resistant, and relatively inexpensive to manufacture. Their downside was that these substances could remain in the environment for decades. Some of the most common synthetic chemicals, such as dioxins and furans, which feature prominently in *The Toxic Ship*, bioaccumulate and biomagnify, building up in the tissues of individual organisms and then becoming progressively concentrated in the food web as these organisms are consumed by others. They are carcinogenic and function as endocrine disruptors, altering the biological processes of living creatures, and their offspring, in fundamental, harmful ways.[26]

Hazardous waste has come to be defined by its chemical characteristics—ignitable, corrosive, reactive, or toxic—and by its chemical classification. In the US, the category of hazardous waste includes a host of heavy metals, asbestos, acids and bases, and synthetic chemicals. Nuclear waste, originating from medical facilities, research labs, and primarily from nuclear power plants and weapons reprocessing operations, constitutes a waste category legislatively, culturally, and historically distinct from hazardous waste. In the United States, the Atomic Energy Act, which governs the disposal of radioactive material, was passed in 1946. Internationally, a number of agencies, such as the International Atomic Energy Agency, are concerned exclusively with radioactive material. It is not discussed in this book.[27]

To a global environmental historian, studying hazardous waste requires more than understanding chemical data from a particular country and from a particular point in time: it also requires familiarity with an accumulating and yet constantly shifting and contested body of knowledge on toxicology, harm, causalities, and interdependencies. Throughout the 1980s, the US EPA was criticized for its politics as well as its science by both national and international actors. Meanwhile, other countries on the route of the *Khian Sea* lacked the technology, the laboratories, the institutions, or the national standards to evaluate its cargo.[28] This book shows that assessments of toxicity, pollution, and modes of exposure are never static. Dose, timing, velocity, and frequency of exposure matter as much as geographic location, nationality, and the ethnic markers and societal positions of those exposed.[29]

Because a global consensus on the definition of hazardous waste was lacking for a long time, any data on waste or the waste trade must be read with great caution. Prior to the Basel Convention, data on the amount of hazardous waste produced and traded was absent or inadequate. In many countries, particularly those of the global South, the category of hazardous waste did not even exist. In industrial countries, such as the United States, different institutions battled over how to classify and regulate hazardous waste.[30] In the early 1980s, estimates of the quantity of hazardous waste by the EPA and the Congressional General Accounting Office (GAO) differed by 150 million tons. State and federal lists of hazardous materials varied, with only about a 50 percent overlap between them.[31] The first statistics from the early 1990s that enabled international comparisons indicated that the United States was responsible for 85 percent of global hazardous waste and the European Economic Community (EEC) for only 5–7 percent. Yet these comparisons were misleading because US definitions of hazardous waste included, for instance, diluted dishwater, while no other nation's did. Moreover, most of these statistics did not integrate data from former Communist countries, where hazardous waste posed a significant problem.[32] When, in the late 1980s, different actors attempted to measure the international waste trade based on these incomplete and conflicting sets of data, their ability to do so was greatly limited. Activists, journalists, and politicians felt they had run into a problem of the utmost significance without being able to estimate its magnitude.[33]

A Ship's Tale in Seven Chapters

Neither the size of the *Khian Sea*'s cargo—fifteen thousand tons is very little—nor its chemical characteristics—even US protagonists were divided over whether the incinerator ash was hazardous waste—were typical of the everyday business of the unequal trade in wastes. At the time, brokers were negotiating deals involving several hundred thousand tons of material that at least one country in the transaction defined as hazardous waste. Perhaps the *Kirsten*, the *Danix*, and the *Line* might have given a better representation of the implications of the hazardous waste trade. In 1987 those ships transported industrial chemical waste from Milan to Koko, Nigeria, where it was deposited in a field behind a farm. When the containers started leaking, the material contaminated groundwater, making some of the villagers severely ill.[34] The *Khian Sea* also had other counterparts, such as the *Bark*, the *Mobro 4000*, and the *Zanoobia*.

Yet it was the *Khian Sea*—with its journey evocative of the mythical Flying Dutchman, disappearing and reappearing seemingly at will—that became a household name and shaped global environmental history. In its narrative of pursuit and evasion, of externalization and environmental injustice, the United States and Haiti—one of the world's most powerful countries and the world's poorest nation—were battling over waste and righteousness. This plotline made it easy to talk about villains and victims and about right and wrong while ignoring the fact that Philadelphia, too, was struggling. The continuous testing of the *Khian Sea*'s cargo triggered a debate on the relevance and accuracy of scientific evidence that enabled activists to question whether US institutions could be trusted in the first place. From the local to the international level, the *Khian Sea* forced a reconsideration of a trading system with massive loopholes. The story highlighted ideas of morality and development and allowed environmental activists and journalists to play one against the other. Finally, in the words of the journalist Mark Jaffe, covering the story for the *Philadelphia Inquirer*, the ship was "simply a good story" that allowed journalists and environmental activists to influence public opinion in unprecedented ways.[35]

Much of the *Khian Sea*'s story is anecdotal. With two waste-export schemes coming out of Philadelphia and with two ships, the *Khian Sea* and the *Bark*, simultaneously attempting to remain under cover, environmentalists and journalists have at times mistaken one ship for the other. *The Toxic Ship* draws extensively on previously unexamined material, such as materials from and about local protagonists, ranging from the Delaware Toxics Coalition in Philadelphia to Radio Haiti-Inter and Le Collectif Haïtien pour la Protection de l'Environnement et un Développement Alternatif (COHPEDA), based in Port-au-Prince.

Another obstacle to investigating the international trade in hazardous waste is that dealers, always potentially operating on the verge of illegality, avoid opening their archives—if they exist at all. For example, Reilly of Coastal Carriers claimed during legal hearings in the 1990s that most records relating to the *Khian Sea* were discarded when Coastal Carriers moved to a smaller office after filing for bankruptcy in 1989.[36] Much primary-source material on traders comes from other archival compilations, such as contracts, correspondence, and meeting minutes that were disclosed during court proceedings. Many a link would have remained obscure had it not been for material and accounts from witnesses and protagonists in the story.

Chapter 1 takes the reader to Philadelphia, the point of origin of the waste. It explores the pressures and entanglements that induced the city government, led by the city's first African American mayor, to allow waste traders to export Philadelphia incinerator ash abroad. The chapter shows how modern US environmentalism imposed growing pressure on already overextended postindustrial cities and their waste-management systems. The dilemma thus created was heightened by increasing pressure from local citizens' environmental activist groups, rising disposal costs, and a lack of land suitable for waste disposal.

Chapters 2 and 3 center on the voyage of the *Khian Sea* to various destinations in the greater Caribbean, ending with the dumping of some of the ship's cargo in Gonaïves, Haiti, in January 1988. Chapter 2 follows the geographical expansion of Philadelphia waste disposal, from New Jersey to the greater Caribbean, teasing out the historical path dependencies for this shift and its link to postwar policies of development. Chapter 3 traces the emergence of opposition in Caribbean nations to the waste imports in 1987 and 1988. With a particular focus on Panama and Haiti, it shows how protests became linked with growing anti-American sentiments along with internal struggles toward democracy.

Chapter 4 discusses the metamorphosis of Philadelphia's incinerator ash from "harmless" municipal solid waste to *déchet toxique*. It illustrates how US institutions were key actors in producing a situation in which the "objective" assessment of the harmfulness of Philadelphia incinerator ash, by the EPA or any other scientific entity, became close to impossible. Eventually, Philadelphia's incinerator ash became not only the most tested but also the most *contested* ash on the planet.[37]

Chapters 5 and 6 focus on export policies, governance structures, and international activism. Focusing on the US government and its hazardous-waste export policy, chapter 5 explores questions of transnational business conduct, extraterritorial liability, and the extents and limits of national sovereignty. The chapter examines the dilemma that arises when environmental legislation enacted by individual nations comes into conflict with the dynamics of a global economy. Chapter 6 traces the growth of the powerful global campaign that managed to push through the Basel Convention in 1989. The collaboration between Greenpeace and representatives of the African nations helped to conclude a process that had been stalling for a decade: the creation of an internationally binding regulatory system for the trade in hazardous waste.

Chapter 7 focuses on the aftermath of the Basel Convention and return of the ash dumped by the *Khian Sea* in Haiti to a disposal site close to Philadelphia in 2002. The enormous political potential of the *Khian Sea*'s odyssey appears to have vanished completely in the 1990s and early 2000s, as politicians, environmentalists and the public battled over liability, repatriation, cleanup, and the terms of the Basel Convention. While the convention is often seen as a watershed in the history of the global waste economy, it loses much of its significance once its long-term effects, or the lack thereof, are taken into account.

While *The Toxic Ship* begins and ends in Philadelphia, it is not about Philadelphia per se.[38] Philadelphia was no waste city upon a hill but a quintessential example of a postindustrial urban center struggling with diverse crises.[39] Similarly, Captain Arturo Fuentes Garcia of the *Khian Sea* and J. Patrick Dowd and William P. Reilly of Coastal Carriers are not singled out as archvillains: rather they represent opportunity seekers acting (mostly) legally within the flexible boundaries of a neoliberal governance system that enabled them to split and then pass on responsibility to somewhere and someone else, without considering the potential damage to people's health and the environment. In the end, *The Toxic Ship* is also a story for today. The story of the *Khian Sea* and the many ships like it remind us that we still need to come to terms with the same problems—that is, massively rising waste levels on a planet with finite disposal options—while being mindful of vast and increasing social and racial inequalities.[40] Waste is spatial. It will never simply go away.

ONE

"A Classic Situation" | *Philadelphia and the Making of an Urban Waste Crisis*

It stinks. . . . It is making the neighborhood smell and the neighborhood looks horrible.

JO ANN MAURER | quoted in Philip Lentz, "Strike, Heat Leave
Philadelphia in a Stink," *Chicago Tribune*, July 9, 1986

It was in the streets of Philadelphia in the summer of 1986 that journalists first picked up the scent of a story that would lead them and others to the *Khian Sea*. An all-pervasive smell of putrefying garbage, intensified by the July heat, marked the presence of rotten waste structures underneath an economically struggling and socially tense city.[1] That July, Philadelphia's streets were contested territory. The city's sanitation workers were striking for more pay and better working conditions. They stopped collecting trash, clearing the city's incinerators of accumulated ash, and hauling the refuse to landfills in the neighboring counties. Three weeks into the strike, almost sixteen thousand tons of municipal solid waste had accumulated at twenty hurriedly opened emergency dumps, or often simply in front of vacant buildings, where people would drive up and throw their trash out of their cars.[2]

To avoid the sight and smell of the mounting trash, people kept windows and doors tightly shut and blinds down.[3] Mayor Wilson Goode urged Philadelphians to keep their trash at home. Residents were out on the street with brooms and shovels, clearing the waste mounds, while others stood watch to discourage illegal dumpers. Violence was in the air. Goode threatened to bring in private waste haulers as strikebreakers, and Philadelphians revolted at the unequal distribution of waste throughout the city. They all agreed the waste needed to go, without a thought on *where*.[4]

11

A ten-year-old girl covers her mouth and nose while walking through a temporary neighborhood dump site in Philadelphia on July 15, 1986, during the third week of the strike by municipal garbage workers. © Picture Alliance/Associated Press/ Charles Krupa.

To ship Philadelphia waste out of town, and eventually down South, was neither a spontaneous decision nor unprecedented. It resulted from pressures that had shaped the city's waste-handling practices for centuries. Initially, Philadelphia's city council claimed the cause of the waste problem was overly strong workers' unions. Before long, however, the roles of mass consumption, dramatically rising waste levels, new environmental laws, and limited disposal facilities could not be denied.[5] Additionally, more and more citizens had become proponents of environmental protection and were keeping close watch on the city's environmental activities. By the time of the strike, Philadelphia's problem with waste had mushroomed out of proportion. Yet, in comparison with other US cities, it was a "classic situation." A major city had evolved over the centuries "without ever resolving the question of waste disposal."[6]

Philadelphia's Waste-Handling Practices

Philadelphia is one of the oldest European settlements on the North American continent, with even older Indigenous history.[7] Established in 1682 by William Penn at the meeting of the Schuylkill and Delaware Rivers, Philadelphia soon became the fastest-growing and largest city in colonial America. By 1760, its population approached 17,000 people—comprising both voluntary and involuntary arrivals. Between 1840 and 1860, Philadelphia's population mushroomed to 565,529, then grew to one million in 1890 and two million in 1950.[8] Key to Philadelphia's rise was its location as a major Atlantic port and a gateway to Pennsylvania's farmland, the Appalachian Mountains, and the Ohio River Valley. These avenues allowed people to transport resources into the city and to distribute products nationally and internationally from it. Long before Chicago, Philadelphia existed as a metropolis shaped by a hinterland of abundance. In the mid-nineteenth century, the city also became the center of the United States' most highly industrialized region.[9] World War I boosted industrial development. Ships, artillery shells, railroad gun mounts, steel helmets, and military boots were all made in Philadelphia. By 1920, there were 465,000 manufacturing workers in Philadelphia's larger firms.[10] Unlike other American cities where industrial development centered on one particular industry, such as steel in Pittsburgh or textiles in Lowell, Massachusetts, the greater Philadelphia area was home to a range of different industries. There were the glass manufacturers in South Jersey, the iron forges of Hopewell in the west, and the anthracite coalfields north of the city. The chemical and chemical processing industries, among them Rohm & Haas, Dow, and DuPont, formed another important part of the industry of the Delaware Valley region.[11] A mix of small and midsized industries, with a few large-scale producers, shaped the city's waste-handling practices.

Throughout its existence, but particularly after World War II, Philadelphia battled with mushrooming amounts and changing compositions of waste. By 1960, the average American produced an estimated one kilogram of municipal solid waste per day. By 1986, this quantity had almost doubled.[12] Immediately after World War II, Philadelphia's sanitation workers lifted as much as seven tons of municipal solid waste into horse-driven carts on a typical workday—an annual total of 2,555 tons.[13] This figure skyrocketed to 1.36 million tons annually in 1974, or roughly 3,725 tons of trash daily.[14] By the time of the 1986 sanitation workers' strike, the city's trash fleet consisted of 250 waste trucks that collected about 1.6 million tons of municipal solid waste annually.[15]

Until the early twentieth century, paper and food waste formed the major components of Philadelphia's discards. With new synthetic products and rampant consumerism after World War II, this composition changed fundamentally.[16] A massively growing packaging industry created innumerable goods with short useful lives. Many of the trash bags piling up at the emergency dumps during Philadelphia's waste strike contained nonreturnable bottles and cans and plastic packaging from self-service merchandising at the supermarket. By 1986, a range of different heavy metals, plastics in addition to other synthetic materials were common elements in the municipal waste stream, demanding new disposal practices for materials that were nonbiodegradable or could leach toxic compounds.[17]

Philadelphia relied on a combination of waste-disposal facilities and services, ranging from open water-dumping to incineration, without ever having developed a coordinated disposal plan. The Delaware and the Schuylkill Rivers served as major dumping grounds for the city's municipal sewage and industrial runoff.[18] Starting in 1961, Philadelphia also dumped waste into the Atlantic Ocean at a site east of Cape Henlopen, where the ocean currents and the water depth were favorable and the shell fishing was of marginal value. By 1973, Philadelphia had to move its dumping to a larger location southeast of Delaware Bay. The first site had been 5 square kilometers in area; this second site was 130.[19] Between 1961 and 1977, Philadelphia used barges to transport approximately 960 million gallons of sewage sludge to the ocean, most of it contaminated with heavy metals.[20]

On land, Philadelphia relied on open dumps—open pits with no spillage- or leakage-control mechanisms. The open dumps sprung up "wherever city officials could find a willing landlord." Because the sites were usually small, waste disposal required a constant search for new sites.[21] Some large open dumps existed on Fourth Street and Oregon Avenue in South Philadelphia. In its 1924 and 1929 maps, Philadelphia's Bureau of Street Cleaning marked twenty-three city-owned dumps scattered over its twelve waste districts. After 1945, as more people flocked to the city, Philadelphians increasingly considered open dumps a nuisance, observing the stench of vermin, fires from burning garbage, and explosions from the buildup of methane gas.

The model of the sanitary landfill, where refuse was covered with soil to eliminate the putrefaction of organic material and with it the problems of noxious smoke, rats, and mosquitoes, offered an alternative. By 1969, Philadelphia's Bureau of Street Cleaning had consolidated the city's open dumps into three landfills: the sixty-three-acre Penrose Landfill, located in Southwest Philadelphia, the forty-four-acre Swanson Street Landfill in South Philadelphia, and the fifty-one-acre House of Correction landfill located in Northeast Philadelphia on the Delaware River waterfront.[22] Sanitary landfills also caught on in the greater Philadelphia region, and communities started offering their services to the city. In 1951, two sanitary landfills started operating in Montgomery and Bucks Counties in Pennsylvania. Camden started landfilling at a site in the Cramer Hill neighborhood in 1952. In Delaware, twenty-six landfills had opened by 1978. By the end of the 1970s, Philadelphia had closed all its inner-city landfills and was relying on landfills in other counties. Until its closure in November 1985, the city's primary out-of-city landfill was Kinsley Landfill, New Jersey. Kinsley was just across the Delaware River from Philadelphia and about a fifteen-minute drive from Center City. By 1984, it was receiving 1,250 tons of Philadelphia waste daily.[23]

As in other larger cities, burning was the final element in Philadelphia's waste-disposal approach. Reduction was a process similar to incineration; it involved burning garbage but aimed to separate materials in order to extract nutrients from food waste. In the 1970s, Philadelphia was unusual among big American cities in that it still separated its food waste for sale to pig farmers, selling as much as eighty-five thousand tons.[24] The remaining garbage was taken to a reduction plant, where saleable grease and components for fertilizer from food waste were extracted. The unsaleable waste was then incinerated, and everything that could not be burned was dumped.

One of the disadvantages of reduction was that it was expensive. Another was the horrendous odor it produced, which triggered complaints from those living nearby. Philadelphia had two operational reduction plants, the Harrowgate Incinerator in Kensington, and the City Reduction Plant in South Philadelphia, near the Delaware. Both plants were expensive to operate. Despite the revenues from the sale of grease and fertilizer components, it cost more than $100,000 a year to operate the plants.[25]

Incineration—the practice of reducing the volume and weight of waste through burning—was Philadelphia's most controversial disposal method. In the United States, the first generation of incinerators appeared in cities between 1885 and 1908. These proved too smoky and costly to be practical. In the 1920s and 1930s, communities lacking space for sanitary landfills—among them Philadelphia—returned to incineration. By World War II, some seven hundred incinerators were in operation throughout the United States.[26] During the 1950s and 1960s, Philadelphia shifted its inner-city waste management strategy to center on incineration, with the intention of replacing reduction and landfilling. Although incineration was much more expensive than ocean dumping or landfilling,

Philadelphia built four new incinerators between 1953 and 1956. Almost from the start, Philadelphia's four incinerators were working overtime, processing unprecedented quantities of waste. By 1965, two more incinerators were built, with the residual ash being transported to landfills in New Jersey.[27]

Until 1919, when a new city charter was adopted, Philadelphia had contracted out all its waste disposal to private companies. Installed to combat corruption in the waste disposal system, the new charter granted Philadelphia the authority to operate its own street cleaning, waste collection, and disposal services. Garbage disposal moved—on paper—from the hands of private haulers into those of city employees, and a Street Cleaning Bureau was added to the Department of Public Works. It employed between two thousand and three thousand men, primarily African Americans, to collect and dispose of trash. They worked six days a week, providing weekly service for most neighborhoods.[28] Yet despite the new charter, the old contracting system with private waste haulers remained intact. Over the decades, Philadelphia's city council returned to a reliance on private actors, partly motivated by what the council saw as an overly strong sanitation workers' union.[29] In the 1980s, this shared arrangement between city and private services enabled private waste contractors to tempt the city with offers to take Philadelphia's massive amounts of waste beyond city and national borders.

Philadelphia was no pioneer of the sanitary city.[30] Rather, its waste-disposal practices were typical of many large US cities in the second half of the twentieth century. It relied on a mix of disposal facilities, including open-water dumping, landfilling, and incineration, incorporating both public and private services while lacking a plan for coordinating the activities of the different facilities and services. Additionally, the city faced the challenge of dealing with increasing amounts and changing compositions of waste, which in the 1980s included the toxic remnants of US mass consumption, such as plastics, packaging, cans, and other consumer items. Remarkably, much of Philadelphia's waste was disposed of *beyond* city limits from the onset, and the decision to close all inner-city landfills by the end of the 1970s spurred that development: Philadelphia trash was dumped into the Delaware, the Schuylkill, or the Atlantic, or was landfilled in other counties in Pennsylvania and New Jersey. Externalization of waste did not begin with shipping the material to the greater Caribbean on board the *Khian Sea*.

We tend not to think of Philadelphia as a riparian city. Yet its two tidal rivers, the Lenapewihittuk—renamed the Delaware by European settlers—and the Tool-pay Hanna, or Tool-pay Hok Ing—renamed the Schuylkill—have shaped its environment and history. Long prior to European settlement, there was human activity along both rivers. Paleo-Indians were using the rivers as food sources as early as 8000 BCE. Their successors, the Leni-Lenape, followed shad upriver and lived in villages on both sides of the Delaware.[31]

Indigenous peoples had used the waters of the Schuylkill and the Delaware for millennia, but it took the European settlers just a century to poison their own water supplies. The city's wells filled with all manner of detritus, and the small creeks that fed the Delaware served as open sewers. The river became unusable.[32] To solve the problem, the city built the United States' first municipal water system in 1801. Water was pumped from the Schuylkill along a viaduct to Center Square, at Broad and Market Streets, from where a network of pipes redistributed the water to households, breweries, sugar refineries, and fire hydrants. Yet as the city grew toward the Schuylkill and hosted more and more industries, water pollution increased. Not only municipal sewage but all sorts of industrial liquid waste ended up in both rivers. By the mid-twentieth century, the Delaware ran black from coal, oil, tanning byproducts, and waste from other unidentifiable sources. When the Delaware Valley stood as one of the greatest industrial concentrations of industry in the world, "the river had become its sewer."[33]

Those working on or along the Delaware were the first to feel the impact of a dying river. Grease in the water clogged ships' cooling systems. Gases emerging from the water discolored paint on buildings and ships, corroded metal parts in ship engines, and sickened dockworkers. Above all, the river stank. By the 1950s, ground controllers told pilots coming into Philadelphia that the smell they were detecting at five thousand feet was the Delaware. As the fish in the river died, so did commercial fisheries.[34] In 1962, scientists from the marine laboratories at the University of Delaware found that water quality in the Delaware River had undergone rapid changes, possibly irrevocably altering the aquatic environment. Industrial and city pollution, deforestation, and poor land management had resulted in a higher load of silt and dissolved nutrients, resulting in a higher temperature of runoff water, with a reduced capacity to carry dissolved oxygen.[35]

Lacking funds, Philadelphia could do little on its own to save the Delaware. Instead, the State of Pennsylvania and the national government stepped in.

In 1905, Pennsylvania enacted the Purity of Waters Act to limit sewage disposal, followed by the Clean Streams Law of 1937, which expanded penalties on polluters and tightened discharge limits. In 1939, the states of New York, New Jersey, Pennsylvania, and Delaware formed the Interstate Commission on the Delaware River Basin, which over the years sponsored a series of conservation programs.[36] After World War II, the federal government entered the stage. In 1948, US Congress passed the Water Pollution Control Act, which put the federal government in a strong advisory and assistant role, provoking a significant debate over whether the federal government had the constitutional authority to impose air- and water-pollution control mandates. Among other measures, the 1948 act supported local authorities by offering large-scale federal subsidies for building sewage-treatment plants. A 1961 statute expanded federal funding for cities and suburbs.[37] More than three hundred municipal and industrial waste-treatment plants were constructed along the Delaware during the 1950s and 1960s.[38] Between 1950 and 1966, Philadelphia brought three sewage-treatment plants into operation to dispose of waste from the city and roughly two thousand local industries.[39]

While state and federal measures helped the Delaware, Philadelphia lost some of its autonomy to these new governance structures, and both the state and the national campaigns to combat a dying Delaware foreshadowed the increasing pressure that the city would feel to conform to standards imposed from outside. Long before the *Khian Sea* sailed down the Delaware River, it was the river that set the story in motion.

Philadelphia, the Struggling City

In the summer of 1986, Philadelphia's streets not only revealed the story of its long-festering waste crisis; they also exposed its social and economic strains. The decades following World War II had brought profound challenges that the city, once the workshop of the world, had managed poorly. The 1970s and 1980s had brought the global oil crisis, Reaganomics, Watergate, peace accords that ended the Vietnam War, a conservative backlash against the civil rights movement of the 1960s, and the rebirth of the human rights discourse.[40] In line with other industrial and ethnically mixed cities across America, Philadelphia experienced large-scale processes of deindustrialization, white flight to the suburbs, and significant in-migration by African Americans and other nonwhite ethnic groups. These changes transformed the economic and physical landscape of the city.

The first and probably the most pervasive change Philadelphia experienced was economic. Like other industrial centers, such as Detroit, Pittsburgh, St. Louis, and Cleveland, Philadelphia fell into decline in the second half of the twentieth century. Yet this decline had begun in the 1890s, when iron and steelmaking had shifted from Philadelphia to the Midwest. In the 1920s, an increasing number of textile manufacturers left the city for the nonunionized factories of the US South. Philadelphia also suffered severely during the Great Depression. In the 1950s, the city began to lose jobs, population, and revenue as white middle-class Americans moved to the suburbs, taking much of their buying power and their property tax revenue with them. Then, in the mid-1970s, the big wave of plant closings began.[41] From 1970 to 1980, Philadelphia lost 111,756 manufacturing jobs, 44 percent of its manufacturing employment.[42]

The United States as a whole had come out of the 1970s in bad shape. The expansion of worldwide free-trade agreements since the 1960s had been unfavorable to US workers. Industrial goods could now be more cheaply imported from abroad. With more and more plants closing or downsizing, most dramatically in the car-manufacturing center of Detroit, fewer Americans found jobs in the manufacturing sector. During the 1970s alone, the United States lost between thirty-two and thirty-eight million industrial jobs.[43] Additionally, two energy crises had led to a recession characterized by a double-digit inflation and high unemployment rates. In 1980, when Ronald Reagan took office, unemployment stood at 7 percent, rising to 9 percent by 1983. While Reagan promised the remaking of America, for many struggling urban centers, the Reagan administration's turn to deregulation and laissez-faire economics served the death blow to their manufacturing industries.[44]

With major employers closing or leaving and its tax base shrinking, Philadelphia became poorer. By 1972, the city faced a deficit of about $60 million, which had grown to $85 million only four years later.[45] Pennsylvania's House of Representatives worried that Philadelphia's deficit would "degenerate into a billion-dollar catastrophe," leading to insolvency.[46] Matters looked brighter in the 1980s, but the city budget remained tight. In 1986, the year of the waste workers' strike, Philadelphia had a budget deficit of $9.6 million. Predicting a $47 million gap for fiscal year 1987, the city government was forced to cut its staff, laying off 2,400 employees (nearly 10 percent of its workforce), sell city property, and borrow money to cover its debts. Municipal labor unions became recalcitrant when those cuts took hold, as the sanitation workers' strike vividly illustrated.[47]

The financial situation of individual households reflected that of the city. From

1949 to 1979, the household income of Philadelphians fell from almost even with the regional median to only 73 percent of it. In 1980, unemployment was 50 percent higher than the regional average, and more than 20 percent of city residents struggled to survive on an income below the poverty line.[48] A study from 1984 showed that ninety-one thousand households in Philadelphia were struggling to pay for basic services such as electricity and heating.[49] Economic changes had led to an increasing number of abandoned and potentially polluted industrial sites. Meanwhile, the city was obtaining so little revenue from taxes that it could not finance its own municipal services, such as education, housing rehabilitation, and support programs for its low-income population, let alone waste disposal.

On top of these economic and industrial changes, Philadelphia was witnessing a major social transformation. While the population of central cities across the United States grew by 10 million between 1950 and 1970, the surrounding suburban regions grew by 85 million, with a net out-migration of 13 million people.[50] Philadelphia had experienced a first wave of suburbanization in the nineteenth century, when rail and streetcar lines had opened up new residential districts to serve a white upper class.[51] In a second wave between 1950 and 1980, as white families moved out to newly established suburbs, the city lost about 250,000 residents, a quarter of its population.[52] At the same time, the Black population in the city increased. From 250,000 in 1940, it grew to 375,000 by 1950 and 655,000 by 1970, when African Americans represented one-third of the population. This trend continued in the 1980s.[53] These demographic changes exacerbated the racial and social differences as well as the tensions between the city and its wealthier suburbs.

Through deindustrialization, many US cities imploded in the 1970s and 1980s. The disappearance of jobs and the subsequent poverty created problems that included crime, widespread drug abuse, and violence. According to one historian, Philadelphia's Center City became a place "abandoned economically and politically, literally and metaphorically," and in the eyes of many white Philadelphians, the city's suburbs functioned as "defended spaces, bolstering their borders against the urban malaise of the city."[54] Philadelphia's Mayor Frank L. Rizzo (1972–80) heightened racial tensions through his policies. While his supporters praised him for being tough on crime, including taking a tough stance on the city's Black Power movement and tolerating police brutality, his critics accused him of discriminating against minorities. With the election of Wilson Goode as mayor in 1984, the political representation of African Americans changed. Goode became the city's first African American mayor, serving until 1992.[55]

On Goode's watch, however, the ethnic makeup of Philadelphia also became a pronounced issue in the context of the *Khian Sea*. How could a city with a large African American population and an African American mayor end up dumping on Afro-Caribbean Haiti?

[handwritten margin note: kinda presumptious question]

In time for the US Bicentennial celebration in 1976, marking the two-hundredth anniversary of the US Declaration of Independence, Philadelphia attempted to gloss over these financial challenges, social changes, and racial tensions. Three blocks comprising Independence Mall were added to Independence National Historical Park. Two new museums, the Afro-American Historical and Cultural Museum (later renamed the African American Museum in Philadelphia) and the Mummers Museum, opened in 1976, followed by the Port of History Museum on Penn's Landing in 1981.[56] A sense of historic grandeur conveyed itself to those roaming the streets, including those sweeping and clearing the garbage. It foreshadowed a strange parallel to another struggling city with a grand history: Gonaïves, Haiti, the later dumping place of Philadelphia's garbage.

Washington Ends Philadelphia's Ocean Dumping

Philadelphia's Bicentennial celebrations did not fulfill the expectations of city planners and officials. Far fewer than the anticipated one hundred million visitors came to Philadelphia. There were protests, and an outbreak of Legionnaire's disease killed thirty guests at a hotel in Center City. The Bicentennial year was a disaster.[57] The celebrations also compared unfavorably to an earlier mass event that had drawn crowds to Philadelphia: the celebration of the first Earth Day.

On April 22, 1970, approximately twenty million Americans came together to voice their concern about the environmental crisis. Colleges held teach-ins. People gathered in parks and schools, on city streets, and in front of corporate and government office buildings. There were speeches, discussions, and acts of ecotheater. People wore flowers and gas masks and participated in acts of civil disobedience. In San Francisco, activists poured oil into the reflecting pool at the headquarters of Standard Oil. In New York City, marchers held up dead fish to illustrate the pollution of the Hudson River.[58]

While many cities observed Earth Day and perhaps held a few additional events in subsequent days, Philadelphia organized an entire Earth Week.[59] A series of events crystalized how Philadelphians felt about pollution, urban sprawl, nuclear fallout, the harms of pesticide use, wilderness preservation, and waste disposal.[60] They gathered in Fairmount Park to listen to the poet Allen Ginsberg and Senator Edmund Muskie, and in Independence Hall to meet with Senator Hugh Scott and the environmental activist Ralph Nader. These mass rallies were part of a "seven day ecological extravaganza." Participants could take a tour of the city's major polluters and were offered balloons holding "fresh air," filled from compressed air tanks that came from a medical supply center.[61] During "trash-ins," school students collected waste for recycling.[62] In the city where two centuries earlier the Declaration of Independence and the US Constitution had been signed and adopted, Philadelphians enthusiastically signed up for environmental protection.

While President Richard Nixon had taken no official role during Earth Day, he endorsed its activities. He found himself heading a bipartisan consensus on the relevance of environmental protection. It was an issue that had already played a small but fundamental role in President Lyndon B. Johnson's Great Society program of reforms. With public support for environmental reform at its peak, Nixon made it a centerpiece of his domestic agenda, consolidating legislation of earlier decades into one coherent national framework. On January 1, 1970, Congress enacted the National Environmental Policy Act (NEPA), through which the enhancement of the environment became national law. The act also created the Council on Environmental Quality as part of the White House administration.

An estimated seven thousand people jam a quadrangle at the Independence Mall in Philadelphia on the eve of Earth Day, April 22, 1970. © Picture Alliance/Associated Press.

In July 1970, Nixon created the Environmental Protection Agency (EPA) as an independent agency, with headquarters in Washington, DC, and ten regional offices throughout the country.[63] Edward W. Furia, director of Philadelphia's 1970 Earth Week, became one of the regional directors of the EPA.[64]

The new legislation utterly changed cities' approach to environmental protection. It made it easier to enact and enforce strict protection legislation. Earlier, any city that took the lead in passing environmental legislation had risked losing industries to neighboring regions. Now, federal minimal standards put municipalities on an equal footing with their upwind and upstream neighbors and also offered grants to support local environmental programs.[65] Yet the new national legislation also challenged cities' autonomy.[66]

Of all the changes that the 1970s brought to environmental governance, ocean protection was most important to Philadelphia. For decades, ocean dumping had provided a convenient method of waste disposal, since proponents believed that flowing water lent itself readily to dissolving and dispersing whatever was put into it. Protest against the practice built up slowly after scientists started to investigate the potential ill effects of open-water disposal in the 1940s. It came to a climax around 1969, when news broke of the planned scuttling of an old military vessel loaded with roughly twenty-two thousand tons of outdated chemical weapons. The outcry was enormous and global. Great Britain sent official protest notes to the United States government on behalf of the Bahamas and Bermuda. Iceland voiced official concern for its fisheries. The Soviet Union scolded the United States for its anti-environmentalism. In the United States, antiwar and environmental activists formed a coalition against ocean dumping.[67]

In the greater Philadelphia region, these protests persisted into 1971, when the city debated moving to a larger ocean-dumping site because its original site was filling up too quickly.[68] Residents of Philadelphia and a number of coastal towns opposed the plan. The former worried primarily about the ecological effects of sewage sludge dumped in the marine environment, the latter about sewage washing up on shore and its effects on tourism.[69] In 1971, Joseph M. Boyd of Princeton, New Jersey, single-handedly filed a total of twenty-seven citizen suits against the companies barging the waste out to sea, the DuPont Corporation, and the City of Philadelphia as the sources of the material.[70]

Under pressure, Nixon turned ocean dumping from a "neglected environmental problem" to a top national priority.[71] The Council on Environmental Quality conducted a study suggesting that between 1949 and 1968, the average volume of waste dumped into the ocean annually had increased from 1.7 million tons to 37 million tons. Much of the material was "harmful or toxic to marine life, hazardous to human health and esthetically unattractive." Because of the decreasing capacity of US landfills and the comparatively high economic and political costs of opening new landfills, this volume, the report predicted, would increase further.[72] For a US government under the spell of modern environmentalism, the idea that large bodies of water could serve as waste receptacles was fundamentally reversed. In 1972, Congress passed the Marine Protection, Research, and Sanctuaries Act (also known as the Ocean Dumping Act), which prohibited the unpermitted dumping, or transportation for dumping, of radiological, chemical, and biological warfare agents, chemicals, and industrial waste in ocean waters within US jurisdiction. All other ocean dumping was to be phased out by 1980.[73] The EPA formulated an interim permit system to monitor and regulate cities' ocean dumping programs until they were phased out. Philadelphia's permit required that the city reduce the quantity of barged sludge before 1979 and stop ocean dumping by December 1980.[74] In the next eight years, Philadelphia would have to come up with alternatives, submitting quarterly progress reports to the EPA.[75]

Philadelphia responded by taking the EPA to court, arguing that its decisions were based on faulty conclusions reached in a January 1975 report. Philadelphia put forth two alternative studies showing negligible effects of sewage sludge dumping on marine life. The evidence of "adverse impact," the city claimed, was inferential at best.[76] Hearings began on May 19, 1975, before a panel of two scientists and a presiding officer, with the EPA, the National Wildlife Federation, the Environmental Defense Fund, the State of Maryland, and the State of Virginia intervening in opposition to the city. The hearing concluded that there was substantial reason to discontinue Philadelphia's ocean dumping, but Philadelphia's resistance continued.[77] Experts from the EPA disputed with Philadelphia's Water Department as to the scientific evidence for the environmentally damaging effects of ocean dumping. Key to this debate was the assessment of the toxicity and harmfulness of sewage sludge, whose composition depends on the nature of a city's economic and industrial activities. Generally, sewage sludge may contain up to sixty thousand toxic substances and chemical compounds, among them polychlorinated biphenyls (PCBs), chlorinated pesticides (such as DDT), chlorinated compounds (such as dioxin), heavy metals, and microbial pathogens, along with substances like asbestos, petroleum products, and industrial solvents.[78] Because of the composition of Philadelphia's industry, the city's sewage sludge was so high in cadmium and mercury that it was classified as hazardous waste according to the definition established by the Resource Conservation and Recovery Act (RCRA) in 1976.[79]

Still, critics of Philadelphia's ocean dumping were unable to cite actual evidence of damage. Philadelphia's engineers pointed out that when political decisions had been made, the paucity of accurate methods for measuring the effects of ocean dumping made analysis difficult. Although Philadelphia had started ocean dumping in 1961, the first systematic study to gauge environmental effects was not conducted until 1972. Then the Franklin Institute, an independent scientific and educational institute that had been commissioned and paid by the city to conduct the study, concluded that ten years of ocean dumping had done "little or no perceptible damage."[80] The EPA remained unimpressed and continued to wrestle with Philadelphia's Water Department over pollution standards and thresholds. The problem was that if standards were not sufficiently stringent, dangerous amounts of harmful pollutants could be introduced into the marine environment. Conversely, if standards were too strict, or based on unreliable data, the costs of alternative methods of disposal could prove an unnecessary economic burden. Philadelphia's protests were to no avail. Despite four additional court cases, Philadelphia was ordered to stop ocean dumping by December 31, 1980.[81]

Philadelphia was not the sole community in the US struggling with the EPA over ocean dumping. Irrespective of the final deadline, communities were united by the same anxiety: they were already struggling to recycle, burn, export, sell, or bury growing amounts of municipal solid waste, and now they had to find ways to deal with even more of it. Often these cities did not use the time to come up with alternatives. In 1982, Philadelphia started to experiment with incineration at sea but abandoned the project after a couple of months.[82] The termination of ocean dumping brought the waste problem ashore again.

How RCRA Changed the Rules of the Game

As the Ocean Dumping Act effectively washed waste ashore, environmental activists and administrators scrutinized the situation on land. Attention shifted from the marine environment to land and from polluted sewage sludge to a broader spectrum of waste materials, now divided into the categories of nontoxic garbage and hazardous waste. President Johnson had called for "better solutions" for waste disposal and the Solid Waste Disposal Act of 1965 had ushered in a new era of waste management.[83] In the 1980s, the composition of a city's waste truly started to matter.[84] In 1976, Congress had passed an amended version of the Solid Waste

Disposal Act of 1965—the Resource Conservation and Recovery Act. RCRA for the first time defined hazardous waste (subtitle C) as distinct from solid waste (subtitle D). It singled out waste objects that by their composition would pose "a substantial threat to human health or the environment."[85] Standards for the safe treatment, storage, and disposal of hazardous waste, alongside an elaborate tracking system designed to show the whereabouts of toxic substances from "cradle to grave," were due to go into effect on November 19, 1980.[86]

RCRA brought Philadelphia's waste crisis to a new level.[87] Around the city, 380 places were identified as potential hazardous-waste production sites. These included industrial sites associated with the production of textiles, ferrous and nonferrous metals, inorganic chemicals, pharmaceuticals, plastics and synthetics manufacturing, paint and related products, and electroplating.[88] Prior to the enactment of RCRA, industries producing hazardous waste hired outside truckers or chemical brokers to manage disposal. Both would take the waste off the producer's hands for a small fee—together with the liability for the material. Many states, including Pennsylvania, did not require a permit for waste haulers to operate: anyone with a truck could go into the business. Since the state had little control over disposal, hazardous material was dumped wherever these freelance haulers thought "they could get away with it"—in streams, fields, woods, vacant lots, unsafe landfills, abandoned mine shafts, city warehouses, suburban lagoons, and storm drains.[89]

RCRA instituted a strict protocol for disposal of hazardous waste. Waste producers were required to obtain an operating permit from the EPA or an authorized state agency, and any facility involved in the generation, storage, treatment, disposal, or transport of hazardous wastes had to prepare a manifest for recordkeeping and reporting.[90] A group of Philadelphia journalists followed the new cradle-to-grave route of the paper and ceramic filters used to purify a batch of pesticides at the Rohm & Haas plant. The drums containing the waste were first collected at a concrete storage area equipped with underground tanks to collect any spills. Then their content was tested, inventoried, and reported to the government. They were loaded on a truck bound for the region's only hazardous waste incinerator at Rollins Environmental Systems, Inc., in New Jersey, for incineration at two thousand degrees Fahrenheit. Then the wastes were again tested, inventoried, and reported to the government. The new waste products, the ash produced in the incineration, and the sludge from the pollution control systems were also tested, inventoried, and reported to the government before being buried in a hazardous-waste landfill in South Carolina.[91]

This process was both complicated and expensive for landfill operators and waste generators. Across the nation, the number of landfills plummeted by almost 50 percent after 1976.[92] Between 1978 and 1981, fifty waste sites in the Philadelphia area went out of business.[93] The costs of trash disposal exploded. In 1978, landfilling of one ton of toxic material cost $2.50; in 1987, it was $200. For Philadelphia, these changes meant that waste disposal costs skyrocketed from $19.1 million in 1981 to a projected $66 million in 1988.[94] Additionally, the city faced the challenge of safeguarding public health without squeezing the life out of thousands of businesses dependent on chemicals.[95] "Industries [were] becoming 'desperate,'" according to Edward Mullen, head of Folcroft Landfill, to find suitable disposal sites.[96]

Increasingly strict regulations for toxic waste management induced many industries to relocate to an area with cheaper facilities or to dump their waste illegally. In 1973, tons of illegally dumped industrial waste was piling up along 84th Street in a section of Philadelphia that was part of the Tinicum Wildlife Preserve.[97] In March 1977, the Pennsylvania Department of Environmental Resources (DER) discovered a site in Chester, Pennsylvania, where thousands of drums and numerous six-thousand-gallon tankers filled with combustible, explosive, and toxic waste chemicals had been abandoned. Storm drains had carried the wastes directly into the Delaware River. Two major fires in February 1978 had destroyed many of the drums, and the remainder posed a continuing combustion hazard. While the idea behind RCRA and the cradle-to-grave system was to channel all dangerous chemical wastes produced in the United States "into approved treatment and storage," its short-term effect was the dramatic increase of precisely the sort of improper and illegal disposal that the law was designed to halt.[98]

DER's three waste inspectors were responsible for ten northeast Pennsylvania counties and could do little to prevent improper dumping.[99] In 1979, DER proposed a package of bills to punish illegal dumpers, along with a tracking system to monitor the location, movement, and disposal of all hazardous waste in the state. The goal was to determine what became of the millions of tons of hazardous waste both produced by Pennsylvanian industries and trucked into the state for disposal. The legislation also sought to increase maximum fines for violating hazardous waste laws from $300 to $25,000 a day and to mandate prison sentences of up to two years for persons who illegally hauled or disposed of hazardous waste.[100] While this legislation was well-meant, it encouraged organized crime to develop its own hazardous-waste management business.[101] Matters came to a head in 1980, when Philadelphia's grand jury found the owner of a defunct waste-management facility guilty of bribing city officials to let it dump hazardous waste at its facility in Southwest Philadelphia.[102] A year later, another multimillion-dollar court case concerned the illegal dumping of hazardous material on city premises. Between 1973 and 1975, fifteen companies had "improperly disposed" of several thousand tons of hazardous waste material into the landfill in Southwest Philadelphia.[103] Although DER had told Philadelphia officials of possible environmental violations, the city could not close the landfill for lack of an alternative site.[104]

Abandoned and illegal hazardous-waste dumps made news all over the United States. In Toone, Tennessee, investigators in 1978 discovered three hundred thousand buried drums of pesticides that polluted an underground source of drinking water. A case in Louisville, Kentucky, became known as "Valley of the Drums": one hundred thousand drums of toxic chemicals had been dumped into and alongside a river, where they corroded and spilled open, poisoning the river and the underground drinking water.[105] The community of Love Canal, in Niagara Falls, New York, became the best-known symbol of the trouble with unregulated, abandoned, or leaking landfills. For ten years beginning in 1942, Hooker Chemicals and Plastics used Love Canal as a dump for waste, including halogenated organics, pesticides, and benzene. In 1953, the site was covered, and homes were built nearby. Only a decade later, residents had started to complain of bad odors and residues. Problems grew worse in the 1970s as the groundwater table rose and runoff began contaminating nearby residential areas. By 1978, Love Canal had become a national media sensation, and President Jimmy Carter declared it a federal health emergency.[106]

Environmental Citizenship in the Philadelphia Region

Parallel to the congressional investigations of Love Canal, the *Philadelphia Inquirer* ran a week-long "Toxics Series" to discuss the issue of hazardous-waste sites locally. Articles alerted readers not only to the policy changes connected to the implementation of RCRA but also to the dire situation in the greater Philadelphia area. Postwar deindustrialization had left behind "a plethora of hazards," including brownfields, illegal hazardous-waste dump sites, and toxic chemicals in the sediments of the Schuylkill and the Delaware. People in the metropole had to deal with abandoned and hazardous industrial buildings and lead-based paint on the interior surfaces of old homes.[107] After a six-month investigation, the *Inquirer* concluded that while the problem with hazardous-waste was a national one, "nowhere was the situation worse" than in greater Philadelphia. Through meticulous research, Rod Nordland and Josh Friedman, two *Inquirer* journalists, had unearthed dozens of cases of toxic waste dumping. They had found arsenic seeping into the ground, places where villagers had to drink bottled water because of trichloroethylene in the groundwater, PCBs leaking from an abandoned warehouse, and firefighters who were incapacitated as they battled with a landfill that spontaneously ignited.[108]

The *Inquirer's* warning about the omnipresence of toxic sites resonated with Philadelphians. After Earth Day, a number of environmental activist groups began to devote their time to the new topic of pollution. Ian McHarg, a landscape architect teaching at the University of Pennsylvania, explicitly linked environmental issues to urban sprawl and metropolitan development. Through his class "Man and Environment" and his 1969 book *Design with Nature*, he taught students to see the wetlands, rivers, streams, aquifers, and forests in the Delaware Valley as key elements in the hydrological cycle, worthy of protection from both destruction and contamination.[109] In 1967, the Delaware Valley Citizens' Clean Air Council was founded as a nonprofit volunteer group and has since played an important role in lobbying for tougher environmental laws and litigation.[110] In 1979, the Delaware Valley Toxics Coalition (DVTC) was formed. Initially concerned about air pollution, members quickly turned their focus to toxic waste.[111] The group provided assistance to individuals and organizations who were faced with pollution problems or threatened by proposed facilities that might create such problems.[112] One of its biggest successes was the passage of Philadelphia's "right-to-know" legislation, which required companies to publicly disclose any toxic chemicals that they might use, manufacture, store, or emit.[113]

Alerted by the media, citizens in the greater Philadelphia area paid increasing attention to the landfills and waste-disposal facilities in their neighborhoods. They had their eyes particularly on the phasing out of RCRA interim permits, that is, temporary permits for waste disposal that were due to be replaced by a long-term permit program governing all treatment, storage, and disposal facilities, with detailed requirements for all aspects of design, construction, operation, and maintenance.[114] In July 1983, Fran Scullion, codirector of the Delaware Valley Toxics Coalition Education Fund, filed a Freedom of Information Act request with the EPA for "a list of the names and addresses of all companies" in Pennsylvania whose interim permits were under review.[115]

Among the long list they received, one company in particular, Ace Service Corporation from southern Philadelphia, whipped up strong feelings. Ace was one of the independent waste haulers serving Philadelphia.[116] In the summer of 1982, the company had applied for a permit to store hazardous waste at their facility at 19 Snyder Avenue. The property was within an industrial area in the Pennsport–Queens Village neighborhood in South Philadelphia but less than half a mile from residential areas. The company planned a treatment, storage, and disposal facility for hazardous wastes from small industrial generators within the Philadelphia region, such as print shops and tool-and-die companies. Ace would collect the material and haul it to chemical-recycling companies or state-approved toxic-waste landfills.[117] The initiative would serve both the business community and the environment, according to Terry Siman, an attorney representing the company. Until then, Philadelphia's small businesses had difficulties getting rid of their hazardous waste. Without a proper disposal facility, they were "dumping the stuff in the toilets or in a drum out back"—often illegally, was the subtext.[118] Both the DEP and the EPA found Ace's application well thought through. The city of Philadelphia had approved the plan.[119]

The community of Pennsport would have none of it. A first meeting was called in January 1983, chaired by the Pennsport Civic Association and with representatives from the EPA, the DEP, the fire department, and other citizen action groups, such as the Delaware Valley Toxics Coalition Fund. Ace refused to attend.[120] The evening's most famous guest was Vince Fumo, the Democratic Party representative of the district in the Pennsylvania Senate. People were concerned about health risks, spills, emergency evacuation, and the value of their property. Fumo raged that his district would not be "the garbage dump of the City or anywhere else."[121] Pennsport Civic Association established a Hazardous Waste Task Force that coordinated a battle lasting almost two years.[122] Early on, they allied with Frank L. Rizzo, a former mayor of Philadelphia who was setting himself up for a return to office.[123] On May 16, 1984, some two hundred opponents of the facility marched through the streets of South Philadelphia to demand city action.[124] By early summer 1984, South Philadelphia's residents had won the city's support. It opposed the permit.[125]

The sticking point in the controversy about Ace was the proximity of a hazardous waste site to residential areas. The nearest homes were about a quarter of a mile from the site—a distance which, according to federal and national legislation, was permissible. Yet for the people who lived in those homes, this felt too close.[126] "Toxic materials should not be stored in and transported through a densely populated area such as South Philadelphia, nor should a storage facility be permitted within city limits," said Harold S. Levin, a member of the board of directors of the Washington Square West Project Area Committee and Civic Association.[127] Ace defended its choice of site, pointing out that their property was zoned for lease-limited industrial use, surrounded by other industries, and separated from Pennsport by Interstate 95. Additionally, they were not bringing hazardous waste into the city but collecting material that was "already in Philadelphia" for disposal outside.[128] The incident underscored the difficulty of finding sites for new waste facilities at a time when the government was also tightening controls on hazardous waste.

The problem was not unique to South Philadelphia. In 1983, community organizations from Lower Moreland Township, a small community just north of Philadelphia, approached US Senator John Heinz about the Bethayres landfill, which, they alleged, had been "illegally accepting toxic wastes."[129] The same year, a small tract near the Schuylkill River in Upper Merion Township, Tyson Dump, caught the attention of the EPA and the media. From 1962 to 1970, an unknown quantity of different chemicals had been dumped there. Now the closed dump was to become one of the earliest Superfund sites in the United States.[130] In the summer of 1984, Clearview Landfill in Delaware County, about fifteen miles southwest of Philadelphia, became the next hot issue. The fifty-acre private landfill touched the city's borders in a place that, since the late 1970s, had been transformed by urban development from marshland into a patchwork of suburban communities. The landfill had operated from 1958 to 1975, but the dumping of debris and frequent fires had continued after its closure. Now residents feared that chemicals might be leaking from underneath the hill. In 1983, tests on portions of the landfill confirmed that a creek at the western edge of the landfill was polluted with PCBs and chlordane.[131] Almost every month, it seemed, journalists and neighborhood associations uncovered a new toxic-waste dump.

Waste Disposal in a Confined Space

From colonial times onward, Philadelphia relied on lands beyond its city limits for inner-city services. The primary causes for this were geographical and administrational. While enabling growth, Philadelphia's riparian environment also imposed limits on land use. European settlers took the Schuylkill and the Delaware as natural borders for administrative entities. The Delaware divided what was to become the state of Pennsylvania from the state of New Jersey.[132] The Schuylkill created spatial limits that paralleled early conservationist thought and racial and class separation. With the creation of Fairmount Park in 1867, both sides of the river just north of the Philadelphia Water Works were turned into recreational areas, precluding any other kind of land use.[133] Local government measures further limited Philadelphia's inner-city land usage. In 1682, William Penn had divided Pennsylvania into three counties—Philadelphia, Bucks, and Chester. When established, Philadelphia County was framed by the Delaware to the east, by Bucks County to the north, and by Chester County to the south. Its western boundary was undefined, theoretically leaving vast opportunities for Philadelphia's urban growth. But the idea of unlimited westward expansion died with the formation of two new counties, Berks County and Montgomery County, in the eighteenth century.[134] In the nineteenth century, with the massive growth accompanying its industrialization, the city reached its county limits. In 1854, Philadelphia absorbed thirteen surrounding townships, six boroughs, and nine districts, among them the important mill towns of Kensington and Manayunk. Through the Consolidation Act, the city of Philadelphia became geographically identical with its county.[135] The spatial limitations imposed by natural geography and political administration defined Philadelphia's waste-management practices. Given the growing scarcity of waste disposal sites within the city-county limits, Philadelphia was bound to use someone else's territory for disposal.

New Jersey became Philadelphia's primary resource for waste disposal, illustrating how the city externalized waste locally long before exporting it internationally. In the boom years of the sanitary landfill, New Jersey and its vast wetlands had become closely associated with the waste business. *Harper's* magazine dubbed it the "Trash State."[136] Over the course of European settlement, New Jersey's vast wetlands had come to signify a hindrance to economic development. In the industrializing decades from the late nineteenth century onward, they came in handy as dumps for the growing piles of waste from the urban areas near the coast, including Philadelphia and New York City.[137]

For decades, Philadelphia and the surrounding communities enjoyed the mutual benefits of a waste-disposal agreement: one side took care of the waste, the other paid for it. By the 1970s, this relationship was becoming strained. Shortly after the creation of the EPA, New Jersey established its own state environmental agency, the Department of Environmental Protection (DEP). In the early 1970s, the DEP issued a warning that New Jersey was facing a major waste crisis because of lack of landfill space. Still, New Jersey continued importing out-of-state garbage, such as incinerator ash from Philadelphia.[138] The situation escalated in 1973, when Philadelphia considered phasing out waste incineration to meet the EPA's new, more stringent air-pollution standards and to ease citizens' complaints about "garbage fumes."[139] Four of Philadelphia's six incinerators could not meet the standards of the city's air-quality code, and the idea was to close them by mid-1974.[140] City officials anticipated sending all waste to sanitary landfills instead. With no landfills of its own, the city would send all of its waste to New Jersey. Communities across the Delaware responded fervently. Protesters massed at the gates of the Mac and Kinsley landfills attempting to prevent trucks laden with Philadelphia waste from entering. A "Great Trash Rebellion" was rising.[141]

In 1973, New Jersey passed the Waste Control Act, which banned out-of-state refuse.[142] Philadelphia contested the ban in court. The case went all the way to the United States Supreme Court, which issued a 7–2 ruling that struck down the Waste Control Act as an unconstitutional restriction of interstate commerce.[143] Supreme Court justices declared that such a ban must be seen as an "economic protectionist measure." It was "immaterial" whether the legislative purpose of such a ban was "to protect New Jersey's environment or its economy."[144] By declaring waste a commodity in interstate commerce, the ruling allowed interstate disposal practices to continue. This favorable decision, however, allowed only a brief reprieve for Philadelphia.

Philadelphia's waste crisis of the summer of 1986 had been long in the making. Long before the *Khian Sea* left the city, Philadelphia's overextended and flawed disposal infrastructure, its financial precarity, and the geographic and administrative idiosyncrasies of the city-county created the need to dispose of city waste beyond city premises. Meeting this need, communities in New Jersey served as Philadelphia's disposal outlet long before communities in the global South did. The emergence of modern environmentalism in the United States, with ever-stricter waste disposal and environmental protection rules and communities' growing awareness of the hazards in their immediate neighborhoods, tightened the screws on Philadelphia's established waste-disposal system while illustrating the asynchronicity of the global waste trade. In the fall of 1986, the *Khian Sea* sailed down a Delaware River that was much cleaner than it had been half a century before, into an Atlantic that US communities no longer considered as the ultimate dumping ground for all sorts of toxic material, and away from a country where the premises of hazardous waste disposal were legally defined. The *Khian Sea*—and other toxic ships—sailed toward lands where discourses on and practices of (hazardous) waste disposal were differently framed, allowing for a continuation of the cheap dumping no longer possible in the United States.

TWO

"Send It on a Caribbean Cruise" | *The Greater Caribbean as a US Waste Dump*

Q.: What are the four ways to dispose of garbage?

A. Put it in a landfill, incinerate it, recycle it, or send it on a Caribbean cruise.

RALPH HAURWITZ | "With Trash Problems, Who Ya Gonna Call? Junkbusters!"
Pittsburgh Press, June 29, 1987

The cargo ship anchored at Pier 2 was a good fit for the aging industrial setting of Philadelphia's port on the Schuylkill River. The white paint only partially covered the signs of wear and rust resulting from decades of exposure to wind and water. Some parts had been replaced, others repaired. The *Khian Sea,* as the ship was called, had been built in Japan in 1969 as part of the Khian series of ten multipurpose dry-cargo vessels. As cargo vessels, they had once dominated global seaborne trade, but in the past years, bigger and faster tankers had taken their place. Three horizontal slewing cranes enabled the *Khian Sea* to load and unload cargo independent of dockyard facilities and to enter almost any port. A four-cylinder Vee oil engine drove the 142-meter (467-foot) vessel at roughly fourteen knots. The *Khian Sea* was what ship enthusiasts call "basic on board"—a cheap but efficient multicargo vessel. After serving in the buildup of the Greek shipping fleet after World War II, it had recently passed to a new owner, Lily Navigation.[1]

The twelve-acre port facilities at Girard Point where the *Khian Sea* was anchored were less than half a mile upstream from where the Schuylkill flows into the Delaware River. Since 1973, the docks had been easy to make out because of the massive cantilevered truss bridge towering over them that carried Interstate 95 across the Schuylkill into Philadelphia. In better times, Girard Point had boasted one of Philadelphia's largest grain elevators, floating devices that collected grain from ships anchored at the wharves and signified the city's importance in the trade. By the 1980s, the old grain elevator stood abandoned.[2]

Pier 2 was a floating wood, steel, and concrete construction about the size of a soccer field, extending into the Schuylkill. Ships could dock, load, and unload on both sides. Its warehouse housed a highly mechanized waste-processing facility. In September 1986, Pier 2 was owned by Joseph Paolino & Sons Inc., one of Philadelphia's biggest construction companies, founded in 1921 by Joseph Paolino, an Italian immigrant. On his death in 1984, the business had passed to his sons Louis and Joseph Paolino. The company specialized in major construction projects, such as highways, excavation, and asphalt production. One of its prestige projects in the mid-1980s had been the repaving of Broad Street in Philadelphia's Center City.[3] In 1985, Paolino had made headlines after the city's finance director ruled that it had to return $38,665 in profits for breaching the city's "set aside ordinance," which required 15 percent participation by minority-owned firms and 10 percent participation by female-owned firms on all city contracts. For the same reason, the Pennsylvania Department of Transportation had suspended Paolino from bidding on its contracts for a year.[4]

Possibly in response to these rulings, Paolino shifted from street maintenance to waste disposal. In December 1985, the company struck a deal with the City of Philadelphia for the disposal of up to two hundred thousand tons of municipal incinerator ash for fiscal year 1986–87. Paolino suggested using the trash transfer station at Pier 2 to process the ash for transport beyond the city.[5] The *Khian Sea* was the first cargo vessel to be loaded with the material—nearly fifteen thousand tons of it. Contrary to the terms of the company's bid, it did not remain along the US shoreline. In September 1986, the *Khian Sea* sailed for the Bahamas. Its departure brought Philadelphia's established practice of outsourcing waste disposal to other communities' lands to a new level, both geographically and politically.

The Wilson City Government and the Paolino Contract

Philadelphia's waste crisis coincided with the 1983 mayoral election, a turning point in the city's history that reflected the fundamental economic and social transitions Philadelphia had gone through. W. Wilson Goode—a graduate of the University of Pennsylvania and a former managing director of the city—became its first African American mayor. He set out to unify a city that had recently seen major racial tensions.[6] Philadelphia's dysfunctional waste-management system was a key issue in the mayoral race, with the media pushing all the candidates—Wilson Goode (Democrat), John Egan (Republican), and Tom Leonard (Independent)—to declare how they intended to clean up the city. Blaming the city's trash problem on the unions, Egan and Leonard argued that Philadelphia needed to contract out city services. Goode argued for technological and social changes to reduce the amount of trash produced. At the time, Philadelphia was recycling around 1 percent of its waste. Goode favored a waste-to-energy (WTE) incineration scheme and a public information program that would "change people's attitudes about disposal."[7] In the face of dwindling landfill space and mounting opposition to the opening of new landfills, he saw reducing and recycling as the less controversial options.

During his campaign, Goode had thrown his weight behind waste reduction, supporting the building of a WTE incinerator at a US Navy facility close to Girard Point. While he was not opposed to recycling, he saw it as a nice add-on to waste reduction.[8] Goode found the idea of a single public-works project, WTE incineration, easier to embrace than a recycling agenda involving a constellation of operating strategies, new waste-disposal requirements, public education, and the creation of various financial incentives.[9] A majority of Philadelphia's city council, however, disagreed. They sided with the many citizen groups who favored recycling and saw Goode's proposed WTE plant as a threat to human and environmental health. In January 1985, after a year of controversy, the council voted against Goode's initiative, creating a stalemate that would drag on until 1988 and smooth the waters for the *Khian Sea*.[10]

Off to a bad start for his plans for the future of Philadelphian's waste disposal, Goode also had to find a solution for the waste produced in the past. Since 1960, Philadelphia had relied increasingly on incineration, burning about 43 percent of its waste at two city-owned incinerators by the 1980s and sending another 19 percent to Baltimore RESCO, a waste-to-energy plant. Another 29 percent of municipal waste was trucked to the Lanchester Landfill, operated by Chester County, Pennsylvania. Some 8 percent waited at O'Hara Transfer Station for shipment to out-of-state landfills. Only 1 percent of city waste was recycled. When Kinsley Landfill in New Jersey closed its doors to Philadelphia in 1985, the city allowed the residue to pile up next to its Northwest incinerator.[11] By March 1986, the smelly "Mount Everest of ash" had grown to such a size that ash trucks lining up at the gate of the Northwest incinerator had to be turned away for lack of capacity.[12] In December 1985, the City of Philadelphia signed a contract with Paolino & Sons for hauling away and disposing of this residue, starting July 1,

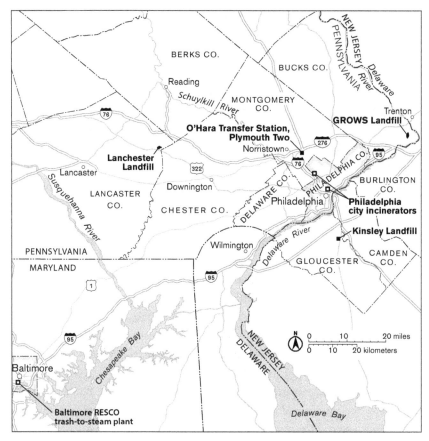

Waste incineration and disposal facilities used by the City of Philadelphia.
Map by Ben Pease, based on data from City of Philadelphia Streets Department.

1986. For $41.75 a ton, Paolino would haul a minimum of fifteen thousand tons monthly and a maximum of two hundred thousand tons overall.[13]

Paolino's contract with the city was an unfortunate arrangement, as the company faced fierce opposition at possible US disposal sites. In their original contract, they had named a landfill in King and Queen County, Virginia. One month into the contract, a court order temporarily barred Paolino from using the landfill, on the grounds that the permit had been issued before sufficient testing had been conducted to determine whether the ash could pollute the groundwater.[14] Facing the risk of losing a $6 million contract, Paolina dug up alternatives: landfills in South Carolina, Georgia, and West Virginia.[15] Again the company faced fierce opposition from local communities to accepting out-of-state waste, reigniting a controversy that had been smoldering since Philadelphia had successfully appealed to the US Supreme Court against New Jersey's ban in 1978.[16] The Supreme Court had ruled that New Jersey could not stop other states from dumping waste because "the right of interstate commerce . . . overruled the right of localities to protect their citizens."[17] Now the issue was back on the table. In March 1986 a landfill in East Liverpool, Ohio, terminated their contract with Paolino within one week after signing it because of violent local protests.[18] In April 1986, South Carolina's governor, Dick Riley, asked South Carolina's Senate and House leaders to prohibit private landfills as a means of stopping the influx of out-of-state waste from Philadelphia. While the General Assembly rejected Riley's plea, Paolino's request to dump a total of 140,000 tons at South Carolina's landfills also went unheard.[19] As more and more options fell through, Philadelphia's incinerator ash continued piling up at Paolino's transfer station on 51st Street, as well as its dock on Pier 2 at Girard Point.[20]

Seeking a solution, Paolino made use of two contractual details: first, its contract allowed it to subcontract with another company. Second, it allowed the company to export the ash, as long as it could prove that its reuse, recycling, or disposal was conducted in "strict accordance with the governing laws of those agencies having jurisdiction over the disposal site."[21] In early summer, Paolino entered into negotiations with John Patrick Dowd and William P. Reilly, president and vice president of Coastal Carriers Corporation in Annapolis, Maryland. Coastal Carriers acted as the US representative of Amalgamated Shipping Corporation, a Bahamian company, whose president and vice president were Robert Cordes, a Bahamian businessman, and Henry Dowd, John Patrick Dowd's father. Robert Cordes was also president of Lily Navigation, the owner of the *Khian Sea*. On behalf of Amalgamated, Coastal Carriers suggested that Paolino export Philadelphia incinerator ash to the island nation of the Bahamas at a cost of $26.75 per ton, $15 cheaper than Paolino's own deal with Philadelphia.[22] Naturally the material would be offloaded "in strict accordance" with Bahamian environmental laws. This requirement appeared easy to fulfill, since at the time the Bahamas had no environment ministry, no environmental legislation comparable to that of the United States, and no distinction between municipal solid waste and hazardous waste, let alone a system for recycling. Waste disposal on the main island, New Providence, happened primarily in uncontrolled and badly vented landfills that often caught fire, producing large amounts of toxic runoff and smoke. The smaller Bahamian islands were served by open dumps, many of them in wetlands, a practice Philadelphia had abandoned in the late 1960s.[23]

On June 23, 1986, Paolino signed a contract with Amalgamated.[24] The plan was to offload the ash on the human-made island of Ocean Cay (104 kilometers from Miami). As part of a major tourist infrastructure and development project, the ash would be used as fill, a century-old practice common in land-reclamation projects around the world, but particularly well suited to land-hungry Caribbean nations.[25] Immediately on signing the contract with Paolino, Amalgamated chartered the *Khian Sea* for a two-year period from Lily Navigation, Cordes's other company. They foresaw a long-lasting business partnership involving multiple voyages moving trash from Philadelphia to the Bahamas. Paolino undertook to deliver material to Amalgamated at a minimum rate of thirty thousand tons every thirty days, which meant that at least two barges the size of the *Khian Sea* would head toward the Bahamas every month.[26]

Although disposing of its waste beyond national borders was a change for Philadelphia, it was only part of a new and flourishing international trade in waste. Canada and Mexico emerged as the first key partners for waste trading schemes that were based on exploiting national differences to make a bargain. By the mid-1980s, about 85 percent of the United States' exported waste ended up in Canada, most of it either at an incinerator in Ontario or at a landfill near Montreal, and another 10 percent was sent to Mexico for recycling.[27] Often waste disposal facilities across the border were closer than the nearest US sites. Tricil Ltd., Canada's largest hazardous-waste handler, ran one of its incinerator-landfill facilities in Sarnia, about fifteen kilometers from the Michigan border. These foreign options also appeared to be cost-efficient because of the strong US dollar, cheaper land, cheaper labor, and less stringent waste-disposal in Canada and Mexico.[28] In 1983 and 1986 respectively, the United States negotiated bilateral agreements with the two nations providing a legislative framework and environmental governance protocol for the international trade in waste. Canada and Mexico had become regular importers of trash.[29]

US waste traders were also opening up other markets in the Caribbean, Latin America, and some parts of Africa. There, differences from the US system were even more profound and bilateral legislative agreements with the US nonexistent. The unequal trade in waste was born. As early as 1979, news emerged of an international waste deal between Nedlog Technology Group, a company based in Colorado, and Sierra Leone.[30] By 1982, rumors had spread in the news and among US foreign-service officials about an Alabama company planning to send paint and pesticide waste to the Bahamas, and another intending to send sewage sludge from Washington, DC, to Haiti.[31] The same year, the City of Fort Lauderdale, Florida, discussed a proposal to ship waste from the city's sewage-treatment system to research farms in the Dominican Republic for use as agricultural fertilizer.[32] The company Atlantic Forest Products Inc. made a similar proposal to the city of Baltimore to dump the sludge from Baltimore's Back River sewage treatment plant on an eighty-thousand-acre tree farm in the Dominican Republic.[33] In 1983, the EPA investigated a scheme to send PCBs from Florida to Honduras for disposal.[34]

Colonial Legacies of Exploitation

To send US waste on a Caribbean cruise represented no haphazard choice of destination. For close to three centuries, the European settlers of North America had looked to the greater Caribbean, with its tropical islands, majestic volcanoes, fertile checkerboard plains, pine-covered mountains, and rainforests with a mixture of desire and disdain. It was the Caribbean islands where Christopher Columbus had first landed in 1492 and from where his arrival nourished an appetite, first among European and then North American colonizers, for possessing these tropical lands, their natural resources, and their people. Since the nineteenth century, ever-larger numbers of Americans had visited this Edenic paradise by boat. Some even maintained winter houses there. Simultaneously, they considered the tropics an environment of danger and discomfort, ridden with snakes, malarial mosquitoes, and dank vegetation.[35] Americans clung to the myth promulgated by writers from Rudyard Kipling to Somerset Maugham that "people living in equatorial climates [were] doomed to moral and physical decay."[36] By 1986, their relationship with their Caribbean and Central American neighbors was marked by a sense of US paternalism interwoven with racism and cultural supremacy.[37] After World War II, Americans viewed the region as rife with economic mismanagement, the drug trade, sex tourism, offshore financing, shady tax havens, and dire expressions of poverty and degradation. These views opened the door for a rhetoric that presented US waste exports as a way to boost economic development.[38]

European colonization had paved the way for this kind of waste colonialism. European powers—first the Spanish and then the Dutch, the French, and the British—fundamentally transformed the Caribbean.[39] Violence, enslavement, massacres, and European diseases depopulated some areas of the Caribbean lowlands of Central America by as much as 90 percent. Many once-cultivated areas reverted to quasi-natural landscapes of second-growth forests and remained that way for three hundred years. To Europeans, these represented ideal plantation sites, particularly for sugarcane. To compensate for the lack of labor, European powers transported millions of African slaves. The plantation system laid the foundation for substantial economic growth in Europe, the emergence of an Afro-Caribbean culture, and the fundamental alteration of the region's ecology. Once the Caribbean had been covered with tropical rainforest. After European conquest, hardwood was logged to construct ships, homes, and furniture. The forests were harvested for fuel and the residue burned to make way for plantations. Since the 1700s, Europeans had exploited the natural resources of the Caribbean for their own enrichment.[40] The toxic ships represented a new form of this practice.

US power politics in the greater Caribbean began in the nineteenth century, following the Monroe Doctrine of 1823, which declared the Western Hemisphere an American sphere of influence. After its victory in the Spanish-American War in 1898, the United States consolidated its influence in the region. The relationship was marked by US attempts to steer and control these countries' processes of decolonization and economic and social readjustment. Different US governments worried that as their neighboring countries broke free from imperial and then dictatorial rule, political instability would threaten US investments and influence. The Cuban Revolution of 1959 and the assassination of the dictator Rafael Trujillo in May 1961, followed by a military uprising in the Dominican Republic, turned the greater Caribbean into a major ideological battleground of the Cold War, one in which the United States regularly exercised military force.[41]

The United States also intervened in the economics of Caribbean and Central American nations. In the nineteenth century, the US "conquest of the tropics" allowed American exploitation of tropical resources.[42] After World War II, when the economic situation of most Caribbean and Central American countries declined significantly because tropical goods could be produced in increasing quantities elsewhere, US economic influence was exerted primarily through investment.[43] With once highly profitable sugar and cacao plantations dwindling into insignificance, greater Caribbean nations sought to expand public-sector spending on infrastructure, public works, health services, communications, education, utilities, and tourism.[44] Frightened by the Cuban Revolution, the United States supported these economic reconfigurations and implemented several "modernization" projects aimed at adapting the economies to new labor markets, transitioning from agriculture to an economy based on the textile, tuna, pharmaceutical, and technology industries. In 1961, the US Agency for International Development was founded to finance such schemes.[45]

Despite these efforts, states in the Caribbean and Central America (and all of Latin America) carried an increasing burden of foreign debt. Initially, this stemmed from the need to take out loans for development projects. In the 1960s, the problem was exacerbated by failures in revenue collection. Many development projects benefited private enterprises without generating commensurate returns for the governments. The accumulation of foreign debt, paired with an increasing inability to pay wages that kept pace with rising inflation, meant that the region became poorer overall. It was soon marked by the associated problems of unemployment, failed educational systems, high crime rates, drug abuse, and alcoholism. This prospect led many governments to consider even more foreign investment or borrowing. The United States increased its financial involvement in the region, as did the World Bank and the International Monetary Fund (IMF).[46]

Economic dependence on the United States became even stronger in the 1980s. In 1982, four years prior to the *Khian Sea*'s voyage, Mexico was the first country to announce that despite its massive oil exports, it could no longer service its external debts. This news sent shockwaves through the international financial world, especially when other nations suggested that they too were having difficulty meeting their external debt obligations. International creditors, such as the United States, the IMF and the World Bank, feared that Mexico's default would set off a chain reaction that might cause a collapse of the financial sector throughout the region. Their joint efforts to ensure that those affected could pay off their foreign debts intensified their economic and financial involvement in the region.[47] In 1983, the United States implemented the Caribbean Basin Initiative (CBI) and created a free-trade zone that included twenty-four Caribbean and Central American nations on the same terms extended in 1992 to Mexico and Canada under the North American Free Trade Agreement.[48] Despite these efforts, for many greater Caribbean countries the Latin American debt crisis sparked a trend of massive economic decline that made them receptive to offers of waste imports.[49]

Not only political and economic but also ecological pathways had been forged in the region long before the toxic ships arrived. Starting with its involvement in the building of the Panama Canal early in the twentieth century, the United States entertained a narrative of the conquest of nature, targeting the region's vast mangrove forests and wetlands as a reservoir of infectious diseases and an impediment to economic growth and development. The drainage of wetlands for the construction of the canal appeared to control yellow fever and malaria.[50]

US influence on the environment also manifested itself in the agricultural sector. Favoring an aggressive capitalist model aimed at maximizing agricultural and industrial exports, the United States supported the expansion of US-based fruit companies, such as United Fruits, alongside the vast expansion of the latifundistas, a Central American plantation oligarchy that since colonial times had wrestled control of land from peasants. By the twentieth century, these actors held almost exclusive control of the most fertile land for the production of cotton, bananas, sugarcane, timber, beef, and various other crops, destined solely to feed growing US and European appetites for "exotic" products.[51] Forced off their lands by the large plantations belonging to the latifundistas or El Pulpo (as United Fruit was called), many peasant families moved onto the surrounding hillsides, clearing them of trees in order to plant subsistence crops. This deforestation resulted in soil erosion, habitat destruction, watershed deterioration, and flash floods.[52]

By the 1970s, US influence on the environment of the greater Caribbean was discernible largely in the form of waste.[53] When pesticides such as DDT, aldrin, and dieldrin were banned in in the United States response to environmental and health concerns, their manufacturers were left with massive stockpiles. These soon made their way to the greater Caribbean to be used on the fields instead of being disposed of as hazardous waste in the United States.[54] In the greater Caribbean, the goal of maximizing export crop yields for short-term profits led to high rates of pesticide use. This created a dangerous cocktail for many low-paid peasant workers, poisoning an estimated seventy-three thousand of them in the 1970s.[55] Additionally, much of the land, water table, and food chain became contaminated. Unrestrained by environmental legislation, industries in the region dumped excess chemicals and their waste products into the environment.[56] By 1970, the United Nations Environment Programme was sounding alarm bells about the contamination of the Caribbean Sea from agricultural runoff.[57] Long before the toxic ships from the United States approached the greater Caribbean, its environment and people were already suffering from disproportionate exposure to environmental harm as a result of US political and economic intervention.

Of Modernization, Wastelands, and Wetlands

On their cruises, the toxic ships plied the seas from Mexico to Colombia and from Guatemala via the Bahamas and Haiti to Puerto Rico, Guyana, and Suriname. These regions exhibited an ethnic and cultural diversity born from a voluntary and forced convergence of people. Today, the largest country of the region is Nicaragua (130,000 square kilometers), the smallest Saint Barthélemy (15 square kilometers). By population, the largest is Guatemala, with 14 million inhabitants, and the smallest Belize, with 400,000 inhabitants.[58] Among the Caribbean islands, Cuba dominates with 11 million inhabitants and an area of 69,000 square kilometers, followed by the Dominican Republic with 10 million inhabitants and an area of 39,200 square kilometers, and Haiti with 11 million inhabitants in 17,200 square kilometers. Some of the island nations consist of only one island—or, as in the case of the Dominican Republic and Haiti, half an island—while others, such as the Bahamas, include many islands.[59]

On the Pacific coast of Central America, the landscape is marked by majestic volcanoes rising above fertile checkerboard plains. The Atlantic coast is defined by rich mangrove swamps. There are pine-covered mountains, freshwater lakes, and cloud forests in the cooler interior highlands of some islands and in Central America, as well as dense tropical rainforests cut through by steaming rivers meandering toward the warm waters of the Caribbean Sea. The region is home to jaguars, monkeys, and manatees in addition to vast numbers of migratory birds.

The decisive factor for human life and twentieth-century notions of urban or agrarian development in the region was the limited amount of arable land permanently above sea level. This made land-reclamation schemes attractive, including the century-old practice of filling wetland areas through the disposal of wastes.[60] Hence, when the *Khian Sea* approached the greater Caribbean, it represented an economic opportunity as much as—or more than—an environmental threat.

The ship left Philadelphia in early September. Initially it was headed for the Bahamas, an island nation that the World Bank then classified as an upper-middle-income developing country, ranking it among the region's wealthiest nations. Even so, it struggled with a dysfunctional education system, inadequate water supply and sewage infrastructure, and a drug and alcohol abuse problem.[61] Tourism, important in the Bahamas' economy since the mid-nineteenth century, had steadily expanded. By 1986, it directly and indirectly accounted for about 50 percent of employment and contributed about 70 percent of the country's gross domestic product. After the US trade embargo on Cuba in 1961, the Bahamas had become the most popular tourist destination for Americans traveling to the Caribbean, with more than 3 million visitors in 1986. Anticipating growing competition from Jamaica, Mexico (particularly Cancún), and cruise-ship tourism, the country's tourist industry sought to increase its appeal by creating more beachfront hotel rooms on what was then mangrove-covered shoreline.[62]

Coastal Carriers, the US representative of the Bahamian company in charge of the deal, had cleverly portrayed Philadelphia's incinerator ash in the language of "modernization" schemes that fit regional desires as well as local imaginaries of wetlands as *wastelands*. A journalist from New Jersey later reported that the ash on board the *Khian Sea* was intended for use as fill material for the human-made island of Ocean Cay.[63] Although details of the deal remain unknown, it is likely that the ash was supposed to act as a foundation for construction that would transform the uninhabited island into a tropical playground for cruise ship passengers and a "Monte Carlo of the Caribbean" for rich North Americans.[64]

Negotiations with Bahamian officials began in the spring of 1986, after Paolino's deal with the landfill in Virginia had fallen through. A Bahamian state official even visited Philadelphia to meet with Paolino, Coastal Carriers (Amalgamated's US representative), and representatives from the Philadelphia Streets Department. It seemed like a done deal. When the Bahamian government halted the import at the last minute in October 1986, claiming that a necessary permit was lacking, it came as a surprise to many.[65] Sources suggest that not enough payment had been put down for a permit, making it sound as if the agreement was a matter of insufficient bribery.[66]

Certainly displeased but not discouraged, the *Khian Sea*'s operators looked for another landing place. Over the remaining months of 1986, Coastal Carriers, represented mainly by William P. Reilly, negotiated with various alternative disposal sites, hoping to get one of them to take at least the *Khian Sea*'s current cargo and, ideally, the two hundred thousand tons of ash detailed in Amalgamated's contract with Paolino, which were piling up in Philadelphia. Under international trade and import laws, the *Khian Sea* could not simply dock at a harbor and unload but needed a local importer of the material. Consequently, Reilly was looking for a deal similar to that entered into with the Bahamas.

The best strategy for disposing of the ash still seemed to be to sell it for land reclamation, a widespread practice. Large parts of the Netherlands and the city of Rio de Janeiro are built on fill, as are parts of Dublin, Saint Petersburg, Helsinki, Beirut, Mumbai, Shenzhen, and Manila. In North America, Toronto,

New Orleans, Chicago, and Boston all relied on fill land to boost their growth. Perhaps the most prominent example is the City of New York. Manhattan saw a massive expansion of its shoreline through excavation-and-fill projects that reclaimed marshlands dating as far back as the seventeenth century.[67]

Although such projects had become less common in industrial countries by the 1980s, the practice continued in the global South. In the greater Caribbean, land scarcity was a major barrier to economic development. Many nations were perched on coastlines open to the sea on one side, with often inaccessible, mountainous interiors and low-lying, deforested plains on the other. On the shorelines, the widespread mangrove swamps—dense thickets of trees and shrubs that tolerate brackish water—had long been used as sources of timber, food, and even medicine. By the late twentieth century, however, they had come to be seen as an impediment to growth and a threat to human health and were targeted as sites for reclamation.[68] In the 1980s the greater Caribbean lost about 10 percent of its mangrove forests: in the Bahamas, about 35 square kilometers were destroyed annually to build tourist resorts, marinas, and residential areas.[69]

The first alternative destinations proposed for the ash were Costa Rica and Honduras, where Reilly and his negotiation partners floated the idea of using the ash for fill on which they would build low-cost housing for workers. Next was Panama, another country with a plentitude of mangrove swamps waiting to be turned into commercial lands, according to Reilly.[70] These plans, however, did not progress as quickly as the Philadelphia side needed them to. As negotiations stalled with clients in Central America, Reilly had the *Khian Sea* sail to Jamaica—officially to get supplies—and then, in December 1986, to the Cayman Islands. Meanwhile, Philadelphia's incinerator ash kept piling up.[71]

To speed up negotiations, Coastal Carriers and Reilly changed tactics. Instead of trying to coordinate with land-reclamation projects, with their cumbersome requirements and schedules, they cast the enterprise as one of actual waste disposal. Reilly started working with Ideal Dominicana SA, established in 1985 to quarry limestone in the Dominican Republic.[72] His idea was to establish a reciprocal trade: importing limestone into the United States and exporting municipal incinerator ash. The ash would be disposed of in a planned landfill on property that Ideal Dominicana leased from the government.[73] Mining had been one of the Dominican Republic's most prosperous industries since its beginnings in the 1970s. By 1980, it brought in as much as 38 percent of the country's foreign exchange, primarily through the export of gold, silver, bauxite, and nickel. Yet with falling international prices and a global economic crisis, mining businesses were struggling, and the government was actively seeking foreign investors to keep them afloat.[74] In 1986, Ideal Dominicana had accumulated a deficit of two million pesos.[75] Coastal Carriers offered a solution. They were ready "to send a shipload of ash to Cabo Rojo [where Ideal Dominicana had a quarry], and use it for demonstration purposes." Naturally they meant the cargo aboard the *Khian Sea*.[76] Reilly also reached out to a Chilean shipping agent and suggested the transformation of "the northern desert areas of Chile" and "perhaps abandoned copper and nitrate open mine stripping sites" into landfill sites that could accept up to one million tons of incineration ash annually from the United States.[77]

During his court testimony years later, Reilly explained the rationale for these projects. He and his business partners sought to develop "a high-scale movement of raw materials for our benefit as entrepreneurs and the benefit of developing countries and the benefit of the United States."[78] Such proposals reflected racist, settler colonial notions of the "proper use" of "untapped natural landscapes." Much as European colonizers rationalized the dispossession of Native Americans because they were not using the land in ways the settlers considered efficient and appropriate—that is, for agricultural and farming purposes—these twentieth-century waste traders looked at the greater Caribbean as lands simply awaiting their proper use for economic development.[79] According to Reilly, the export of Philadelphia ash to countries in the greater Caribbean epitomized the beneficial nature of the waste trade for developing nations, since it "employed people who haven't been employed for five years." Professing the benefits of their business to the people of the poorest nations on earth, Reilly declared that they had "nothing to be ashamed about on that particular note."[80]

The notion that lands of the greater Caribbean needed to be developed caught on among Reilly's negotiation partners, at least initially. A potential Honduran business partner, Edgardo A. Pascall, expressed his utter conviction that the import of Philadelphia ash would bring progress to the Atlantic coastal lowlands of Honduras. Communicating with the Honduran port authorities, he described the scheme and enumerated the opportunities it might bring to the region around Puerto Castilla, a port on the Caribbean approximately twenty kilometers north of Trujillo, the capital of the region of Colón. Until the late 1930s, Puerto Castilla had been the site of a division of United Fruit. When Panama disease (a fungus) infected the local banana plants, United Fruit had left, and Puerto Castilla had become impoverished. Pascall claimed that Puerto Castilla could again serve as

Image taken by Greenpeace activists showing strip mining in Haiti in 1988.
© Greenpeace/Jay Townsend.

Honduras's link to the world if the port could attract foreign investment. The ash deal, he declared, would enable authorities to expand the port, stabilize lands, build roads, generate jobs, and combat malaria through draining wetlands. It would also secure Honduras's access to global markets.[81]

While Reilly and Pascall both asserted that dumping US waste in mangrove swamps was a productive use of the material, Reilly would never have suggested the same deal for a US wetland area. With the emergence of modern environmentalism in the United States, wetland areas were seen as worthy of protection. In 1971, a group of primarily industrial nations had negotiated the international Ramsar Convention for the conservation of wetland areas, with the United Kingdom, Australia, Finland, Denmark, Bulgaria, Germany, Greece, Italy, and Iran among the earliest signatories. It took effect in 1975. Although the United States did not sign until 1986, US wetlands were already protected to some degree by the Clean Water Act of 1977 and provisions of the 1985 US Food Security Act. The latter included "swampbuster" provisions that penalized farmers for filling wetlands in order to expand their acreage. Panama was the first greater Caribbean to join, in 1990. The Bahamas did not join until 1997.[82]

City under Pressure

Despite the enthusiasm expressed by Pascall and others for importing the ash from Philadelphia, months went by without a contract materializing. The deadlock caused ripples back in Philadelphia. By March 1987—six months after the ship had set sail—Amalgamated and Coastal Carriers had still produced no viable alternative to the Bahamian deal or done much to get rid of the Mount Everest of Ash. Paolino filed a $500,000 lawsuit against Amalgamated for its failure to fulfill its contract obligations, charging that Amalgamated had lawfully declared that it would receive the necessary import permits from the Bahamian government, which it turned out not to possess.[83] Paolino acted under pressure, because the city of Philadelphia was withholding the agreed payment of $6 million to Paolino until the company provided proof that the ash had been lawfully disposed of.[84]

The deadlock was also making life difficult for city officials. Citing budgetary constraints, Goode's government had to announce to Paolino that it could not extend its ash-hauling contract beyond the original $6 million, despite rising amounts of ash. Paolino had already announced in January 1987 that they had provided $6 million worth of services and would stop their disposal services by the end of the month. This meant that for the next five months, until the start of the new fiscal year, there would be no waste services for the city's incinerator ash. Instead, it would accumulate at collection sites throughout the city. In February 1987, the streets commissioner, Harry M. Perks, sent an alarmist note to the press. Philadelphia had only "a few days—four, five, maybe eight days—of storage left."[85] In the end, some eight hundred thousand tons of incinerator ash were piled up next to the Northwest incinerator alone.[86]

Philadelphians were fed up with the ongoing waste-disposal crisis. Memories of what the city had been like in the summer of 1986, during the sanitation workers' strike, still rankled, and the incinerators had for years been a cause of complaints. Germany Hill Civic Association, an environmental neighborhood initiative, sued the City of Philadelphia for not providing proper waste services. Those living in the neighborhood of the Northwest incinerator had grown weary of the smell, runoff, and other potential hazards coming from the mound of ash.[87] The association was successful. The court issued a consent order stating that the City of Philadelphia could dump ash at the Northwest incinerator only with the association's permission and only in an emergency.[88] Environmentalists had Goode's government on a leash.

As the question of where to put the city's ash became ever more pressing, Philadelphia partnered with new contractors for the upcoming fiscal year. A Norwegian-American company, A/S Bulkhandling, proposed a scheme that would target the greater Caribbean as the destination for Philadelphia waste. Bulkhandling planned to send a ship, the *Bark*, to Panama.

THREE

"We Exist for the Good of Others" | *The Rise of Opposition in the Greater Caribbean*

Our problem is that, in the eyes of other nations, we do not exist for ourselves, we exist for the good of others. And it's not only this field of dumping garbage. Think, for example, political life in Haiti.

Think, for example, of what happened with the last election. Haitians are not allowed for their own good. They have to serve others. . . . The way it is, we are a small nation, at the service of the so-called Big Brother. That's the way it is. Garbage, economy, politics. You name it.

HAITIAN INTERVIEWEE | speaking with Greenpeace toxics campaigners, January 1988, Gonaïves

With long and sinuous coastlines and numerous sheltered estuaries, Panama had extensive mangrove forests. The province of Bocas del Toro was home to the country's third largest.[1] In contrast to the mangrove communities in the south of Panama, where large tidal ranges allowed trees to grow as high as forty meters, Bocas del Toro's mangroves reached only about five meters. But Bocas's mangrove communities were important ecosystems, covering large areas in the waters surrounding the numerous islands and keys in the Bay of Almirante. Together with vast seagrass meadows and extensive coral reefs, they kept the coastal zones healthy. They provided essential habitat for thousands of species, stabilized shorelines, prevented erosion, and protected the land from waves and storms.[2] For the human population, the coastal forests supported important shrimp and crab fisheries as well as providing a source of timber.[3] For the Ngäbe, Panama's Indigenous population, which lived mainly in the western Panamanian provinces

51

of Veraguas, Chiriquí, and Bocas del Toro, the mangrove forests were sacred and alive with many spirits. Some said the visible, tangled root systems were a hiding place for Anansi, an Afro-Caribbean folktale character full of mischief, and home to the goddess Orisha Nanã and the spirits Matinta Pereira, Boiúna, and Mãe-do-caranguejo, folktale characters said to protect the forests by causing agony to those who interfered with them. Such unfortunate souls were doomed to lose their way and forever wander in this liminal zone between land and water.[4]

Settlers from within Panama and European and American expatriates liked to claim they had found a "lost paradise" in Bocas.[5] Although Panama's tourist industry showed great interest in the region, the lack of infrastructure made development difficult. Not until 1987 would a road, originally built for the maintenance of an American oil pipeline crossing the isthmus, reach the Caribbean coastline of Bocas del Toro. Within the province, most transport was by boat, and even that could be difficult because the extensive root networks of the mangroves often made it impossible to land onshore. Roads were few, particularly on the islands of the Bay of Almirante. A single road connected Bocas, the capital town of the province, located on Isla Colón, with the island's interior.[6]

A/S Bulkhandling, a Philadelphia-based subsidiary of a Norwegian shipping company, had its eye on Bocas del Toro precisely because of this lack of infrastructure when they submitted their bid for the disposal of Philadelphia's waste for fiscal year 1987–88. Using the incinerator ash as landfill, in a plan similar to that proposed by Paolino and Coastal Carriers, offered a win-win-situation for the company and the government of Panama.[7]

Yet, in contrast to Coastal Carrier's Caribbean disposal plans for Philadelphia incinerator ash on board the *Khian Sea* a year earlier, the projected voyage of this second toxic ship, the *Bark*, did not go unnoticed. Activists and journalists had gotten wind of the city's contract with Bulkhandling shortly after the ink had dried. From January 1987, they observed closely the progress of Philadelphia's incinerator ash toward Bocas del Toro. Eventually, when activists also traced the *Khian Sea* and the remnants of Philadelphia's ash cargo in Haiti, it dawned on them how big a problem they had stumbled on.

Bulkhandling's Waste Deal with Panama

By 1987, waste appeared to be constantly piling up in Philadelphia, first during the sanitation workers' strike in the summer of 1986 and then with the failure of Paolino and Coastal Carriers to come up with a disposal option for the

Northwestern incinerator's ash. Revolted by the sight and smell, Philadelphians pilloried Mayor Goode for his inability to deliver on his election promise to clean up the city. Given the stalemate with the *Khian Sea*, it was no surprise that Philadelphia's current ash disposal contractor, Paolino, did not win the bidding for the next fiscal year. Instead, the contract went to Bulkhandling. Its parent company, A/S Torvald Klaveness, was one of Norway's leading shipping companies. Starting out with refrigerated ships in 1946, Klaveness had become a leader in international bulk transport—the transportation of goods in large quantities loaded directly into a vessel. In 1960, Klaveness had led the creation of Bulkhandling, a group of several Norwegian shipping companies.[8] The company operated its shipping business from a pier at an old sugar refinery in South Philadelphia, at Pier 60 on the Delaware River. In December 1986, Bulkhandling had won Philadelphia's disposal contract by offering to take the city's ash to Panama for $37.60 per ton (a lower price than Paolino's winning bid of $41.75 per ton the previous year).[9] Bulkhandling had undercut three other competitors who had also proposed foreign disposal grounds, among them the Bahamas, the Dominican Republic, and an unspecified place in North Africa.[10]

Under the Bulkhandling scheme, Philadelphia's incinerator ash would be used in a land-reclamation project in Bocas del Toro. A new road would cut right through Bocas's vast mangrove landscape and make travel and transport easier for foreign tourists. Once the trees were cut, filling the swamp with Philadelphia incinerator ash would create firm ground for infrastructure and a resort hotel on one of the islands in the Bay of Almirante. Winding along Bocas's scenic coastline, the road would come within one hundred meters of the water and bring tourists to the "paradise" of Bocas del Toro. The Panamanian city of Changuinola, Bulkhandling's contract partner, would receive a payment of US $30 million from Bulkhandling.[11]

In their dealings with Changuinola, representatives at Bulkhandling followed the same logic as William P. Reilly of Coastal Carriers a year earlier, when he was attempting to get rid of the ash on board the *Khian Sea*. They picked an importer in a country marked by political instability, eager to implement modernization projects, and lacking effective environmental legislation. Like many other countries in the region, Panama had a long history of struggle between the military and a white oligarchy that had controlled the country since 1903. In 1968, General Omar Torrijos had established a military junta in Panama. Responding to a major economic downturn triggered by the collapse of the building boom in Panama City in the mid-1970s, Torrijos had pursued policies of social reform and modernization. Bocas del Toro came into view as part of his scheme to "conquer the Atlantic," which included infrastructure expansion and the resettlement of Latino Panamanians into what was then almost exclusively Ngäbe country. In the end, Torrijos's effort to fix everything at once broke the country's fiscal budget and incurred heavy foreign debt. He died in a suspicious airplane crash in 1981, and rumors that he had been murdered further destabilized the country. In 1983, General Manuel Noriega emerged as the new leader, firmly controlling the Panamanian military and its government and using paramilitary groups to suppress opposition.[12]

When Bulkhandling negotiated the deal with Changuinola in the summer of 1986, Panama had little in the way of effective environmental legislation or practices. On paper, it had been the first country in Latin America to incorporate environmental protection into its constitution, in 1972 (almost simultaneously with the founding of the EPA in the United States). Inspired by the United Nations Conference on the Human Environment in Stockholm, Article 118 of the constitution obligated the state to guarantee "a healthy environment, free of contamination (pollution), and where air, water, and food satisfy the requirements for proper development of human life." Article 119 promoted economic and social development that would "prevent environmental contamination, maintain ecological balance, and avoid the destruction of ecosystems."[13]

Often coupled with political transitions toward more democratic regimes, a number of countries in the Caribbean and Latin America incorporated green ideas into their new constitutions in the 1970s and 1980s, among them Cuba (1976), Peru (1979), Ecuador (1979), Chile (1980), Honduras (1982), Guatemala (1985), and Haiti (1987). Additionally, some countries established national agencies dedicated to environmental protection. Uruguay's was the first, in 1973, followed by Cuba's Comisión Nacional de Protección del Medio Ambiente y del Uso Racional de los Recursos Naturales (National Commission for Environmental Protection and Rational Use of Natural Resources). Similar commissions were set up in Panama in 1985, Guatemala and Bolivia in 1986, and Argentina in 1987.[14]

Despite this green constitutionalism, environmental policies in Panama and these other countries had remained primarily a philosophical expression of intent, an intent that faltered when confronted with the cross-sectoral nature of environmental protection and the difficulties of implementation. Waste management was a leading problem for many communities.[15] Although waste disposal was not entirely unregulated, Panama lacked rules that would make possible the application and enforcement of environmental principles.[16] It had established its

Metropolitan Sanitation Office, the Dirección Metropolitana de Aseo (DIMA), in 1984. The agency was charged with the collection, transport, and disposal of waste generated in several of Panama's municipal districts. Yet the country had only one sanitary landfill, Cerro Patacon, opened in 1987. In addition, DIMA left the corridor between Panama City and Colón with no official waste collection service, encouraging a practice of burning waste in yards and dumping it into rivers, at unofficial dumps on back roads, or near Panama City–Colón highway. Waste in Panama was categorized not as municipal solid waste or hazardous waste but rather according to whether it could be burned, with plastics often included in waste destined for open-pit incineration. Organic waste was used as fertilizer or animal feed.

Like the ash headed for the Bahamas a year earlier, the ash on board the *Bark* was characterized not as a waste product but as material for reuse. Changuinola had signed a deal with Bulkhandling for the import of up to 660,000 tons of ash per year for the next ten years.[17] Clearly, this amount was not to come solely from Philadelphia's incinerators. The contract symbolized a long-term business relationship between Changuinola and Bulkhandling, in which, most likely, Bulkhandling already had several other US cities lined up as possible clients. As Bruce Gledhill, Philadelphia's deputy streets commissioner, pointed out, the *Bark* and the *Khian Sea* were "no isolated occurrences" with respect to their destinations or the intended purpose of their cargo.[18] In August 1987, for instance, while facing a December 31 deadline to halt ocean dumping, Los Angeles negotiated a deal to ship more than 350 tons of sewage sludge a day to Guatemala for fertilizer rather than dumping it in the Pacific.[19] The Philadelphia ships were part of an armada of trash-carrying vessels going south, ostensibly to foster development.

The Awakening of Opposition

After Philadelphia's Streets Department struck the deal with Bulkhandling in December 1986, word about an unethical disposal deal spread around the city, and opposition started to form. In January 1987, Jerome Balter, an environmental attorney at the Public Interest Law Center of Philadelphia, became the first to publicly raise concerns. Having represented the Germany Hill Civic Association in its battle against the Northwest incinerator, Balter was familiar with the city's incinerator ash situation. Worried that the transport of ash to Panama would leave the city legally liable for the costs of contamination, Balter leaked the news to the *Philadelphia Inquirer* and the *Philadelphia Daily News*, where the reporters

Mark Jaffe and Ramona Smith, among others, were already covering Philadelphia waste.[20] On January 4, 1987, the *Philadelphia Inquirer* ran a short item noting how, "shunned by landfills from New Jersey to Georgia," Philadelphia's ash would soon be traveling to Panama.[21] Meanwhile, Balter attempted to ascertain whether the city had taken steps "to ensure an environmentally sound use of incinerator residue in Changuinola, Panama."[22] In response, the Streets Department sent a delegation to Changuinola to inspect the site.[23]

For a while, nothing happened. Four months later, however, the story blew up in Panama. In May 1987, Panama's national public radio and leading newspapers picked up the story of an imminent waste shipment from Philadelphia to Bocas del Toro. Somewhat surprisingly, given the general acceptance of the depletion of mangrove forests in Panama in connection with infrastructure and tourism projects, health and environmental groups all over Panama organized in opposition.[24] A local group spray-painted the walls at the Changuinola airport with ecological slogans. La Fundación de Parques Nacionales y Medio Ambiente, a coalition of twenty-four Panamanian environmental organizations, made an official demand to the government for the disclosure of all information about the shipment and announced a bigger campaign against foreign waste shipments. They urged environmentalists to join forces to thwart plans "to turn Panama into the garbage dump of industrialized countries."[25] Environmentalists were aided by farmers and businesspeople in Bocas del Toro who feared soil and water contamination from the ash. Eventually the Panamanian Ministry of Health joined the foundation's criticism of the shipment.[26]

From Panamanian sources, information trickled back into the United States. A researcher from the Smithsonian Tropical Institute (located in Miami) wrote to US Greenpeace Southeast in Jacksonville, Florida, to alert the group to the imminent shipment of ash.[27] Another researcher, from Florida Agricultural and Mechanical University, had picked up the story on Caribbean radio and reached out to Rainforest Action Network, an environmental organization based in San Francisco, to inquire if they could "put this on the front burner."[28] The cargo of the *Bark* became a matter of national concern.

Information moved slowly in the preinternet era, and environmentalists in the United States were trying to learn more about the ash shipments from Philadelphia by letter, phone, and fax. They also relied on the services of information providers, such as ECS Marine Information Services—a company that tracks vessels and investigates the shipping industry—and Lloyd's List. At the time, ships could be identified only once they reached a port and signed in with port

The barge *Mobro 4000* is towed from New York in August 1987, carrying 3,186 tons of solid waste. Greenpeace activists displayed a banner on the barge reading "Next Time Try Recycling." The skyline of New York City, where the waste originated, is visible in the background. © Greenpeace/Dennis Capolongo.

authorities. Of particular interest to US activists was the Panamanian perspective. Had people in Panama "any awareness or potential opposition" regarding the shipments?[29] Over the summer of 1987, several environmental groups and individuals in the United States were independently piecing together the details of Bulkhandling's shipment to Panama. Some wondered if the story had enough substance to justify a larger environmental campaign. Soon it dawned on them that Philadelphia's deal with Bulkhandling was one of many examples of the US export of waste.

While US environmental activists focused their attention on Philadelphia, another toxic ship hit the national news: the *Mobro 4000*, New York's version of the *Khian Sea* and the *Bark*. In spring 1987, the small community of Islip ran out of landfill space to accommodate waste sent up from nearby New York City. Seeking an alternative to building an expensive incinerator, New York City officials hired a private consortium to ship the waste to North Carolina by barge. There, residents protested against out-of-state waste. After North Carolina officials turned the barge away, it meandered through the Atlantic and the Gulf of Mexico during April and May. The captain of the *Mobro* unsuccessfully tried to offload his cargo in Louisiana, Texas, and Florida before taking the barge to Belize and on to the Bahamas. Denied entry there, the *Mobro* sailed on. Authorities in Mexico and Cuba threatened to fire artillery should the barge try to dock there. News of the *Mobro* and its two-month "Caribbean cruise" attracted attention in US national media, primarily because it concerned New York City. The barge made an appearance on the *Tonight Show,* and stores along the shore of New Jersey sold commemorative T-shirts.[30]

The *Mobro* prompted the first public intervention by Greenpeace in the international waste trade. Established in Vancouver in 1971 in response to US nuclear testing, Greenpeace founders took an international approach to environmental activism. Since nature did not recognize the artificial boundaries of nation-states, they believed the organization had a mandate to address global environmental issues, such as waste shipped to global South countries, irrespective of the presence or absence of Greenpeace activists in those countries.[31] Despite having roughly 1.5 million members worldwide in 1987, Greenpeace was far from a global brand with a unified corporate identity or agenda. Regional and local chapters had considerable autonomy in choosing issues for their campaigns. As news spread about the toxic ships, diverse Greenpeace chapters took note and responded. Some protested toxic incinerator ships in the North Sea.[32] Others climbed the chimneys of waste incinerator plants in Detroit and cities in the US Northeast.[33] In August 1987, Greenpeace activists from New York used the *Mobro* to highlight the social injustice of sending US hazardous waste abroad. They boarded the waste barge after it had returned to New York and unfurled a banner reading "Next Time Try Recycling."[34] Building on this event, Greenpeace USA decided to mount a national campaign in conjunction with the organization's existing anti-toxics campaign, which operated out of Washington, DC, to oppose Philadelphia's waste shipment to Panama. A first set of actions was planned for September 7–11, 1987.[35]

Greenpeace was eager to garner support for this campaign in Panama, where it had no local chapter.[36] They reached out to the Panamanian ecologist Wilberto Martinez and the popular Panamanian singer and actor Ruben Blades, who had moved to the United States in 1974, to support their events and serve as ambassadors to the Panamanian people.[37] Concurrently with their action week in Philadelphia, they published the bilingual report *Offers of Poison/Ofrendas envenenadas.*[38] The report detailed the concentrations of heavy metals and toxic substances found in the ash and described their possible effects on Boca's wetlands if it was used in the land-reclamation project. The Greenpeace campaign

Greenpeace activists hang a forty-by-forty-foot banner from City Hall Tower in Philadelphia to protest the city's plan to ship incinerator ash to Panama. © Greenpeace/ Jay Townsend.

significantly added to the pressure that Panama's media and activists had brought to bear since May.[39] Early on the morning of September 8, 1987, two Greenpeace climbers scaled Philadelphia City Hall and unfolded a forty-by-forty-foot banner that read "Don't Export Toxic Ash to Panama/*No envenene Panama.*" Meanwhile, a group of activists stood below carrying placards reading "Incineration is a Pain in the Ash!" or "Return it! Don't burn it!"[40] Activists attempted to gain access to Philadelphia Mayor Wilson Goode, chanting, "No Goode, No Ash!" Mayor Goode refused to speak to them.[41]

In Panama, Bulkhandling's ash import project had initially enjoyed strong support from the country's ruling elite. One leading supporter was a rich Panamanian senator and member of the opposition party who had a stake in a proposed tourist center in Bocas del Toro.[42] But the deterioration of US-Panamanian relations, which had started in 1986, accelerated. In June 1987, an anti-American demonstration—supposedly orchestrated by the Noriega government—caused an estimated $106,000 worth of damage to the US embassy in Panama City. In response, the Reagan administration froze a $26 million aid program for Panama.[43] Rising anti-Americanism boosted support for the Panamanian environmental groups opposing the ash import. On September 10, 1987, following Greenpeace's protest in Philadelphia, which was duly noted in the Panamanian press, Noriega's government put the waste deal on hold.[44] It announced that the existing certificates provided by Bulkhandling and the City of Philadelphia, attesting the ash to be harmless, were invalid, and it ordered Panamanian defense forces to prevent the ship from entering territorial waters.[45]

Both Bulkhandling and the city of Philadelphia were caught unprepared by the opposition to the ash shipment and the rapid decline of US-Panama relations.[46] For Philadelphia, these developments were catastrophic. Bulkhandling refused to accept any further ash until the situation stabilized, and the next bidder's offer was $5 million more expensive.[47] To make things worse, the Germany Hill Civic Association, represented by Balter, refused to extend the emergency permit for storing ash next to the Northwest incinerator.[48] Because of lack of space for the ash, the Street's Department shut off the city's two incinerators for some days. But Bulkhandling was not off the hook. According to their contract, they were responsible for the disposal of the ash they had already collected.[49] And then, as if the situation had not been complicated enough already, the *Khian Sea* reappeared.

The Flying Dutchman Reappears

"Haïti n'est pas la poubelle de l'extérieur!" (Haiti is not the world's garbage can!) the voice of Jean Dominique proclaimed from the radio, before his rage echoed from the walls of the colorful houses typical of Caribbean architecture and lost itself in the humidity of the tropical climate. Philadelphia's ash from on board the *Khian Sea* at Sedren Wharf, a berthing facility in a small town on Haiti's west coast, "constitue un camouflet pour la population" (represents a snub for the people), Dominique continued; the unloading and illegal abandonment of the ash showed a disrespect for human rights and international relations. Addressing the people in the local vernacular, Haitian Créole, Dominique reached thousands of listeners throughout the Caribbean with his station Radio Haiti-Inter.[50] Still, it would take weeks before Dominique's rage about Coastal Carriers' activities in Haiti was heard in the United States.

News of the *Khian Sea* had been scarce after its deal with the Bahamas had fallen through. Although William P. Reilly of Coastal Carriers was in touch with potential importers from Costa Rica and Jamaica to Honduras and the Cayman Islands, none of the schemes materialized. However, a US businessman from outside Philadelphia, whose name William P. Reilly would later claim not to remember but who appeared to have connections to the Paolino company, had a permit from Haiti's military government to dispose of nontoxic and nonhazardous ash, and he was willing to transfer this permit to the *Khian Sea*.[51]

Singling out Haiti as the recipient of US refuse was dumping not only on the poorest of the poor nations but also on one of the most politically unstable countries in the Caribbean.[52] Two hundred years back, Haiti—then Saint-Domingue—had been home to a plantation system creating enormous fortunes for French colonists. The plantations, primarily sugar and coffee, had consumed the landscape and the people. Large areas of forest had been chopped down for construction and the timber exported to Europe. When the slaves working the plantations died in large numbers, they were simply replaced. In 1791, slaves arose in violent opposition to the colonial plantation system. André Rigaud, the leader of the revolution, forced the British to withdraw, only to face a French invasion. Eventually, the tide turned in favor of the former slaves, who declared independence in 1804. Despite this success, it was almost impossible for the young republic to recover from its brutal colonial legacy. Jean-Jacques Dessalines, one of the heroes of the revolution, became Haiti's first ruler, proclaiming an empire in 1804, only to be overthrown in a coup d'état in 1806. Haiti was then divided into two regions, controlled by rivaling regimes, before it descended into political chaos by the mid-nineteenth century, with a succession of short-lived emperors and generals.[53]

By the early twentieth century, Haiti appeared close to anarchy, with a population mainly poor, uneducated, and hungry. Little remained of the prosperous sugar plantations of the French colonizers. Coffee represented the only cash crop. By 1908, governmental rule broke down completely, with no fewer than seven men attempting to gain control until 1915 and each meeting a gruesome end: one hacked to pieces in the streets, one killed by a bomb, a third supposedly poisoned. By then, Haiti was regarded as the poorest nation in the Western Hemisphere.[54]

Worried that the German Empire would seize control of Haiti, the United States occupied the country in 1915, returning to white Haitians the right to own property. Partly motivated by economic depression at home, the United States government opted to leave Haiti in 1934. This period was followed by a series of comings and goings of Haitian presidents. Élie Lescot, in power between 1941 and 1946, had attempted to extend his rule indefinitely, but he fled the violent public response and left the country to military rule. From then on, the Haitian military largely controlled the island: it overthrew presidents, held provisional power for a while, anointed another leader, and started anew.[55] In 1957, its chosen presidential candidate was François Duvalier, also known as Papa Doc. Duvalier installed one of history's most corrupt and repressive dictatorships, using violence, voodoo, and a civilian force called the *tontons macoutes*—named for a folklore character who carries away disobedient children—to suppress opposition. During his presidency an estimated thirty thousand Haitians were killed. In 1964, Duvalier assumed the title of president for life, and on his death in 1971 he was succeeded by his son Jean-Claude Duvalier. For a while, many observers hoped that "Bébé Doc" would end his father's dictatorship. He eased the level of repression and implemented new economic policies. He managed to revive the coffee, sugar, and tourism industries and secured aid to improve roads and infrastructure. The United States started pouring financial aid into the poverty-stricken land. Meanwhile, Bébé Doc increased his own wealth through embezzlement of public funds.[56]

In the 1980s, the Duvalier regime became vulnerable. In 1978, Haitian pigs were diagnosed with Asian swine fever, and the nation's entire stock of pigs was culled. As a result, many Haitians lost their main source of food and income. Deprived of prospects, many fled the country. Reports of "boat people"—refugee Haitians prepared to risk drowning rather than starve—started appearing in the US press. The outbreak of HIV/AIDS in the United States additionally stigmatized Haitians. Early in the AIDS pandemic, a number of Haitians who had emigrated to the United States and Canada developed symptoms of the new syndrome. The Haitian patients denied homosexual activity, intravenous drug consumption, or blood transfusions, all of which had been associated with transmission of the disease. By 1982, scientists in the US declared all Haitians to be at risk, suggesting that HIV was an epidemic Haitian virus that had been brought back to the homosexual communities of the United States.[57]

In 1983, Pope John Paul II visited the island and condemned the Duvalier regime. The visit had a catalyzing effect on the Haitian clergy, including the liberal Catholic priest Jean-Bertrand Aristide, who began agitating for social justice.[58] In 1984, in response to mounting food prices, riots broke out in Gonaïves. Angry crowds invaded a warehouse stocked with provisions from the aid agency CARE and launched assaults on the local prison and police. Throughout 1985, Gonaïves erupted in student protests over government efforts to control Haiti's young people. On November 28, 1985, when army troops fired on hundreds of protesters and killed at least three, the United States suspended foreign aid to Haiti. In February 1986, following a mass insurgency, the military forced Jean-Claude Duvalier into exile.[59]

The end of the Duvalier dictatorship encouraged many exiled Haitians to return, establish democratic parties, and revive trade unions. In March 1987, a new constitution was ratified, and elections were scheduled for November 1987. Elections were stopped and the new constitution suspended when massive violence erupted and the military was alleged to have massacred voters. Two hundred people died that day. New elections took place on January 17, 1988, but these were neither safe for voters nor truly democratic. The Haitian military essentially installed Leslie Manigat, a returned Haitian exile who had worked in France as political science professor at the Sorbonne, as president. Manigat's rule lasted only four months.[60]

At the end of the Duvalier regime, Haiti's unemployment rate stood at 60 percent. The average annual per capita income was US $300.[61] Haiti's poverty, its economic dependence on foreign investors, and the atmosphere of political renewal after the end of the Duvalier dictatorship allowed Reilly to secure smooth sailing for the *Khian Sea* into the harbor at Gonaïves. Haiti's 1987 constitution contained provisions for environmental protection. It even included a ban on the import of wastes. But with the constitution being suspended and reinstated, these provisions were of little significance.[62]

After more than a year at sea, the incinerator ash from Philadelphia would be discharged. Equipped with the import permit that the mysterious US business-man had transferred to the *Khian Sea*, Reilly managed to find a Haitian import partner. On December 3, 1987, Antonio Paul, a brother of the military officer Jean-Claude Paul and a resident of Port-au-Prince, applied to Haiti's port authority for an import permit. Antonio Paul represented the company Eleveurs de l'Ouest (Cultivators of the West), which planned to import two hundred thousand tons of "topsoil fertilizer" in powdered form from Philadelphia.[63] On December 22, 1987, the *Khian Sea* anchored at Sedren Wharf in Gonaïves. Amalgamated hired about thirty local Haitians to discharge the cargo. By means of a ramp installed on the barge and a crane on board the ship, the ash was loaded onto trucks for transport about three hundred meters inland.[64] With a permit allowing for the importation of over two hundred thousand tons of ash, it appeared as if Amalgamated and Paolino could fulfill their contracts to dispose of all Philadelphia's ash.

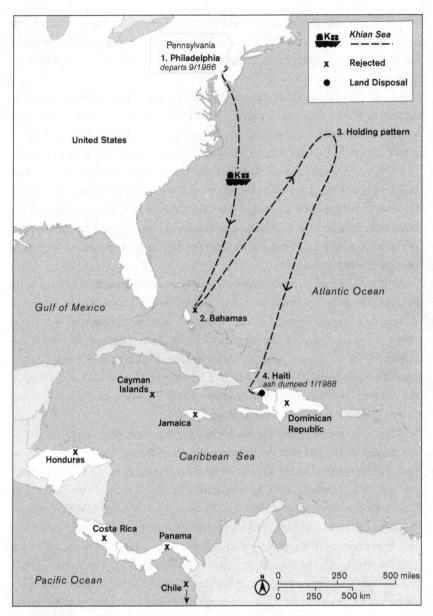

The *Khian Sea*'s voyage through the greater Caribbean before landing its cargo of ash in Gonaïves, Haiti. Map by Ben Pease.

Waste Protests as a Test for Haitian Democracy and Beyond

The Haitian radio stations Radio Haiti-Inter and Radio Lumière were the first to politicize the story of the unloading of the Philadelphia ash in Gonaïves. On January 2, 1988, Radio Haiti-Inter aired a lengthy report in Créole about the landing of a ship loaded with toxic ash, called the *Khian Sea*. This ship, according to Radio Haiti-Inter, had set up at a private dock "yon waf yon ansyen konpayi ki te konn cheche richés anbaté" (of a former company that used to search for wealth) and was now unloading garbage. The radio also reported that protests had erupted, although the situation and the government's position was still unclear.[65]

News institutions, particularly radio—the *presse parlée*, the spoken word—had played a fundamental role in nourishing the democratic movements. Broadcasting in Créole rather than in French, the language of the elite, they soon became the voice of resistance in a country where the illiteracy rate was as high as 50 percent in the 1980s and less than 10 percent of the population spoke French fluently. (Créole was not recognized as an official language until 1987.)[66] The Duvaliers had sought to tightly control the news media, and there was little that resembled a free press under Duvalier *père*. With the change of power from father to son, some restrictions had been relaxed.

In 1980, Haitian journalism, spearheaded by *Le Petit Samedi-Soir*, Radio Haiti-Inter, and Radio Soleil, became more critical of the Duvalier regime. Radio Haiti-Inter, founded in 1935, was Haiti's first and most prominent independent radio station. In 1968, Jean Dominique, an agronomist turned charismatic journalist, bought the station. He became the station's news anchor, speaking out against oppression and corruption while advocating for human rights and celebrating Haitian culture and heritage.[67] In the weeks and months following the landing of the *Khian Sea*, Radio Haiti-Inter and the Catholic church-funded radio station Radio Lumière served as a network for the initiation and communication of protest. Their coverage of the situation in Gonaïves and the government's lack of response alerted listeners all across Haiti to the drama.

With about fifty thousand inhabitants, Gonaïves, in the northwest of Haiti, was the country's fourth largest city. It was also one of its most economically depressed cities. The port at Gonaïves had once been used by international trading vessels and local fishing craft, but in the 1960s François Duvalier closed it down in a move to concentrate shipping in Port-au-Prince. The port reopened in February 1986 but was little used. Aside from the port, the only industry was some unprofitable limestone mines around Gonaïves. Gonaïves was wedged between a region of fertile, irrigated rice fields to the south and the northwest peninsula, an area frequently suffering from drought. The city is surrounded by a desertlike area, made so in large part by the indiscriminate cutting down and burning of trees to produce charcoal. Farmers could barely make a living. Many people in Gonaïves had taken the arrival of the *Khian Sea* as a good sign, bringing jobs and money. For many of the locals who helped unload the ship, the work was their first paying job in months. When, in late January, Haiti's Ministry of Commerce put a temporary stop to the discharge of the cargo, many of the workers protested.[68] Yet as more became known about the *Khian Sea* and the potential toxicity of its cargo, this initial support for the undertaking disappeared.

Haitian opposition against US waste imports became closely entangled with the country's processes of political, economic, and social realignment after the fall of Duvalier. People from all social sectors, including returning expatriates, came forward to exercise their right to participate in political life.[69] Residents formed neighborhood committees to address issues ranging from urban improvements such as street cleaning, planting trees, and painting colorful graffiti and murals to water and power supply and the construction of schools and medical care centers.[70] In this outbreak of participatory citizenship, the Créole-speaking and agrarian population of Haiti living outside the capital of Port-au-Prince—about 80 percent of all Haitians—took an active role. Throughout much of the Duvalier dictatorship, this population had shown little interest in politics, assuming that one elite government would be as good or bad as any other. Yet the ousting of Duvalier in 1986 was their achievement. "Aba lan mizè, aba Duvalier" (down with misery, down with Duvalier) had been the war cry that resounded all over the country, and particularly from Gonaïves.[71]

In 1988 those neighborhood committees opposed the unloading of the *Khian Sea* as an exercise in environmental citizenship. Among them were the Komite Tet Ansanm pou Onè Respè Konstitisyon an (Joint Commission for Honoring the Constitution) and Jeunesse Ouvrière Chrétienne (Young Christian Workers). The environmental group Fédération des Amis de la Nature–Haiti Verte (FAN), founded in 1986, became the key partner for Greenpeace on the *Khian Sea* issue before the Collectif Haïtien pour la Protection de l'Environnement et un Développement Alternatif (COHPEDA) took a more prominent role in the 1990s.[72] For people in Gonaïves, the ash from Philadelphia quickly turned from an economic opportunity into the epitome of environmental racism born from foreign intervention and the ineptitude of Haiti's political leaders.[73] Activists from Gonaïves interpreted the *Khian Sea's* waste as a sign that the United States "did not respect Haiti."[74] The problem was, one activist said, that "in the eyes of other nations," Haitians did not exist for themselves: they existed "for the good of others."[75]

Political protest had a long history in Gonaïves. It was the city where Haiti's Declaration of Independence was issued in 1804, where protests had ushered in the fall of Duvalier, and also where substantial violence had overshadowed the election of November 1987. In early 1988, a controversy had erupted over the import of rice, as well as tomato paste, bicycles, and appliances from the US to Gonaïves. This trade had continued illegally after being banned by the government. For three months at the end of 1986, a "small civil war" had raged between peasants growing rice in the Artibonite Valley south of Gonaïves and the dockworkers from Gonaïves, in the course of which one man was killed and many more wounded. One side had built barricades along the national highway to stop imported "Miami rice" from reaching Haitian markets and undermining domestic prices. The other side responded with its own street barricades to stop locally grown rice from Artibonite, which was more expensive than the rice from the US, reaching the northern provinces. Both the local authorities and the army stationed at Gonaïves simply stood by and watched the drama unfold. In the end, most people blamed the situation on Americans seeking to destroy the local economy by flooding the market with cheap imports.[76]

The arrival of the ash from Philadelphia deepened the anti-American sentiment in Gonaïves, and the antipathy soon extended to all foreign investors. On February 18, 1988, the executive vice president of First City Development, an American-owned corporation active in Haiti, sent a letter of "formal complaint" to the assistant secretary for inter-American affairs at the US State Department, declaring that a "yet to be named US Corporation and/or other entities" had both "damaged our property and embarrassed us in the eyes of our host country," Haiti. Gonaïves was part of a mining concession granted to First City Development by the Haitian government; the company used the port as a transit station before shipping materials to Japan. First City Development had no wish to jeopardize its relationship with the Haitian government through association with "those who are trying to make Haiti a dumping ground for US garbage." Moreover, Haiti had already "enough problems without also becoming the trash dump for the City of Philadelphia."[77]

On January 31, 1988, the Haitian minister of commerce, Mario Celestin, ordered a stop to the discharge of the *Khian Sea*'s cargo, referring to Article 258 of the Haitian constitution, which forbade the importing of any kind of wastes to Haiti. Additionally, he ordered the crew to reload the ash and find a different dump site.[78] On February 4, 1988, Haiti's minister of justice and the government commissioner to the Civil Court of Gonaïves met with William Reilly and Drew L. Latham, the operations manager of Amalgamated, to discuss the reloading of the *Khian Sea*. They were granted until February 16, 1988, to complete the task.[79] Meanwhile, Haiti's immigration service kept the passports of the ship's crew.[80] Testifying later before a US court, the captain, Arturo Fuentes Garcia, recalled an increasingly threatening attitude toward the crew. Haitian soldiers came "and told me to pick up the cargo back, what we had already put outside, to put it back on board and leave."[81] On the night of February 4, the *Khian Sea* clandestinely left Gonaïves. According to Fuentes, he had received instructions "from the company to leave as soon as possible."[82] A small part of the ash had been reloaded. Some three thousand tons of it remained on the beach for someone else to deal with.

After Haiti's national elections in January 1988, the neighborhood committees of Gonaïves had asked the newly elected government to take care of the ash. This request crescendoed after the *Khian Sea*'s departure. On February 18, 1988, President Leslie Manigat announced that he wanted to build a wall around the ash and get it tested for toxic chemicals and heavy metals. He formed a commission within the Ministry of Health to investigate the ash. The population of Gonaïves was afraid President Manigat, a returned expatriate dependent on the goodwill of Haiti's military, would have neither the power nor the resources to follow through with his plan.[83] Following the fall of Duvalier, people had watched their new, well-meaning, but often inept interim government fail to ease their poverty, to curb police abuses, or to purge wealthy Duvalier cronies from bureaucracies.[84] The "Miami rice" episode had illustrated the indifference of the government in Port-au-Prince. Why should things now be any different with the ash still lying around at Sedren Warf?

Haiti's new political opposition used the incident to discredit the government of President Manigat. On February 3, 1988, the Bloc Unitaire Patriotique, a coalition of three Haitian opposition parties, published an official statement in Créole demanding the "respect of all other peoples and nations" for Haiti and calling on the Manigat government to prosecute the people who had dumped the toxic waste.[85] Some days later, Louis Dejoie II from the National Agricultural and Industrial Party (PAIN) used the opportunity to make himself the spokesperson of the "vast majority of the population" that condemned the dumping of foreign waste on Haitian shores.[86] Likewise, Mobilization for National Development, the runner-up to Manigat's party in the 1988 election, remarked on this "new form of genocide, conceived and carried out with the complicity of some senior national officials," at Gonaïves.[87] According to the political opposition, the situation showed that the Manigat government was only a "puppet government" made up of "fake nationalists" that in their search for "land, for power, for money, for food, for relationships" had been turning "against the people."[88]

The municipal government at Gonaïves attempted to quiet its citizens by employing repressive methods recalling those of the Duvalier dictatorship, such as "spying and prosecuting."[89] Yet, by the end of February, when the government had still not offered any proposal for removing the ash, and rumors were spreading about another waste ship, the *Bark*, heading toward Haiti, people's outrage could no longer be suppressed. Radical, even violent measures were suggested, targeting the United States, foreign waste traders, and its own indolent government.[90] According to Haiti's central workers' union, the Centrale Autonome des Travailleurs Haitiens (CATH), the "hatred of Haitian authorities" and of "foreign capitalism" hung "over the heads of the people of Gonaïves, who are already living in misery, in mud, in disappointment, in shame despite our historical past."[91]

In response to the rumors about the arrival of the *Bark*, an alliance of neighborhood committees, labor unions, Christian youth groups, women's rights groups, and conservationists organized a protest march in Gonaïves on March 25, 1988.[92] The galvanizing moment for all of these groups was less environmental or health concerns than the obvious defiance of Haiti's new democratic structures, including the constitution, and the inability of the Port-au-Prince government to do anything about it.[93] The discharge of Philadelphia incinerator ash had become a test of Haiti's democracy.

The protests in Gonaïves were highly politicized. Protesters had chosen a significant date for their march: March 25 marked the first anniversary of Haiti's new democratic constitution.[94] Gonaïves's military commander, Colonel Gambetta Hippolyte, worried that violence and uproar would again spread from Gonaïves to the rest of the country. The military started interrogating the march's leaders and intimidating residents. A military training exercise was conducted in plain sight, and a revolver was placed at the steps of Radio Soleil to intimidate the staff.[95] Hippolyte warned the organizers against moving forward with their march. At the last minute he intervened "by force of arms" to prevent it from taking place. A second protest march scheduled for May 8, 1988, was similarly suppressed.[96]

On May 10, Manigat finally addressed the situation, promising that the ash would be removed. Later a report reached Greenpeace activists about a "man from Long Island, New York," who had "taken it upon himself to clean up the ash pile" for free. The man had allegedly been donating his company's services to the Haitian government and brought his own vessel down to Haiti. Over the summer, he shoveled the ash into individual barrels and developed plans to return the ash to the United States for disposal at a site in northern New York State.[97] When, in the fall of 1988, a delegation from the Young Christian Workers investigated the situation, they encountered a mess. They reported finding 655 barrels of ash, 268 of them "very badly closed," 28 "only covered with a simple little plastic," and 61 barrels "fully open without any protection whatsoever." Their protests went unheard, however, as Haiti was by then battling once again for the survival of its democracy.[98]

Leslie Manigat, brought to power in early 1988, soon fell out of favor when he attempted to govern Haiti without military intervention. In June 1988, Manigat was overthrown by General Henri Namphy, who, in turn, was overthrown in September 1988 through the coup of General Prosper Avril, a former member of François Duvalier's Presidential Guard and a political adviser to his son.[99]

Haiti's political instability was central to the story of the *Khian Sea*. Instability created the legal loophole that allowed for the import of Philadelphia incinerator ash, despite Article 258 of the 1987 constitution. Instability also gave rise and lent momentum to the various popular committees and organizations, including FAN, that cast the disposal of the ash as a challenge to Haiti's democracy. In the end, it was this instability that eliminated any chance of having the ash removed or restoring "respect" for Haiti and its people.

FOUR

"The Most Tested Ash on This Planet" | *Producing and Discarding Standards of Toxicity*

Orange rinds, beer bottles, day-old newspapers. Junk mail, aluminum foil, chicken bones. Cigarette butts, old shoes, dead batteries. Coffee grinds, half-eaten hot dogs, tin cans. It was trash, like all trash, the refuse of everyday life collected door-to-door and trucked to an incinerator in Philadelphia's Roxborough neighborhood.

JERRY SCHWARTZ | "Ship Filled with Garbage Ash Still Sits off U.S. Coasts after 14 Years," Associated Press, September 4, 2000

The camera shows a long close-up of the man's white sneakers, his stomping movements, and the way black dust particles swirl up and cover the shoes with a dark, greasy film, before it zooms out to capture the entire scene. In blazing sunlight, a tall white man (Western, to judge by his clothes) and his Afro-Caribbean guide are walking on a mound of black ash about three meters high and fifteen meters long, covered with limestone rocks. Every now and then the white man bends down to pick up small items from the mound. Eventually he finds something he recognizes, a half-burnt snippet from the *Philadelphia Daily News.* "There is no mistaking," he says, "whether this is Philadelphia ash. An apartment for rent at Eleventh. A two-bedroom, door-to-door carpeting, US $385 a month."[1]

In late January 1988 US journalists, politicians, and environmentalists following the Bulkhandling's attempted disposal of ash in Panama realized that another waste ship, the *Khian Sea*, had long since left Philadelphia. A Philadelphia news team set out to search for the ash that had disappeared from Paolino's pier on the Schuylkill in September 1986, as did Greenpeace activists. Eventually they found it at a "remote beach" in Gonaïves, Haiti. The footage of the ash dump, shot by a crew from WPVI, a Philadelphia TV station, showed unpaved roads, made slippery and muddy by oily runoffs, and close-ups of Caribbean children's faces with runny noses, swarmed by flies. Then they turned to views of Caribbean beaches, palm trees, and glistening white sand, casting Gonaïves as an "unspoiled spot, before the ash arrived." An off-screen voice says that one of the villagers "told us sarcastically to say thanks to the people who sent this down here, for what the villagers call *déchet toxique*—the toxic ash."[2]

International price disparities for waste disposal made it attractive for US waste haulers to seek offshore disposal sites. This system worked as long as no party in the transaction questioned the differences in the valuation of human life and the environment that underpinned these disparities. The cargo of the *Khian Sea* and the *Bark* could simply have been handled like any other trash: collected from homes and businesses and trucked to one of Philadelphia's two incinerators. From there it could have been burned and carted away as refuse to a landfill in New Jersey, as fill material to a land-reclamation project in Panama, or as fertilizer to farms around Gonaïves, Haiti. But when Philadelphia's ash was transformed into *déchet toxique*, it became unwelcome anywhere.

In the fall of 1987, first Panama, then Haiti, and then other nations in the global South began to question the scientific evidence offered to them that certified Philadelphia incinerator ash as nontoxic. Their refusal to accept what the American traders presented as objective knowledge shook the foundations of Philadelphia's waste deals, along with many others. It discredited not only the traders but also the scientific and administrative institutions and laboratories involved, Philadelphia's city agencies, and even the EPA. As these actors attempted to regain credibility, Philadelphia's incinerator ash became not only the most tested, but also the most *contested* ash on the planet.[3]

Dioxins and Incinerator Ash

The troubles with Philadelphia ash abroad had their roots in the rise of waste incineration across the United States. In the early 1980s, multiple cities, the waste industry, and the EPA had all considered a new generation of waste-to-energy (WTE) incinerators as a solution to municipal waste crises. WTEs reduced the weight of waste by two-thirds and generated energy.[4] Proponents claimed that

WTE was a "proven technology" with "no health effects."[5] Given Mayor Wilson Goode's assertion that there was "no way" recycling could eliminate the waste crisis, WTEs appeared to be Philadelphia's only alternative to landfilling.[6] Goode projected that the new WTE incinerator in South Philadelphia would burn as much as 70 percent of Philadelphia's trash, and unlike curbside recycling, it would require no changes to the city's trash collection procedures.[7] Nationwide, some experts predicted that WTE would handle half of all US waste by the end of the twentieth century.[8]

WTE incineration sounded like the ultimate panacea, except for some of its byproducts—dioxins and furans. These endocrine-disrupting chemicals did not originate in the collected waste, as heavy metals did. They were created during the process of incineration when lignin, a component of wood and paper, was burned with garbage that contained chlorine, which is present in almost anything made of plastic or vinyl. Dioxins and furans are toxic and carcinogenic. Both persist in the environment for a long time. They are virtually insoluble in water but accumulate in fat tissues and so bioaccumulate in the food chain.[9]

These chemicals came into public awareness in the United States after World War II as trace compounds found in herbicides, and particularly from their presence in Agent Orange, a defoliant heavily used by US forces in Vietnam.[10] They gained notoriety in 1983, when the CDC evacuated the entire town of Times Beach, Missouri, because of dioxin contamination.[11] Municipal incinerator ash as a source of dioxins gained attention as scientists developed the technology to measure concentrations of chemicals in parts per trillion. While dioxin contamination levels had been very high in areas sprayed with Agent Orange and at Times Beach, they were comparatively low in incinerator ash.[12]

A key question concerning Philadelphia's incinerator ash was whether it counted as hazardous waste under the provisions of the Resource Conservation and Recovery Act (RCRA) of 1976. At the time, almost all incinerator ash in the United States came from incinerators burning municipal solid waste—that is, household waste, which typically included food waste, newspapers, plastic bottles, cans, food packaging, foil, and household batteries. With the proliferation of single-use plastics, however, household waste was becoming a more problematic category.[13] RCRA offered guidelines on how to classify waste as hazardous based on the material's ignitability, corrosivity, reactivity, and toxicity, but it also provided exemptions from these rules. Household waste and the incinerator ash created from it were exempted.[14]

The EPA was aware of the issue but slow to take a position on it. In 1980, when

RCRA went into effect, the agency acknowledged that incineration concentrated some substances, such as heavy metals, and that it created other toxic compounds, such as dioxins. The agency announced that it intended to regulate incinerator ash as hazardous waste in the future. In 1984 Congress amended RCRA through the Hazardous and Solid Waste Amendments (HSWA), but it continued to exempt household waste from classification as hazardous and did not clarify the legal position on incinerator ash. Incinerator operators were left guessing whether their product constituted hazardous waste and, if it did, whether it qualified under the household waste exemption.

In 1985, after the HSWA amendments, the EPA maintained the exemption for household waste, which also applied to incinerator ash as long as there were no "toxic characteristics . . . found in ash residue." While acknowledging that some incinerator ash might count as hazardous, the EPA did not specify any testing procedures for incinerator operators to follow. In 1987, at a hearing before the Senate Subcommittee on Hazardous Waste and Toxic Substances, EPA spokesperson J. Winston Porter declared that incinerator ash would generally be considered nonhazardous. In 1988, after the storm over the *Khian Sea*'s cargo, the institution went back to its vague and unclear statement of 1985.[15]

The EPA's intentions in this policy were deregulatory and pro-recycling. Were the EPA to declare incinerator ash as toxic, went the reasoning, disposal costs would increase dramatically. This would induce cities to return to already overused landfills rather than to focus on incineration, a practice that the agency encouraged as "recycling" given that the latest incinerators functioned as WTE facilities.[16]

US scientists were divided on the harmfulness of incinerator ash. Most experts contended that incinerator ash was nontoxic after a complete burn, that is, incineration at 1,800 degrees Fahrenheit or higher, as this would destroy furans and dioxins. Some disagreed, among them the biologist and environmental activist Barry Commoner, a prominent figure since Earth Day 1970, and the chemistry professor Paul Connett from St. Lawrence University in upstate New York.[17] Among the US public, suspicion grew about the harms of incinerator ash.[18] Under Commoner's leadership, protests were held in New York City in 1985, followed by protests in New Hampshire, Vermont, and Massachusetts.[19] In the greater Philadelphia area, two proposed WTE incinerator plants—one in Plymouth, Montgomery County, and Mayor Goode's project in Naval Yard, South Philadelphia—attracted fierce opposition.[20] A group of angry citizens from Plymouth founded an organization "to fight trash with T.R.A.S.H. (Township

Residents Against Scandalous Hazards)." South Philadelphia activists organized under the name of the Trash to Steam Alternative Coalition and joined forces with the Clean Air Council of Delaware Valley, the Delaware Valley Toxics Coalition, the Public Interest Law Center, and about nineteen other community groups from South Philadelphia.[21] As the Goode administration continued its efforts to expand WTE incineration, opponents bused thousands of people to Philadelphia City Hall with signs, gas masks, and other props to participate in the city council's public hearings.[22]

The protests reflected an erosion of trust in scientific evidence produced or validated through state institutions. Connett contended that the waste industry was "run by the Mafia," and activists complained about a lack of transparency, alleging that institutions kept information locked up.[23] Vince Termini, head of a neighborhood initiative from South Philadelphia, announced that his group was "not going to trust any health experts the Mayor hires."[24] The roots of this distrust went back to the administration of Ronald Reagan, who had moved the United States government away from the pro-environment stance of the 1970s.[25] Anne Gorsuch, Reagan's appointee as EPA administrator, used her tenure to significantly roll back environmental legislation. She shifted responsibility for policymaking and implementation back to the states and proposed significant cuts to the agency. Key positions remained unfilled, hampering the agency's ability to fulfill its regulatory and scientific duties.[26] Press reports about an irregularity in the EPA's hazardous-waste program, dubbed Sewergate, eventually led to an official investigation, in the course of which Gorsuch resigned. Attempting to limit the political damage, Reagan brought William D. Ruckelshaus, the EPA's first administrator, back to the agency. But public trust in the EPA was only slowly regained.[27]

The EPA also struggled in its scientific assessment of incinerator ash. When the agency was founded, its primary concern was pollution—environmental harms considered as "real and observable, capable of abatement." During the 1970s, according to the researcher Sheila Jasanoff, "risk, or the possibility of adverse effects, displaced pollution as the watchword for the new regulatory era."[28] In a landmark case in 1976, installing a form of the precautionary principle, the Court of Appeals for the DC Circuit ruled that certainty of harm was not a prerequisite for regulation. This decision allowed the EPA to restrict industrial activity even on the basis of imperfect knowledge.

While this change from a focus on observable pollution to the possibilities of adverse effects allowed the EPA greater regulatory authority, it also led the agency into gray areas of scientific inquiry. It was now responsible for assessing the possible harms of hundreds of pollutants that were widespread and detectable at minute concentrations, with limited understanding of how to determine safe levels of exposure. Meanwhile, seeking to prevent effects that were largely hypothetical, it employed methods of demonstrating risk that were novel, untested, and frequently controversial.[29]

Wrestling over Data

In Philadelphia, the controversy about dioxins and possible new WTE incinerators merged with a controversy about the city's existing two incinerators. Citizens around the Northwest incinerator in Roxborough had complained since the 1960s about the odors, vermin, and smoke created by the ash pile.[30] In 1983, the notion was raised that something in the ash might be making people sick. The US Centers for Disease Control and Prevention (CDC) conducted a study that indicated a 5 percent excess incidence of cancer among the population exposed to emissions from Philadelphia's Northwest Incinerator.[31] A year later, as fingers were pointed at dioxins, New Jersey's Department of Environmental Protection issued a ban on the landfilling of Philadelphia's incinerator ash.[32] Congressman Lawrence Coughlin (R-PA) initiated a congressional debate, and a Virginia group called Concerned Citizens launched a campaign against Philadelphia ash being trucked to their county.[33]

Addressing these concerns, EPA's Region III office worked with the City of Philadelphia to investigate possible contamination. Between 1984 and 1986, both organizations conducted tests to determine the levels of heavy metals and trace organic chemicals in Philadelphia ash. They used the method standard at the time: the extraction procedure (EP) toxicity test or leachate test. This entails dripping a mildly acidic water through the ash, which causes compounds to leach into the water. If the collected leachate exceeds certain levels of any one of eight heavy metals or six pesticides, the ash is considered hazardous. In a series of seven tests run by the city between December 1984 and February 1986, only one reading of the incinerators' ashes was in excess of hazardous waste thresholds. This was the reading for lead, which was 31 percent above the threshold. Since tests did not consistently show hazardous waste readings, the city concluded that the ash was nonhazardous and safe to deposit in a wetland area in Bocas del Toro, Panama.[34]

The EPA's tests turned up a conundrum concerning dioxin levels in the

Northwest incinerator's fly ash, that is, ash collected in the incinerator chimneys. A 1984 test showed TCDD, the most toxic form of dioxin, present at an alarming rate of 13.1 parts per billion (ppb). This was ten times higher than levels ever detected elsewhere. A task force with representatives from EPA Region III, the Commonwealth of Pennsylvania, and the City of Philadelphia ordered a new study of the ash, including an air-quality risk assessment, soil analysis, ash-pile analysis, water-quality analysis, and evaluation of incinerator operating procedures. Samples from the ash pile *next* to the Northwest incinerator returned readings of 26 to 89 parts per trillion (ppt) for TCDD. Soil analysis within a two-mile radius detected no dioxins or furans. Similarly, water-quality analysis showed no measurable dioxins in edible fish tissue two miles downstream from the sampling site, supporting EPA Region III's conclusion that "there was no water quality problem."[35] Concerning the dioxin in the ash pile next to the incinerator, EPA Region III consulted with the Centers for Disease Control and received assurance that dioxin levels of less than 90 ppt did not pose a significant health threat. Dismissing the much higher dioxin levels in fly ash from the earlier testing as insignificant, EPA Region III announced in January 1986 that Philadelphia incinerator ash was "harmless" and "no threat to public safety."[36]

When Bulkhandling approached the city of Changuinola in Panama about accepting incinerator ash from Philadelphia, they cited these test results certifying that the ash contained levels of heavy metals and dioxins "well below levels deemed hazardous under US toxic waste regulations."[37] The assessment lost currency when environmentalists pointed out the delicate nature of the wetlands and mangrove forests around Bocas del Toro where the ash would be deposited. Greenpeace had Philadelphia's ash retested. Testing now employed not only the standard EP toxicity test but also a more aggressive leaching method. For those already opposing the deal, the results added to the suspicion that something was wrong with Philadelphia ash, the EPA as a regulatory institution, and its testing methods. The independent analysis of the waste detected up to 260 ppt of dioxin, significantly higher than the "negligible" 89 ppt detected by the earlier tests. Additionally, Greenpeace's tests showed that 250,000 tons of ash contained more than 5,900 tons of heavy metals: aluminum, arsenic, chromium, copper, lead, mercury, nickel and zinc.[38] According to the Greenpeace report, such quantities in the ash were enough "to pose a danger if it were used in a road project" through marine and freshwater environments that were the chief breeding ground of the white shrimp, Panama's chief food export.[39] Alerted by protests in Panama, the Agency for International Development (USAID) and the US embassy in Panama made inquiries about the ash. The US ambassador in Panama wired the US State Department warning of the chilling effect it would have on international relations if the United States shipped dioxin-laced ash to foreign allies.[40]

Finally, EPA officials at the highest level became involved. Following Greenpeace's publication of the new test results in September 1987, half a dozen EPA branches and other institutions hurriedly collected and reevaluated existing data from the 1984–86 tests, cited new studies in environmental toxicology in aquatic environments, and brought their conclusions before the EPA's inspector general, the agency's internal watchdog.[41] Two weeks later, the inspector general published a report titled *Flash Report: Philadelphia Incinerator Ash Exports for Panamanian Road Project: Potential Environmental Damage in the Making*. Contrary to the assessment of EPA Region III, the report concluded that Philadelphia incinerator ash would "potentially endanger human health and the environment if it [were] dumped into Panamanian wetlands." Concentrations of dioxins were "higher than some of those identified at Times Beach, Missouri, in 1983," and the retested samples contained levels of lead, cadmium, and benzene, a substance newly included in testing, that occasionally exceeded hazardous-waste thresholds. The inspector general publicly urged the EPA to disclose all the test results so that Panamanian authorities could make a "a fully informed decision."[42] Internally, the inspector general recommended against exporting the contaminated ash to Panama.[43]

EPA's senior officials noticed the hidden accusations of irresponsibility embedded in the report and went back to the 1984–86 test results themselves. Contrary to the inspector general's report, a report from EPA headquarters determined that Philadelphia's ash was "a non-hazardous waste" and that the agency's "original assessment of no imminent danger to human health and the environment is accurate."[44] Meanwhile, EPA headquarters also sent a private ten-page memorandum to its inspector general that went through the *Flash Report* point by point, indicating where information was "factually correct, but misleading," sentences "factually incomplete," or statements simply "incorrect."[45] The atmosphere was frosty between the executives of the EPA and its inspector general.

The most important difference in the two reports was that while both considered the same object—Philadelphia incinerator ash—and the same scientific evidence, they did not consider them in the same context. The inspector general's report considered the use of incinerator ash in a land-reclamation project in a mangrove and wetland area in Panama. EPA headquarters analyzed and responded with their eyes on incinerator ash awaiting its disposal in a US sanitary landfill, where the key concern was leachate, and its potential harmfulness to local residents. In the latter context, means were available for the monitoring and control of leachates and gas emissions. Moreover, the site for a sanitary landfill is selected in part on the basis of geology that minimizes the possibility of wastes leaching out of it.[46] In contrast, in Panama the dioxin-contaminated ash would have been deposited as material for a road built through a wetland area that provided a source of food. The road itself might stimulate local development and draw even more people to settle, exposing a higher number to the contaminants.[47]

Trusting Your Senses or Trusting US Data?

For actors in the greater Caribbean, it was difficult to contextualize the scientific, administrative, and foreign policy aspects of the debate on Philadelphia's incinerator ash taking place in the United States. An "air of uncertainty" rose, according to Augustin Luna, an official at the Panamanian Ministry of Health, which made it more and more "unlikely that [Philadelphia] ash would be permitted to be shipped."[48] But almost all greater Caribbean nations were forced to work with the scientific evidence presented to them by US vendors. Few had the resources to conduct their own tests for heavy metals or other chemicals in parts per billion, much less parts per trillion.

In the US, environmental toxicology was a relatively young scientific field that had developed as an independent discipline in the late 1950s. By the 1980s, it owed much of its reputation among the public, activists, and policymakers to environmental scientists and activists, among them Rachel Carson, who had introduced Americans to concepts such as acute and chronic toxicity, parts per million, reproductive effects, and carcinogenicity.[49] Other industrial nations had also developed capacities in environmental toxicology, but in the greater Caribbean, only Cuba and the French overseas territories of Guadeloupe and Martinique had much science infrastructure. In much of the region during the postwar era, governments struggled to provide even basic education.[50] When William P. Reilly approached businessmen in Honduras to negotiate the import of Philadelphia ash on board the *Khian Sea*, the Hondurans asserted that no laboratory in the country "was qualified to make the proper lab analysis of this material."[51]

Possible import partners attempted to improve their negotiating position by asking for additional tests on the waste material. The contract between Paolino and the Bahamas-based company Amalgamated, for instance, stipulated that

Paolino arrange for tests in an "independent testing laboratory acceptable to Amalgamated so as to ensure that the nature and characteristics of the material comport with the written representation and test analysis reports of the City of Philadelphia as to the nonhazardous, non-toxic, inert nature and characteristics of the material."[52] When Reilly negotiated with potential import partners in Honduras, he provided them with a sample of the ash and an analysis of the material made by an independent laboratory in Philadelphia. He planned for representatives from Honduras to visit the US so that they could assess the incineration process and inspect places where incinerator ash was similarly used as fill material. Edgardo Pascall, the potential Honduran partner, in turn planned to have another lab test the ash, with results being sent "directly to the undersigned. . . . All with the purpose of assuring us of the harmless nature of this material."[53] Finally, should evidence prove that "material when tested in accordance with applicable EPA procedures, fails to meet EPA standards for non-reactivity, non-corrosivity, non-ignitability, and non-toxic leachate," the Americans would be held liable for the ash and would return it to its source.[54]

Despite all these measures, greater Caribbean nations lost trust in US data. Their suspicion was grounded not in differing interpretations of the scientific data but in their observation of public reactions in the United States. "If [the Americans] thought that this waste wasn't dangerous," asserted the Honduran Ecological Association, "then they wouldn't be sending it to us in the first place."[55] Luna of the Panamanian Ministry of Health announced that Panama would not accept Philadelphia incinerator ash "for the same reason six states in the United States won't accept it."[56] It did not help the situation when the Philadelphia streets commissioner, Harry M. Perks, responded patronizingly that he did not know "what kind of standards [they were] using down there," but Philadelphia considered the ash to be safe.[57]

Overseas concern about the harmfulness of US incinerator ash in turn undermined Philadelphians' trust in official scientific evidence. Local groups who had been fighting against the city's existing incinerators argued that if the ash was bad for Panama, "what about the people up here?" The EPA inspector general's comparison of the ash to the soil of Times Beach was not lost on Philadelphians.[58] At an emergency meeting in November 1987, about sixty people crammed into the 5th Police District headquarters to meet with EPA officials to discuss the removal of a 150,000-ton mound of incinerator ash at the site in Roxborough.[59] A local reporter covering the meeting noted that she had talked to people who felt that "if EPA does not come out and say there is a hazard posed by the ash, then they will feel that the report is a whitewash."[60] The discussion in the United States was fueled by a report published by the Environmental Defense Fund (EDF) in November 1987.[61] The EDF had conducted independent studies of incinerator ash at nineteen incinerators all around the United States, including Philadelphia's. Their analysis confirmed that burning trash concentrated toxic substances contained in the waste stream and that incineration itself led to the formation of other toxicants. It supported the EDFs position that, contrary to the EPA's assessment, incinerator ash should be classified as hazardous waste.[62]

In the greater Caribbean, the result of this shift in attitudes was to cast deep suspicion on any waste deal proposed by US American waste traders. Reports by the EPA and independent US laboratories were equally discredited. It no longer mattered whether the proposed imports consisted of treated rather than untreated incinerator ash (that is, ash from which most contaminants had been removed), whether the trader was Paolino or Bulkhandling, or whether the cargo was untreated waste from New York City, sewage sludge from Los Angeles, or incinerator ash from Baltimore. It was all unwelcome. Amalgamated and the *Khian Sea* were the first to experience this shift when, in the fall of 1987, Reilly approached Panama about importing waste, possibly unaware of the country's dealings with Bulkhandling. At the time, the *Khian Sea* was anchored in Panama to take on food and fuel. Informed that the ship might also leave its cargo behind, the Noriega government acted swiftly. Soldiers of the Panamanian Defense Forces boarded the *Khian Sea* and told the captain to leave immediately.[63]

Reinventing Philadelphia Ash as Topsoil Fertilizer

Paolino and Bulkhandling both responded to the new hostile atmosphere with a new tactic. Using the loopholes provided by weak environmental governance in most Caribbean and Central American nations, they changed the description of their cargo. As Reilly entered successive negotiations with different nations, he transformed "incinerator ash" into "general cargo" and then into "bulk construction material." By the time the *Khian Sea* reached Haiti in December 1987, the ship was carrying "topsoil ash fertilizer."[64]   *rebranding toxic waste*

This tactic might have worked had it not been for local environmental groups. In the midst of the discharge, local conservation groups, among them the Federation of the Friends of Nature (FAN), condemned the hauling and scattering of US waste on Haitian soil. News of citizen protests in Gonaïves reached Haiti's capital, Port-au-Prince.[65] By January 15, 1988, the Haitian Ministry of Commerce had officially requested the Haitian Bureau of Mines and Energy to inquire into what was going on with the "possible import of products . . . by the Mining Company called 'First City Development.'" On arrival in Gonaïves, they found no sign of First City Development but only the *Khian Sea* discharging incinerator ash that, according to a manifesto signed by the captain, contained "potentially toxic detritus"—not "top soil fertilizer," as noted on the import permit.[66] According to Article 258 of Haiti's 1987 constitution, which prohibited "the introduction of waste of any kind on national territory," the discharge of the *Khian Sea's* cargo was illegal. On January 21, 1988, the Haitian Ministry of Commerce issued a press notice reminding "the public in general and traders and importers in particular" of the provisions of Article 258.[67] Although the communiqué did not explicitly mention the *Khian Sea*, the context was clear. Still, the ministry took no action.[68] The indecisive response was due to underlying political and economic considerations, as well as the possible complicity of Haitian government officials in the deal.[69] Although the constitution banned waste imports, General Henri Namphy's interim military government had not been indifferent to the economic benefits that came with such deals.[70]

Yet public attention made it nearly impossible for the Haitian government to ignore Article 258. Put on the trail of the ship through Haitian protests, first the attaché of the US embassy in Port-au-Prince and then a local TV team from Philadelphia and a team from Greenpeace descended on Gonaïves.[71] The US attaché reported to Washington that he had found incinerator ash with "bits of plastic in it" and a ship that "looks like a derelict" with the exterior "completely rusted."[72] Greenpeace activists undertook a more detailed investigation of the site. Supported by FAN, they took samples from the ash and its surroundings, which they sent to laboratories in Germany and Guadeloupe, in addition to taking some home to the United States. They spoke with Haitian activists and politicians, organized a press conference for the people of Gonaïves, and unfurled a banner in Créole, French, and English with their interpretation of the material. It read, "Danje: Danger . . . Toxic Garbage from USA."[73]

As the situation escalated, Coastal Carriers' president, John Patrick Dowd, came to Gonaïves.[74] He carried three thousand copies of the scientific reports on Philadelphia incinerator ash that Paolino had commissioned in 1986. Dowd planned to distribute these reports at a press conference where he intended to "clarify any misunderstandings."[75] Additionally, Dowd offered his own body as living proof of the harmlessness of the *Khian Sea's* cargo. Filmed by FAN activists and surrounded by Haitian dock workers, local press, and activists from FAN,

Dowd staged a scientific demonstration with himself as the guinea pig: "It's not toxic waste. It's not radioactive. . . . It's household ash, it's burned incinerator. You can come over and look for yourself what it is," he invited the audience. "We are not sick, there is no smell, and there are no flies," he announced. The grand finale came when Dowd popped a handful of the ash into his mouth, ate it, and boasted: "See, it's edible! No danger. . . . That's how worried I am about its toxicity."[76]

In his imitation of the food tasters of antiquity, who sampled foods to detect poison before their employers ingested them, Dowd reduced the scientific complexity of modern risk assessment—thresholds and doses, acute and chronic toxicity, and the timing of an organism's exposure—to one quick and simple test. Would he exhibit an immediate and acute reaction from eating the ash? His performance was intended to send the message that dioxins, furans, and heavy metals were as readily detected as poisons.[77] If a toxic substance did not have immediate effects, it did not pose long-term risks.[78]

Soon after the unloading of the *Khian Sea*, however, locals reported changes in their community and environment. One of the workers said his daughter was sick and that there were rumors the ash was "killing goats and chicken." Local farmers were afraid "to eat fish from nearby waters."[79] The findings of Greenpeace investigators appeared to confirm Haitian suspicions. Although some parts of the ash heap had been covered with limestone gravel, others had not. The wind was blowing directly from the ash to the nearest human settlement across the bay, exposing the residents to the risk of inhaling very fine airborne particles. In addition, the ash contained mercury, which might be entering the marine ecosystem.[80] "I know this ash is no good," a local environmentalist told Greenpeace, "if not now, then in six, eight, ten years."[81] By the end of January, the people of Gonaïves had formed their own view about the *Khian Sea*'s cargo, one that Dowd could not alter. They called it *déchet toxique*—the toxic ash.[82]

Greenpeace toxics campaigners soon realized that the term *déchet toxique* carried many possible meanings. To local people, it translated as "venom," an immediate and acute threat.[83] At a Greenpeace press conference, people's main concern was radioactivity. Greenpeace struggled to communicate the possible ranges of toxicity and risk to the people of Gonaïves in a moment when even US science and environmental governance was divided on standards and thresholds. Patiently, the Greenpeace spokespersons tried to describe the potentially harmful characteristics of the ash. "We don't have any reason to say that there is any radioactivity in this ash. . . . Otherwise, I wouldn't even have it." They were going to test it in different laboratories in Germany, Guadeloupe, and the

United States and expected to find "heavy metals, dioxins, furans, and some other chemicals. We doubt very much that there is radioactivity."[84] Years later one of the Greenpeace spokespersons remembered the anxiety and tension at the press conference. Part of Greenpeace's campaigning strategy was the arousal of emotions, yet in Gonaïves there was "so much concern that we even felt [we] had to downplay it. . . . Saying it was toxic, it might as well have been plutonium. There might have been a panic. We had to be moderate."[85]

NEW MARKETS, NEW EXPERTS

While the *Khian Sea*'s Haitian drama was playing out, Bulkhandling was involved in its own drama in Philadelphia. After the company had lost the deal to ship ash to Panama, it was forced to let ash from the incinerators pile up on its pier on the Delaware, an old sugar refinery in South Philadelphia. This sparked local opposition. Greater Media, Inc., and a number of other businesses adjacent to Pier 60 filed a lawsuit against Bulkhandling involving the roughly thirty thousand tons of incinerator ash held there and the noxious fumes and smells coming from it. The resulting consent order allowed Bulkhandling to continue using the site as an ash transfer and processing facility until March 15, 1988.[86] After that date, the company would have to pay a fine of $10,000 a day—more than an average day's operating cost for a ship at sea.[87] Bulkhandling opted for two alternatives. It arranged to dispose of half the ash at a landfill in Ohio. The other half was loaded onto a ship for transfer to a destination abroad. On February 4, 1988, Bulkhandling's ship, the *Bark*, left Philadelphia without a clear destination. News of this departure caused great anxiety in the Caribbean. Numerous countries threatened Bulkhandling should the ship attempt to land there.[88] More than a month after the *Bark* had left, Bulkhandling's parent company, Klaveness, announced that Philadelphia ash was destined for the West African nation of Guinea.[89]

This selection of a destination across the Atlantic brought in new experts to assess the situation and the harmfulness of Philadelphia's incinerator ash. Aluko International Society (Société Internationale Aluko Guinés, SIAG), a Guinean company with an established partnership with Klaveness, had bought the cargo for US $117,450. SIAG's main business was shipbreaking and the production of steel sheets and rebar. The company intended to use the ash for a new product, similar to concrete, which it would market in West Africa as fill for roads and railroads. The Klaveness group was to deliver the ash and the production technology, while SIAG intended to build a factory near Guinea's capital, Conakry.

The cargo of the *Bark* would be the first shipment in an arrangement that involved the import of up to one hundred thousand tons of incinerator ash.[90] The Guinean government had issued import licenses to SIAG despite a two-year prohibition against foreign wastes entering Guinea. Bulkhandling had apparently assured officials that the *Bark*'s cargo of "bulk construction material," as it was described in the shipping papers, was nontoxic, nonhazardous, and nonwaste.[91] On February 16, 1988, the *Bark* arrived at Kassa Island, a small island off the coast close to Conakry. Its population of about five thousand people lived primarily by farming and fishing.[92] The crew and local workers unloaded the shipment in a bauxite quarry some twenty-five meters from the seashore. Then the *Bark* left for Freetown, Sierra Leone.[93] The Guinean government apparently did not know that its cargo of "construction material" was in fact highly controversial incinerator ash from Philadelphia.[94]

When the *Bark* left Philadelphia without disclosing its destination, however, Greenpeace was on its trail, using international shipping services and its own extensive network to trace the ship. When they found the ash on Kassa Island, they informed Guinean officials about the potential contamination of the ash with heavy metals and dioxins, the fact that other nations had already rejected the cargo, and the likelihood that the workers involved in the manufacture of the new product would be at risk.[95] Greenpeace passed on information from the US Agency for Toxic Substances Disease Registry (ATSDR), which in the wake of the EPA inspector general's investigation had released a "health consultation" recommended for anyone who came into contact with Philadelphia ash. The agency recommended that "on-site workers . . . wear proper personal protective equipment and exercise proper personal hygiene."[96] But a photograph documenting the unloading of the *Bark* by *Jeune Afrique*, a weekly magazine, showed four men standing in front of a mound of ash, their backs to the viewer. Instead of the recommended full body suits, working boots, goggles, gloves, and other protective gear, three of the men wore gumboots and another sneakers, with baseball-style caps.[97] On the island, locals reported that what they had taken to be sand smelt foul and that trees and other vegetation were dying.[98] Guinea officials responded by isolating the mound of ash, taking extensive samples from both the ash and the bricks already manufactured from it, and setting up a government committee to vet all similar chemical imports. The president of Guinea, Lansana Conté, asked islanders who had come into contact with the ash to register with the government, saying, "They may be able to claim compensation if they develop illnesses."[99]

Guinea consulted international experts to assess the toxicity of the ash and its harmfulness. Lacking scientific resources, as many Caribbean countries did, the Guinean government turned to the United Nations. Since Guinea's independence in 1958, international institutions and aid and development programs from both sides of the Cold War had been sending experts to assist with the development of its economy, agriculture, and health and educational systems. The United Nations Environment Programme (UNEP) now helped Guinean officials find laboratories abroad that could perform tests for heavy metals and trace contaminants. Guinea drew on UNEP's INFOTERRA and its International Registry for Potentially Toxic Chemicals (IRPTC). Both programs were pillars of UNEP's strategy to "pool knowledge, information, and experience . . . all over the world" for "containing and combating" environmental problems.[100] INFOTERRA, set up in 1973 as an international system for environmental data exchange, started operating in 1977.[101] The IRPTC was set up in 1976 and collected political and scientific information, including the chemical characteristics of certain elements, their uses, and products that contained them. UNEP also kept a record of products were banned or restricted in participating countries and the reasons why.[102]

Through these channels, experts from the Harwell Laboratory in the United Kingdom, the US EPA, Greenpeace, and the Canadian, Irish and Swedish national focal points of INFOTERRA responded within days to Guinea's request. British specialists advised Guinea to move the ash onto an impenetrable rock layer and surround it with drainage ditches to prevent winds blowing it around until a permanent solution was found. A toxicologist based in Europe informed them that ash with low concentrations of dioxin and heavy metals could be dumped safely only in specially created landfills where impervious clay linings prevented seepage—which Guinea did not have.[103] Another expert contended that the ash, "although it can contain heavy metals and dioxins, if properly disposed of does not present a public health or environmental hazard."[104] All this advice, however, was issued from a distance, without inspecting the site on Kassa Island or testing the ash. Since the potential toxicity of any incinerator ash varied depending on the input and the source, the advice was in any case of limited use.

In the event, the Guinean government took these recommendations, combined with local observations about the changing environment on Kassa Island, to mean that the *Bark*'s cargo was harmful. Designating it as toxic waste, in April 1988 they ordered Bulkhandling to immediately remove the ash and return it to the United States.[105] Bulkhandling responded that it no longer owned the ash and was not responsible for its removal. Meanwhile, SIAG, the Guinean company that

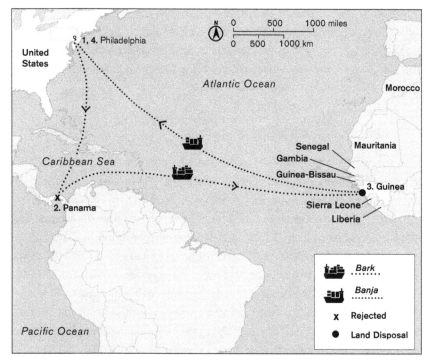

The voyage of the *Bark* from Philadelphia to Kassa Island, Guinea, and the return journey of the rejected ash on board the *Banja*. Map by Ben Pease.

technically owned the ash, had disappeared.[106] Matters stalled for some weeks, allowing Bulkhandling to believe that it was off the hook. But on June 4, 1988, after other waste import scandals had shaken West Africa, Guinean police arrested Sigmund Strømme, the honorary Norwegian consul general and Bulkhandling's agent, along with two Guinean trade ministry officials. Another ten government officials, many of them from the Guinean Department of Commerce, which had signed the deal, were arrested a week later.[107]

Strømme's arrest finally prompted a reaction from Bulkhandling and Klaveness. Company officials held discussions with the EPA about an ocean dumping permit, along with the EPA's possible assistance in returning the material to the United States.[108] Klaveness quickly buried their plan to import the ash to Norway (where Strømme's arrest had also made headlines) to be used in the manufacture of construction material in a factory in Bergen. Norwegian building and cement workers all across the country had joined in a protest against receiving toxic waste from Philadelphia.[109] Despite the intervention of the Norwegian foreign office, the Guinean government declared that it would release Norway's honorary consul only after the removal of the ash.[110] Klaveness and Bulkhandling gave in. On July 6, 1988, the ash was reloaded onto a Klaveness barge, the *Banja*, and began its journey back to the United States.[111]

"Hysteria" versus Market Rule

The story of the *Bark*'s cargo did not end with its return to the United States. The return of the material allowed the EPA to attempt to regain its scientific credibility in the United States and abroad. US laws stipulated that any imported material needed to be proved harmless. Given the contractual situation, the ash on board the *Banja* originated from Guinea, and existing lab reports on the material were now invalid.[112] As the *Banja* approached Philadelphia in mid-July 1988, it was greeted by a team of toxicologists and waste management experts from the EPA Region III office and the Pennsylvania Department of Environmental Resources (DER). A number of tests were run to assess the amount of heavy metals, trace contaminants, furans, and dioxins. The agencies would use these results to determine once and for all whether the ash was hazardous.[113]

In contrast to the Guinean dock workers with their baseball caps, sneakers, and gumboots, US officials arrived in full protective clothing. From a helicopter, Philadelphia's WPVI TV station filmed half a dozen figures in white jumpsuits, protective headgear, and footwear, goggles, gloves, and respirators boarding the *Banja*.[114] On July 22, both environmental agencies announced that "the ash cargo of the *Banja* has tested non-hazardous under the applicable Pennsylvania and Federal regulations." Particular attention had been paid to cadmium and lead, two elements of significant concern in incinerator ash, and both were below the regulatory threshold. EPA Region III's director, Leon Gonshor, stated that "based on the tests of the ash residue samples, the cargo has been determined to be non-hazardous and will not be required to be disposed of as a regulated hazardous waste."[115] The underlying message was that the EPA had been right all along.

This statement enabled the traders involved to claim that they had been judged according to an environmentalist agenda based on faulty scientific analysis. Representatives of both Bulkhandling and Coastal Carriers criticized the EPA, which they claimed had failed to protect US companies through its inability to vouch for the validity of its test results. Bulkhandling asserted that it had shipped Philadelphia ash to Guinea only after the EPA had certified "that said municipal incinerator ash was not hazardous or a threat to human health or the environment." Hence, the company had fallen prey to "unfounded allegations . . . made to the Guinean Government" by Greenpeace and others, which led to the imprisonment of Sigmund Strømme, and to "strenuous demands by the Guinean Government." Meanwhile, they had been abandoned by the EPA, which had refused to recertify the harmlessness of the cargo. In his letter to the EPA, Bulkhandling's lawyer concluded: "A grave, painful, costly injustice was groundlessly inflicted on both Bulkhandling and its representatives in Guinea by the grossly misleading erroneous inflammatory statements which caused the Government of Guinea to react as it did after the Philadelphia ash was unloaded in good faith."[116]

Coastal Carriers sang a similar tune of unfair treatment and financial hardship. The company stated that it had paid out close to $1 million on behalf of the *Khian Sea*'s charterer, Amalgamated. As expenses amassed, it had received no repayment from Amalgamated, which, in turn, had received no payment from Paolino. In March 1989, Coastal Carriers filed for bankruptcy. According to its vice president, William P. Reilly, Coastal Carriers had been driven to insolvency by the inaccurate assessments of the toxicity of the ash. "We were entirely confident," said Reilly, "but it's the first time in the 30 years of my business experience that I ever saw a business completely destroyed and nullified by hysteria and misrepresentation in the press, and by perhaps some pressures from environmental groups."[117]

Reilly asserted that traders had relied on the EPA's original judgment that the cargo was nonhazardous. The EPA's further inspection of the *Khian Sea*'s cargo in March 1988 had also determined the ash to be nonhazardous according to US thresholds. Yet "the cargo was represented in the media as being hazardous and toxic" because the press did not listen to scientific facts but rather to "rumors" spreading from Philadelphia. "Once a story gets in the world media and world press, it has a life of its own," complained Reilly. In response, "absolute hysteria set in on behalf of the government authorities" of the foreign countries approached about receiving the ash.[118]

Reilly blamed the situation not only on the press but also on environmentalists, some of whom had "very great goals," such as an international ban on waste exports. He asserted that these groups employed dirty tricks and treated the *Khian Sea* "as a particular whipping boy." Coastal Carriers and Amalgamated "got caught in the middle."[119]

There was no winner in this dispute. The EPA had done everything by the book, from using testing methods, such as the EP toxicity test, that were standard at the time, to assessing incinerator ash according to US regulations for its disposal in a sanitary landfill. Environmentalists and the EPA inspector general looked at the particular contexts the ash would be discharged in, which in their view called for stricter standards. The waste traders felt mistreated by environmental activists and the media and betrayed by the EPA. Ultimately, the journey of Philadelphia's incinerator ash reveals the political, economic, scientific, and moral controversies inherent in the task of producing global standards and thresholds of toxicity. It is emblematic of the state of environmental science and governance in the 1980s, battling internally over risks and future possible effects while battling externally with public and corporate expectations about setting and enforcing standards for hazardous waste disposal.

FIVE

American Rules in a Global Environment | *US Hazardous Export Regulations, from Caveat Emptor to Prior Informed Consent*

We know that you don't have the power to stop a transaction, but
for goodness sake, we are all on the same planet.

CONGRESSIONAL REPRESENTATIVE JOHN CONYERS | to EPA representative
Sheldon Meyers, House Government Operations Environment, Energy, and Natural
Resources Subcommittee, July 14, 1988

On July 14, 1988, the heat and humidity in Washington, DC, were relentless. Two nights previously, powerful thunderstorms had swept through the area, ending a weeklong period of record heat and a string of unhealthy air quality readings. The storm had uprooted trees, toppling them onto cars. Power had been cut to more than forty thousand homes, two police stations, and a prison in Montgomery County, Maryland. The storm had struck during rush hour and knocked out lights in Red Line metro stations from Friendship Heights to Shady Grove, so that passengers had had to stumble down stalled escalators lit only by emergency illumination. The rain had come down so fast that most of the water had just run off, doing little to end an unusual drought in the Washington area.

More than forty-eight hours after the storm, traces of its destruction were still visible, as Capitol Hill staffers, Congressional representatives, and invited experts all rushed through the Rayburn House Office Building, equipped with what little information they had on US waste exports. As of the morning of July

14, 1988, there had been no news from the *Khian Sea* since it had illegally left its anchorage in lower Delaware Bay on the night of March 22. No one—least of all Amalgamated and Coastal Carriers—would or could give details of its whereabouts, let alone the fate of its waste cargo. The boat's last known location was somewhere near the Cape Verde islands, off the northwest coast of Africa. Meanwhile, the *Bark*'s cargo of Philadelphia incinerator ash was due to be returned to the United States on board the *Banya*.[1]

In Washington, DC, Representative John Conyers (D-MI) was about to address the situation before the House Government Operations Environment, Energy, and Natural Resources Subcommittee, consisting of more than fifty congressional representatives, staffers, and invited experts. They had invited the assistant secretary for oceans, international environment, and scientific affairs at the US State Department, members of the Greenpeace Global Toxics Campaign, staff of the Philadelphia Streets Department, the inspector general for the US Environmental Protection Agency (EPA), and fellows of the Federation of American Scientists. Subcommittee members also intended to interview the director of environmental affairs at Waste Management, Inc., and the representative of the Office of International Affairs at the EPA. They sought to speak with everyone available who had been involved in the export of Philadelphia ash, yet the invitation list showed signs of arbitrariness. Waste Management, the United States' largest waste disposal company at the time, had had no dealings with the *Khian Sea*. Yet, because the actual waste haulers involved—Paolino, Amalgamated, Coastal Carriers and Bulkhandling—had made themselves unavailable, Waste Management seemed to be there to represent the business side of things.

The House Committee on Government Operations, its members, and its subcommittees were powerful agents in the US political arena, with oversight jurisdiction over the entire government, and legislative authority.[2] The committee's function was to study government operations with a view to economy and efficiency. In 1988, it had seven subcommittees, dealing with topics ranging from health care, national security, and information technology to energy and the environment.

In an emotionally charged statement, Conyers opened the session by observing that as they were meeting, children were playing "on mounds of Philadelphia incinerator ash in Guinea, West Africa," which, "as was well known," contained heavy metals and dioxins, substances that could "cause learning disabilities, cancer, congenital defects, and the rest." American companies that exported hazardous waste were "taking advantage" of countries that had "no ability to handle [the] problem." The importing nations were "debt-ridden countries" where "corrupt officials are easy payoff targets for exploiters seeking cheap and easy outlets." Moreover, in such countries, "inadequate port facilities . . . , substandard roads with children and farm animals," and possibly "little understanding of the health hazards involved in these substances" made the safe handling of toxic wastes a challenge. The subcommittee had not assembled to discuss the "international export of US hazardous waste," insisted Conyers. They were there to discuss US "toxic terrorism."[3]

Outside Rayburn House, where the meeting was in session, protests were erupting. With presidential elections coming up in November 1988, the contest between the Republican candidate, Vice President George H. W. Bush, and the Democrat, Massachusetts governor Michael Dukakis, was already heating up. Initially, Bush had focused on environmental issues to set himself apart from President Ronald Reagan. Dukakis had a stronger record on environmental issues and was not burdened by association with Reagan's almost anti-environmental stance. But Dukakis had unresolved environmental issues in his own backyard, such as the pollution of Boston Harbor.[4] Meanwhile, Greenpeace's Toxics Campaign, with activists wielding banners, drums, and flyers, was exerting pressure on local and national politicians and traders in exporting and importing nations to revisit the practice of the unequal trade with waste.

Officially, the purpose of the House subcommittee meeting was to review the United States' waste-export program. Unofficially, some of those present were using it to advance their own political agenda. On June 29, Republican Senator Robert Kasten had introduced the Waste Export Control Act, S. 2598, into the Senate to prohibit the export of US waste unless it could be proved that transport, treatment, storage, and disposal were done in a manner providing environmental protection no less strict than required in the United States. On July 12, only two days prior to the subcommittee's meeting, Conyers had introduced his Waste Export Prohibition Act into the House of Representatives as a more far-reaching alternative. If Kasten's bill was passed, current legislation on the export of hazardous waste would be refined. Conyers's bill would amend the Solid Waste Disposal Act of 1965 and fundamentally alter the principles of US export policy on hazardous material to prohibit all exports to any country around the world, except for those with a bilateral agreement existing before the act, that is, Canada and Mexico.[5]

Foreign Liability and the Export of Banned Pesticides

The subcommittee's discussions had a political and ideological legacy that reached back decades. Legal experts, environmental and human rights activists, administrators, and congressional representatives had long wrestled with the moral and legal issues involved in the export of consumer products, drugs, pesticides, and chemicals that a US regulatory agency had determined to be unsafe for domestic use or consumption.

This issue had its roots in the mid-1950s, when the United States public became increasingly aware of the environmental and health hazards of the country's nuclear capabilities.[6] Concerns about chemical pollution gained prominence throughout the 1960s with the publication of Rachel Carson's *Silent Spring.*[7] Skillfully, although not single-handedly, Carson alerted her readers to the misuse of pesticides and herbicides, with tales of invisible chemical poisons contaminating the world.[8] The book brought to public attention scientists' concerns over chlorinated hydrocarbons (such as DDT, aldrin, dieldrin, and chlordane), organophosphates (such as parathion and malathion), and other synthetic chemicals. Farmers had used these substances after World War II to control mosquitoes, lice, and insect pests on crops, understanding little about their effects on human health and the ecosystem. *Silent Spring* explained how organophosphates bioaccumulated in the environment and biomagnified in the food web until reaching toxic levels in top predators such as the bald eagle, and how exposure to organophosphates, functioning as potent neurotoxins, inhibited the function of cholinesterase, an enzyme critical to nerve function.[9]

Debates on the indiscriminate use of pesticides had led the EPA to ban the use of several synthetic chemicals in the United States. Among them were the infamous pesticide DDT (banned in 1972), but also less well-known substances such as Kepone (chlordecone, banned in 1975) and Phosvel (leptophos, banned in 1977).[10] In 1975, the EPA suspended the sale of the pesticides chlordane and heptachlor, which had been widely used on farm crops, including corn and tobacco.[11] The Consumer Product Safety Commission also expanded its list of substances banned for use in consumer products, such as the chemical flame retardant tris(1,3-dichloro-2-propyl) phosphate (TDCPP). Little did these agencies realize that their bans would lead to the stockpiling of the banned substances in massive amounts all over the United States—on farms, in shops, and on the premises of chemical manufacturers. Salable products had been transformed into hazardous waste. Moreover, the bans had not ended the production of these chemicals or prohibited their export abroad. In their mission to protect US residents, the agencies were complicit in creating an unequal system of global hazard distribution.[12]

Throughout the 1970s, US companies exported large quantities of nonsalable products, chemicals, and other hazardous substances to countries where these items were still legal commodities, primarily in the developing world. In the 1970s and 1980s, these countries collectively imported about US $500 million worth of chemicals annually (of a total international trade in bulk chemicals of US $90 billion annually). Additionally, banned or nonsalable pesticides found their way to the global South through humanitarian aid agencies, such as USAID and the United States Export-Import Bank, under the umbrella of the Green Revolution.[13] Since 1941, when the Rockefeller Foundation had sent three scientists to Mexico to study how to improve the nation's food production, the idea of bringing modern industrial agriculture to developing countries had formed part of the agenda of Western scientists and policymakers.[14] Pesticides banned in the United States were part of the technology transfer intended to convert the people of the global South to a Western way of life. Two years after DDT was banned in the United States, USAID bought old stockpiles of the pesticide and shipped it to India, Ethiopia, Nepal, Indonesia, South Vietnam, and Haiti for malaria control and agricultural development projects.[15]

Many countries in the global South had no legislation governing the importation, domestic use, or disposal of potentially toxic chemicals. Few maintained the facilities to monitor the effects of these products on human health or the environment. Even if laws were in place, governments still faced problems in implementing them.[16] Pesticide registration, where it existed, required little to no preliminary government testing and was largely based on information supplied by the manufacturer—who was not obliged to disclose that a substance had been banned or suspended from use in the United States.[17] Overall, 29 percent of all pesticides exported in 1976—161 million pounds—had never been registered for use in the United States because their dangers had become apparent during the registration process.[18] US companies did not produce these toxic products specifically for export abroad: rather, export was a convenient way to legally empty warehouses of massive amounts of stock of chemicals suspended from sale in the United States that had turned almost overnight into hazardous waste.[19]

Until 1978, US export transactions in hazardous substances were subject to little regulation. Under US law, three administrative agencies were responsible for monitoring the manufacture and distribution of potentially hazardous products and their regulation in both foreign and domestic markets: the Consumer Product Safety Commission (CPSC), the Food and Drug Administration (FDA), and the EPA. Each agency had jurisdiction over particular products and was charged with the administration of a particular statute, such as the Federal Insecticide, Fungicide, and Rodenticide Act (FIFRA), the Toxic Substances Control Act (TSCA), or the Federal Hazardous Substances Act (FHSA).[20] Prior to 1978, hazardous exports from the United States followed the principle of caveat emptor (let the buyer beware). It was the foreign recipient's responsibility to check the quality and suitability of the substances for their purposes—and to come up with remedies for ills resulting from the substances' use.[21]

In the 1970s several cases of pesticide poisonings challenged the notion of caveat emptor. In 1973, the World Health Organization (WHO) reported that an estimated 250,000 cases of pesticide poisoning occurred annually in the global South, of which about 6,700 were fatal.[22] Workers were often unaware of what chemicals they were using, how to apply them properly, or the hazards the chemicals posed. Labeling requirements did not include detailed warnings about the hazards of a product, and manufacturers usually did not provide information in any other language than English.[23] In 1971, the US-manufactured pesticide Phosvel killed over one thousand water buffaloes and an unknown number of people in Egypt. In 1972, the consumption of grain coated with a mercurial fungicide banned in the United States (intended for use as seed grain) caused the deaths of several hundred people in Iraq. In 1976, malathion, used to control malaria-carrying mosquitos in Pakistan, poisoned some 2,500 workers and killed five of them.[24] By 1978, WHO identified pesticide poisonings as a serious problem in many nations in the global South.[25]

Information about the harms of US pesticide exports spread slowly in the United States, until a group of environmentalists saw it as an opportunity to expand the US National Environmental Policy Act (NEPA) of 1969. To challenge US federal actions abroad, they followed the example of civil rights activists and used the tool of the citizen suit. In 1975, a group of environmental advocacy groups, led by the Environmental Defense Fund, sued USAID under NEPA, seeking the preparation of environmental impact assessments with respect to *all* USAID activities affecting the environment and specifically with respect to pesticide exports.[26] When President Richard Nixon signed the act, Congress had not intended it to apply to US actions abroad. With the lawsuit, environmentalists pushed the question of what role NEPA played in protecting the global environment. USAID agreed to prepare environmental impact statements for its pesticide exports.[27] Other court cases, including one against the Export-Import Bank, were less successful. US federal courts largely avoided extending US environmental policies, concluding that NEPA was procedural rather than substantive—that is, it did not prescribe an outcome.[28]

President Carter's Hazardous Substance Export Policy

Congress appeared unconcerned about the foreign-policy implications of NEPA until the tris sleepwear scandal of 1977–78. Tris(1,3-dichloro-2-propyl) phosphate (TDCPP) is a chlorinated organophosphate with a variety of applications ranging from pesticides and plasticizers to nerve gases. In the United States, it was used as a flame retardant in garments, including children's pajamas. Growing evidence suggested that tris could cause cancer in children exposed to it. Children wearing fabrics treated with a similar compound were found to have mutagenic byproducts in their urine.[29] The Consumer Product Safety Commission banned the domestic sale of tris-treated sleepwear and fabric in April 1977 and required US manufacturers to repurchase distributed garments. The ban left unresolved the disposition of these garments, in addition to hundreds of thousands of yards of tris-treated fabric that could no longer be sold in the United States. For more than a year after the ban, suppliers legally shipped approximately 2.4 million sets of children's pajamas to Asia, Africa, and South America.[30] News about these exports caused a national and international outcry. *Mother Jones*, an investigative journalism magazine, called them "the corporate crime of the century."[31]

In response to the scandal, Congress amended most of the statues that regulated the export of hazardous substances in 1978. The amendments introduced new standards for the collection and dissemination of data. The amendments now required exporters to inform the appropriate US administrative agency, be it the EPA, the FDA, or the Consumer Product Safety Commission, that products banned in the United States were to be exported. The respective agencies then had to inform the foreign governments about these exports.[32] The seeds were sown for a new US foreign trade policy concerning hazardous materials, one based not on caveat emptor but on prior informed consent. Theoretically, the exchange of information between buyer and seller would allow the foreign government to make an informed decision about any hazardous substances coming its way. In practice, as the members of the House Government Operations Environment, Energy, and Natural Resources Subcommittee learned during their meeting on July 14, 1988, ensuring prior informed consent was no simple task.

In addition to these amendments, President Jimmy Carter initiated the In-ter-Agency Working Group on a Hazardous Substances Export Policy (HSEP) to review US export policy more generally. The group was convened by Esther Peterson, a women's and consumer advocate, who in 1978 directed the Office of Consumer Affairs. It included representatives from the State Department and the Departments of Agriculture, Commerce, Energy, Health, Education and Welfare, Justice, Defense, Labor, and the Treasury. The EPA, the Consumer Product Safety Commission, the Export-Import Bank, the Overseas Private Investment Cor-poration, the Nuclear Regulatory Commission, the Office of Management and Budget, the Council on Environmental Quality, and other White House groups were also represented.[33] The diversity of the group demonstrated a political will to address the problem from every angle. It also raised the question of whether so many cooks might spoil the broth.

The key question for the HSEP group was how much consumer and envi-ronmental protection free trade could tolerate. Free trade—that is, the idea that restrictions on exports and imports should be minimal—had dominated US foreign trade policy for much of the twentieth century. In 1934, Franklin D. Roosevelt had signed the Reciprocal Trade Agreements Act, which that gave the president the authority to negotiate bilateral tariff agreements between the United States and other nations.[34] In 1947, the United States was the driving force in the creation of the multilateral General Agreement on Tariffs and Trade (GATT). By 1980, US tariff rates on imports had fallen from 60 percent in 1930 to 5.7 percent.[35]

The trade in hazardous substances challenged this liberalizing trend. A growing number of US politicians worried about the integrity of the label "Made in the United States," asking how foreign consumers could trust the quality of US chem-icals if they were the basis of environmental and health scandals.[36] The question had not only economic but also political implications. In the 1970s, the Soviet Union's reputation for aiding developing nations had suffered a blow when the Aswan High Dam in Egypt, a project financially supported by the USSR, had been associated with a major health hazard. Prior to its completion, epidemiologists warned that the dam would increase the incidence of schistosomiasis, a blood disease caused by a water-borne parasite whose effects range from abdominal pain and diarrhea to liver damage, kidney failure, infertility, and bladder cancer. Epidemiologists argued that the impoundment of the Nile River would increase the population of the snails that were the intermediate hosts of the parasite. Moreover, the regulation of water levels downstream from the dam would make the Nile more accessible to people, which would increase the risk of exposure to the parasite.[37] The US Council on Environmental Quality cited studies showing that infections among farmers had jumped from 5 percent to 65 percent since the dam became operational.[38] Although later epidemiological studies would prove that schistosomiasis in Egypt had actually decreased, the scare was real, and the harm to the Soviet Union's image was done.[39] US politicians were keen that the United States should not suffer damage to its reputation as a result of toxic exports.

Meanwhile, free-trade advocates warned that the introduction of tariffs, regulatory measures, or a ban would threaten the liberal international trading order. They argued that the application of US environmental and consumer protection standards to exported goods would hamper the ability of US companies to compete in international markets.[40] These arguments were persuasive at a time when US exports were low: by 1984, the US trade deficit had reached US $123.3 billion.[41] Advocates of free trade feared that a restrictive export policy would exacerbate the trend. Regulatory measures to protect foreign buyers' health and the environment would adversely affect domestic manufacturing output, jobs, and prices.[42] Pressure on the HSEP working group to reconcile these two positions rose as importing nations demanded more information on and regulation of the export of hazardous substances.[43] At the United Nations Environment Programme Governing Council meeting of 1977, the Kenyan minister for water development, Julius Kiano, warned that "developing countries [would] no longer tolerate being used as dumping grounds."[44] In May 1977, UNEP issued a resolution calling on nations not to permit the export of hazardous substances without the knowledge and consent of the importing nation.[45]

For two and a half years, the HSEP working group met with representatives of affected industries, labor, and public interest groups, and discussed five successive drafts of its policy recommendations.[46] The fundamental problem it identified was that the United States had no consistent export policy regarding hazardous substances. Different government agencies acted under different and often conflicting statutory mandates. Confusion existed as to whether the agencies had the authority to halt a trade scheme on health or environmental grounds. In August 1980, the working group recommended that the US Congress clarify the agencies' powers over hazardous exports once and for all.[47] It proposed a multistage review of all products, processes, and substances banned or restricted in the United States and a program under which exporters would have to notify the government of their intention to sell hazardous goods abroad.[48]

Neither the HSEP working group nor environmental activists called for an export ban on hazardous substances that were produced but not marketed in the United States. Both parties reasoned that while such a ban could prevent harm to foreign users, it would not stop US companies from manufacturing the same substances abroad or deter foreign users from purchasing such substances from a third-country source.[49] Environmental advocacy groups, politicians, and administrators argued that an outright ban would hamper foreign governments in obtaining products they needed and would shift the decisions about what was best for foreign sovereign nations from foreign governments to the US Congress.[50]

At the end of his tenure, President Carter implemented the working group's policy recommendation to universalize the United States' hazardous-substances export policy. It was a final pro-environmental act in a presidency that had been characterized by frugality, environmentally sensitive retrenchment (Carter had solar panels installed on the roof of the White House), and an attempt to enforce an energy policy that required Americans to pay more for energy while consuming less of it. Carter had signed a bill regulating strip mining; the Comprehensive Environmental Response, Compensation, and Liability Act (Superfund), which gave the EPA new powers to go after producers of toxic waste; and the Alaska Lands Act, which protected over 100 million acres of land as wilderness areas, national parks, or wildlife refuges.[51] On January 15, 1981, he signed Executive Order 12,264, titled "On Federal Policy Regarding the Export of Banned or Significantly Restricted Substances." The order created a uniform notification system governing exports of "banned or significantly restricted" products and substances. First, it required the improvement of export notice procedures and the annual publication of US government actions banning or severely restricting substances for domestic use. Second, it directed the State Department and other federal agencies to help develop international hazard-alert systems. Third, it required agencies to institute formal export-licensing controls. Carter's executive order significantly strengthened the information collection and dissemination processes needed for a hazardous export policy based on informed consent.

One month later, on February 17, 1981, the new president, Ronald Reagan, revoked Carter's executive order. To the conservative Reagan, it represented another example of government interference in commercial affairs.[52] Reagan had based his election campaign on the question of how much health and environmental protection the US economy could afford. Once in office, he set out to dismantle US environmental regulations. Reagan's revocation of the executive order had support from many potentially affected industries, such as the Pharmaceutical Manufacturers Association, which warned that the order would cause sales to go to foreign firms.[53] As part of a strategy to first delay and then bury the issue altogether, Reagan asked for yet another review of the existing US hazardous-substances export policy. This review called for further market liberalization through a number of changes, the most controversial being the withdrawal of a ban on drugs and potential biological warfare agents that had not been approved for use in the United States.[54] Under Reagan, according to one Democratic representative, US companies could continue to export "whatever they [could] convince unsuspecting people abroad to buy."[55]

The Introduction of Prior Informed Consent

Reagan's overhaul of Carter-era policies was not primarily concerned with waste exports. In the midst of its deliberations, the HSEP working group had decided to exclude hazardous waste from its policy recommendations. This was a decision that had tremendous impact on future policy implementation: it irrevocably differentiated waste from consumer products, creating a policy path dependency that made it impossible for future campaigners or policymakers to link the two issues, irrespective of their similarities. In the shorter term, however, the split created an opportunity to reform the Resource Conservation and Recovery Act of 1976 (RCRA), which governed the management and disposal of waste in the United States, with a view to addressing foreign environmental policy concerns.

For the HSEP working group, this split had been a deliberate decision. Those working on hazardous waste had feared that the work on consumer products, let alone a combined approach, would close a window of opportunity.[56] By 1980, the tris sleepwear scandal had faded from the news, but the catastrophe of Love Canal made national headlines and reinvigorated people's worries about hazardous waste. In the small neighborhood in Niagara Falls, New York, partly built on landfill, chemicals from the fill leached into the groundwater and resurfaced, harming the health of hundreds of residents.[57] The scandal drew attention to the flawed regulation of hazardous waste in the United States and allowed the HSEP working group to also draw attention to the international implications of such mismanagement. The Love Canal incident occurred just as RCRA was coming into effect. RCRA substantially tightened rules on the management and disposal of hazardous waste in the United States, and administrators and politicians feared an increase in shady disposal and export cases. Stricter domestic laws, they reasoned, would increase the pressure to search for alternatives beyond the regulatory system of the United States.[58]

In the fall of 1979, US American diplomats began sounding alarm bells about the US chemical industry offering multimillion-dollar deals to countries in the global South to secure disposal grounds for hazardous wastes. Undisclosed industry sources had revealed proposals made to Nigeria, Liberia, Senegal, Haiti, and Chile, among other countries.[59] US embassies were directed to inform the State Department of any reports of hazardous-waste exports.[60] In October 1979, the State Department learned about a scheme that Nedlog Technology Group of Arvada, Colorado, was negotiating with high officials in Sierra Leone. Sierra Leone would receive US $25 million for accepting the company's hazardous waste. Nedlog, a company formed in 1977, was involved in recovering minerals from mining and smelting waste, and Sierra Leone was one of half a dozen countries they were considering as potential partners. According to a *Washington Post* interview with Nedlog's CEO, James Wolff, the company planned to export a million tons of hazardous waste for processing and dumping abroad. Sierra Leone's president, Siaka Stevens, showed "great interest," according to Nedlog's spokesperson.[61] At the time, the West African country was in economic free fall. The country's oil import bill had more than doubled since 1978, while its alluvial diamond fields, which provided about 70 percent (US $154 million) of government's revenue, were drying up, and domestic agriculture was declining. The situation forced Western creditors to reschedule loan repayments of US $350 million, and experts estimated a US $100 million fiscal deficit for 1980.[62] Nedlog's offer of US $25 million annually for the disposal of all sorts of hazardous waste would have gone some way toward plugging Sierra Leone's financial gap.[63]

Washington diplomats frantically cabled to their colleagues in Freetown to stop the deal. Federal officials worried that US hazardous waste would "poison US foreign relations along with the environment of developing countries around the globe." Should the shipment become controversial, Sierra Leone would join in with other "Africans to condemn the United States for dumping its wastes in the black man's backyard."[64] In the end, the US ambassador to Sierra Leone officially warned President Stevens not to accept the deal.[65] In early 1980, reports about the imminent deal in the *New York Times* and the *Washington Post* unleashed public uproar in Sierra Leone and elsewhere in West Africa. Prominent Sierra Leonians living in the United States expressed their objections. Students organized demonstrations at Njala University in Freetown and at the Sierra Leone embassy in Washington. The governments of neighboring Liberia, Nigeria, and Ghana also announced concerns. Under extreme political pressure, Sierra Leone's president, Stevens, went on state TV to deny the scheme.[66]

In the United States, the scandal led to a change of heart. An ad hoc committee was formed of members from the State Department, the EPA, and the Council of Environmental Quality to come up with legal regulations to stop such exports.[67] Yet a split between the EPA and the State Department overshadowed the committee's work. The State Department wanted to see strict export regulations in the form of a permit system.[68] The EPA was hesitant to limit the trade in hazardous waste too strictly, given that there were "some superior disposal sites abroad and recipient foreign states might be planning to recycle [US] waste." The EPA was thinking of countries such as Canada, the largest importer of US hazardous waste. Diplomats were worried about the much smaller percentage of wastes that would go to countries that "lack the facilities and expertise to protect their populations from hazardous waste disposal," such as Sierra Leone.[69] The disagreement mirrored discussions in the HSEP working group. While the EPA wanted to protect US waste businesses and their foreign recycling schemes, the State Department was worried about US foreign relations.[70]

In 1980, the EPA for the first time formally recognized that "improper management of hazardous waste can extend beyond the Nation's boundaries" and so met the State Department halfway.[71] Initially, RCRA had not expressly addressed exports of hazardous waste. Now export requirements were specified in additions to two sections of RCRA: Section 3002, which dealt with standards applicable to generators of waste, and Section 3003, which dealt with transport of waste. These addenda were limited in scope and relatively weak. The regulations required exporters to (1) initiate a manifest, (2) use proper labels and containers for waste, (3) comply with the record-keeping requirements of RCRA, and (4) notify the EPA four weeks prior to the first of possible multiple shipments of the same material. Theoretically, the notification requirement allowed the EPA to monitor international shipments of hazardous waste. In practice, the notification requirements were limited. Generators had to identify only the waste and the consignee. They were not required to specify the quantities of waste, the frequency of shipment, or the manner in which the waste would be transported, treated, or stored. Additionally, the foreign country was not required to provide evidence of written consent to the EPA *prior* to the shipment. Exporters could simply make up the information on the form. In any case, the EPA had no authority to prohibit the export of hazardous waste, even if a foreign country objected to the shipment.[72]

These regulatory loopholes continued to haunt Congress. Neither environmental interest groups nor the press would let the issue drop. News stories about possible export schemes from the United States to the global South continued unabated in the early 1980s: an Alabama-based company wanted to send paint and pesticide wastes to the Bahamas, another to ship sewage sludge from Washington, DC, to Haiti, a third to transfer paint waste from New Jersey to Haiti. In Mexico, officials jailed an American expatriate after he had illegally imported toxic wastes, including polychlorinated biphenyls (PCBs)—highly carcinogenic compounds, structurally and toxicologically similar to dioxins that function as endocrine disruptors and neurotoxins and are highly persistent in the environment. They were banned in the United States in 1979. An EPA official reported a rumor about a scheme to send hazardous waste from the US East Coast to Latin America in TV boxes.[73] In May 1981, World Information Systems, a small environmental information agency, detailed an increased flow "of waste from [the United States] into developing countries."[74]

Although the HSEP's decision to separate the export of waste from that of suspended consumer products was intended to speed up the policymaking process, it would take Congress four more years to reach a conclusion on the issue. On November 8, 1984, Reagan signed into law the Hazardous and Solid Waste Amendments (HSWA) to RCRA, which took effect in August 1986. The regulations subjected the export of hazardous waste to a stricter policy of prior informed consent. Exports required not only a prior informed consent (PIC) form completed by the exporter but also written proof of the consent of the foreign government prior to the shipment. These documents needed to be attached to the cargo throughout the journey. Violators of these rules could be fined up to US $50,000 a day and be imprisoned for up to two years. Repeat offenders could face up to four years of prison time. The new regulations said nothing, however, about the ways in which hazardous waste should be disposed of or managed in the importing country.[75] The *Khian Sea* set sail on September 5, 1986, only days after the HSWA amendments had come into force.

Rallying for Systemic Change

Congressman Michael Synar (D-OK), chair of the House subcommittee, had started preparing for the July 1988 meeting six months earlier. He identified and called expert witnesses and gathered background information. His information package included a recent internal audit of the EPA and its waste export program. Citing a long list of regulatory violations, mishaps, and loopholes, the audit concluded that RCRA needed "major improvements."[76] The most serious problem was violation of the PIC principles. Auditors had found dozens of instances where hazardous waste had been exported without notification, where exporters stated they had been unaware of the notification requirements, or where the liberal use of the terms *recycling* and *reclamation* suggested sham recycling or other illegal treatment methods. Concerning the right to refuse a shipment, a key element in the PIC principle, auditors found no records indicating that the EPA had informed exporters of any objections made. Moreover, since there was only one person in the EPA responsible for monitoring international shipments of hazardous waste, exporters could disregard EPA regulations "with little chance of detection."[77]

Following the chain of command and responsibilities, subcommittee members learned that the EPA was not the only weak link. The other actors involved in the cases of the *Khian Sea* and the *Bark*, ranging from the US Coast Guard to the State of Pennsylvania and the City of Philadelphia, had little control over the situation. Synar concluded, "These boats are just coming and going at their will."[78] The job of the committee was to investigate how to avoid such a lack of control, given that cities were likely to continue exporting toxic waste.

For Synar and John Conyers, who succeeded Synar as chair of the subcommittee, the timing seemed to be ideal for initiating a fundamental shift in US hazardous-waste export policy. The *Khian Sea* and *Bark* incidents had washed up just in time for discussions of major policy changes. The year 1989 would see substantial political changes. RCRA was up for renewal.[79] The impending change in leadership in the White House might also open up new possibilities for bipartisan solutions. For the first time in more than a decade, the environment had figured positively in a presidential campaign. During the presidential race, both Bush and Dukakis agreed that not enough had been done to protect the environment during the Reagan administration, and each vowed that he would be more aggressive in environmental protection.[80] But the possibility of bipartisan agreement was still jeopardized by deep ideological divisions about the trade-offs between environmental protection and economic growth.

Of those present at the subcommittee meeting, Conyers was the harshest critic of the current state of US hazardous-waste export regulations. As the first to speak, he set the tone for the day. He fervently addressed and interrogated almost every single expert witness, NGO representative, and government administrator present. He cleverly exposed the loopholes in the present system and eloquently countered the positions of those opposing his idea of a ban. Conyers rarely held still, and together he and Synar dominated the meeting. It was high time to act, declared Conyers, lest one of these shipments of ill-regulated hazardous-waste exports "exploded into an exported Love Canal."[81]

Conyers, born in Detroit in 1929, had a long track record on civil rights issues. When he first ran for Congress in 1964, Rosa Parks endorsed him. In 1970, Conyers fought for the release of the imprisoned activist Angela Davis, and in April 1988, he had introduced the Racial Justice Act, prohibiting the carrying out of the death penalty in a racially discriminatory manner.[82] Environmentalism for Conyers was less about conservation or opposing pollution than about social justice, and in that respect he clearly understood the positioning of Haitian and Panamanian activists. In 1984 he wrote the preface for a report of the Urban Environment Conference (uec), a nonprofit corporation founded in 1971 by Michigan Senator Philip Hart to provide a forum to join discussions on urban reform, environmentalism and organized labor. In the report, titled *Reagan, Toxics, and Minorities*, Conyers argued that minorities in the United States experienced disproportionate harms from toxicants, in both their workplaces and their homes, and that Reagan's policies had little done to alleviate their plight.[83] Instead, Reagan had brought about a time when "birds fall from the skies, rivers are poisoned and deer die in the forests, all because of the white man's greed."[84] In the 1980s, Conyers belonged to a small cadre of African Americans who saw environmental harm as a civil rights issue.[85]

In the months leading up to the subcommittee meeting, Conyers had been approached by representatives from the greater Caribbean and other countries in the global South to tell him their worries and to try to convince him to become their spokesperson.[86] In 1971, Conyers had been the cofounder of the Black Caucus, which included almost all African American congressional representatives. In the 1970s members of the caucus had been particularly outspoken in their criticism of Duvalier's dictatorship in Haiti and their support for the impoverished, primarily Black population of the Caribbean nation.[87] Conyers appeared sympathetic to those targeted by racism and ready to acknowledge the connection between racist policies and environmental degradation.

Conyers had the support of Mike Synar, an up-and-coming star in the US Congress twenty years his junior. Synar was a lawyer, rancher, and real estate broker from a prominent ranching family in northeast Oklahoma. He was first elected to Congress in 1978, at the age of twenty-eight, and became chair of the House Government Operations Environment, Energy, and Natural Resources Subcommittee in 1983. He died in 1996, at the age of forty-six, from cancer. In Congress, Synar stood for tough and controversial issues; he did not mind that his views might pit him against his opponents, his party leaders, his own state, or powerful representatives of special-interest groups, such as the tobacco industry or the National Rifle Association.[88] Synar believed strongly that government should help the poor and protect the environment, and he championed social justice, gender, and equity issues.[89] As the chair of the House Government Operations Environment, Energy, and Natural Resources Subcommittee, he was familiar with the problems of waste management in the United States. In 1983, he investigated the illegal dumping of toxic waste from US military bases.[90] In 1986, he banged heads with the EPA after stockpiles of recalled liquid pesticides had started leaking in a warehouse in St. Joseph, Missouri, and created a substantial environmental health threat for nearby residents.[91] In 1987, Synar and his subcommittee were again targeting the EPA after his team learned of a company's illegal dumping of PCBs and other toxic substances into the Missouri River.[92]

Conyers had come into contact with Synar through a prominent case in his own constituency, Detroit, involving the activities of the lawyer A. Robert Zeff and his company, Lindaco. Zeff had formed the company to negotiate a deal to ship nearly fifteen million tons of hazardous waste to Guinea-Bissau in West Africa.[93] Once investigative journalists and Greenpeace activists brought this deal to light, "an uproar ensued" in Detroit, and "people were up in arms" against the deal.[94]

During the subcommittee meeting, Conyers and Synar formed a team that was difficult to beat. They fed each other lines and supported each other's arguments. It was a well-orchestrated performance in support of their shared goal, a waste-export ban.

Two days prior to the subcommittee meeting, Conyers introduced his Waste Export Prohibition Act into the House of Representatives. The bill proposed to alter the Solid Waste Disposal Act of 1965 by adding a section prohibiting the export of solid waste from the United States to any other country unless (1) there were bilateral agreements established prior to the act, (2) it concerned small quantities of personal household waste carried by individuals traveling abroad, or (3) the transaction was covered by specific exceptions concerning substances for reuse and recycling. Canada and Mexico, with which the United States had had bilateral agreements regarding waste exports, would be exempt from the ban. If it passed, the bill would fundamentally alter US export policy on hazardous material. The ban would overhaul the principle of prior informed consent. No longer would foreign countries decide for themselves whether they wanted to import US hazardous waste: in banning these substances from export, the United States would decide for them.[95]

Conyers's bill represented the Democrats' response to a Republican bill that was currently pending before Congress. On June 29, 1988, Senator Robert Kasten (R-WI) had introduced bill S. 2598 to "ensure that waste exported from the United States to foreign countries is managed so as to protect human health and the environment."[96] Kasten was chair of the Senate Appropriations Committee on Foreign Relations. Like Reagan, he was an outspoken conservative, although he seemed less of an anti-environmentalist. In 1984–85, he had successfully taken on the World Bank in a battle to reform its environmental performance.[97] Under Kasten's proposed bill, hazardous-waste exports would be generally allowed, as long as the importer demonstrated that foreign waste treatment, storage, and disposal were in accordance with US environmental standards.[98] While the Democrats aimed to curb the US waste trade through government intervention, the Republicans favored the self-regulation of the market.

As the witnesses at the subcommittee hearing were questioned about how things might be done differently, discussions kept returning to the divide between government intervention and market regulation, a ban or no ban. There was little common ground between the two sides. Rather the debate reiterated the same questions that had been asked in 1980: How far should US environmental policy reach? Should the export of hazardous waste be regulated by government or rely on market forces? And should policy recommendations be based on the exception or the rule?

At the time, most US hazardous waste went not to Haiti, Guinea, the Philippines, or Guinea-Bissau but to other "advanced countries" such as Canada, Great Britain, and West Germany. The *Khian Sea*, the *Bark*, and the Lindaco deal were all exceptions rather than the general rule. And in the majority of waste transactions, the receiving country had a facility capable of handling waste, and it was "economical to both countries to help each other either way," according to Peter Christich from the EPA's Office of International Activities.[99] Given this situation, William Clinger (R-PA) argued that the "the existence of some bad apples should not unfairly penalize those who are acting in a proper and environmentally sound way."[100] Conyers and Synar, however, prompted witnesses to focus on the problematic exceptions. Even one case of hazardous-waste export to a country in the global South, Synar declared, might "ultimately come back to tarnish [the] Nation's image as a responsible trading partner and respected member of the international community."[101] Other members of the committee and expert witnesses backed this assumption. "Few things could be more damaging," said Louise Slaughter (D-NY), "than to be perceived as a nation which conspicuously overconsumes the world's resources and then foists off its dangerous waste products on nations unprepared to properly dispose of them but desperate for cash to meet their needs."[102] The stakes for the United States' image abroad were high, as protests in the greater Caribbean against the *Khian Sea* had illustrated.

The approach of prior informed consent assumed that each importing nation would be able to make sense of the information that the exporter provided. If asked about it, the EPA provided information on the shipment but left it to the importing nation to evaluate. If the paperwork was correctly filled out and the importing nation declared itself willing to accept a shipment, the EPA had no legal mechanism to stop it. Yet, as the case of Philadelphia ash had illustrated, prior informed consent was not always "as informed as it should be," according to Synar.[103] Not every importing nation had the ability or resources to evaluate the information supplied by exporters in a way that enabled it to make sound environmental and public-health-related decisions. If technical advice and assistance was needed, should Congress take regulatory and legal steps to provide it? This question opened a Pandora's box. It moved the subcommittee's discussion to focus on issues of the mandate of the EPA, its financial and staffing limits, and the definition and extent of national sovereignty.

The subcommittee hearings seemed to suggest that a profound reform of prior informed consent would not stop at burdening the EPA with providing technical assistance to countries in the global South; it might also require direct financial assistance. Several nations in the global South had repeatedly demanded financial assistance from the industrial countries to deal with the imports of hazardous wastes. One idea was to establish a fund that would pay for technical experts to visit countries in the global South to provide systematic assistance in hazardous-waste management. On the part of the United States, there was considerable concern about the financial burdens that this might entail.[104]

There was one more thing that needed to be said, declared Sheldon Meyers of the EPA, and so finally named the elephant in the room. "There are some developing countries," he went on, "that just don't like to be talked down to by big brother Uncle Sam."[105] Almost immediately, Conyers refuted the remark. There existed a profound difference, he said, between talking *with* leaders of Third World countries and talking *down to* leaders of Third World countries.[106] Synar smoothed emotions and at the same time pressed the issue by telling Meyers that he would not "get off the hook" by saying that it was up to the importing country to tell the United States when it could intervene. The United States had a much greater responsibility.[107]

Throughout the 1980s, Meyers's point about US paternalism had served as justification for actors from all sectors of the hazardous-waste trade to oppose the tightening of legislations. The brothers Charles and Jack Colbert brothers had built up a multimillion-dollar trade empire over the course of the 1970s and 1980s through the export of chemicals that the United States had banned, but which were legal in other places. Why, they demanded, should anyone claim that the EPA knew better than 165 other countries in the world?[108] Similarly, James Wolf, who had negotiated Nedlog's Sierra Leone deal in 1980, argued that the United States was" paternalistic in telling the Africans what they can and can't do with US hazardous waste."[109] Essentially, these actors cast the United States as complicit in re-creating structures of violence and dependence by implementing regulatory structures that implicitly violated another nation's sovereignty. Although this rhetoric was well established, at that particular meeting it could not stand up to the persuasiveness of Synar and Conyers. At least for the time being, their opponents lost the battle against a ban right there during the meeting of July 14.

When Synar adjourned the meeting that afternoon, he joked that five-hour meetings usually dealt with issues of impeachment rather than with the territorial reach of US hazardous-waste regulations. The participants left without reaching conclusions on most of the questions they had touched on that day. Although this particular meeting was the subcommittee's last before Congress adjourned, its members would come back to the issues it raised in the next session of Congress. By then a lot of things would be different. John Conyers would be the subcommittee chair, a new president would have been elected, OECD and the United Nations discussions on hazardous-waste regulations would have progressed further, and perhaps there would even be news of the missing *Khian Sea*.

The content of the subcommittee meeting, said Synar, would make neither the five o'clock nor the ten o'clock news. It was not that kind of story.[110] The *Washington Post*, in fact, remained silent about this congressional hearing and gave preference to the Washington Redskins' intention to renegotiate the contract of their quarterback and the announcement of a concert by the Cathedral Choral Society. The upcoming weekend promised to be nice, mostly sunny, breezy, and less humid.[111] The storms, it seemed, had passed.

SIX

Stop "Garbage Imperialism" | *A Global Campaign against the Unequal Trade in Waste*

The goal of the International Waste Trade Project is a global ban on
transboundary movements of all toxic wastes. The existence of such trade poses
a formidable obstacle to the primary goals of the Greenpeace toxics campaign—
the implementation of waste minimization and clean technologies.

JIM VALLETTE et al. | "International Waste Trade Project Proposal 1990/91" to
Greenpeace International, 1989

Fax and telephone were never silent in the Washington, DC, office of Greenpeace
USA in the summer of 1988, as Jim Vallette was pulling together information
on the transboundary movements of hazardous wastes all across the globe.
While Greenpeace was still interested primarily in the whereabouts of the *Khian
Sea*, they were adding to their radar more and more ships carrying potentially
hazardous waste. Eventually, all these ships would be listed in *A Greenpeace
Inventory*, which the activists made available in English, French, German, and
Spanish and in multiple editions.[1] Meanwhile across the Atlantic, Andreas Bernstorff, campaign manager for the German Green Party in Baden-Württemberg,
reported to Greenpeace International in Amsterdam that his organization, too,
had witnessed a massive "influx of information about schemes to export wastes
from industrialized countries to Third World countries."[2] Greenpeace was about
to vastly expand its geographic scope of action.

In March 1988, after Greenpeace campaigners had returned from their investigation of Philadelphia ash in Haiti, Jim Vallette had put together a proposal
for a Global Waste Patrol Campaign that would synthesize the organization's

work of the last decade. Since the trade in waste was now global, Vallette argued, Greenpeace's campaign needed a global reach. The campaign would have offices in both Europe and North America and aim to lobby international government bodies, such as the Organisation for African Unity (OAU) and the Organization of American States (OAS), along with encouraging "grassroots opposition to the waste shipments in the countries of import and export."[3] Effective January 1989, Greenpeace expanded its campaign, renamed it the Global Toxics Trade Campaign, and hired a number of additional campaigners, among them Andreas Bernstorff, Annie Leonard, and Jim Puckett.

Their timing for globalizing the campaign on the unequal trade in wastes was opportune. With the *Khian Sea*'s illegal departure from Haiti the night of February 4, 1988, and the *Bark*'s unhappy unloading of Philadelphia ash on Kassa Island at the end of February 1988, a morally questionable but legal form of business was transformed into a politicized and highly visible issue of environmental injustice. A chorus of outrage swelled across the global South. The story of the ash on board the *Khian Sea* and the *Bark* was no longer simply about Philadelphia and the Bahamas, Panama, or Haiti. It was a story about Norway and Guinea, about Italy and Nigeria, about Portugal and Guinea-Bissau, about Western Europe and East Germany. It was a story of the poorest countries of the world serving as the industrialized nations' garbage dumps, of the "recolonization of the world through trash," and of the power and violence—both immediate and slow—of "garbage imperialism."[4]

Throughout 1988, the voyage of the *Khian Sea* became a symbol of growing resistance and the forging of a global environmental alliance between local and international, Western and non-Western activists. Together these groups managed to bring about a conclusion to a process that had been stalling for a decade: the creation of an internationally binding regulatory system for the trade in hazardous waste.[5] This form of global governance, however, would not bring about the end of the trade.

Africa United against Global Waste Dumping

As the greater Caribbean became a less welcoming place for US waste, waste traders looked across the Atlantic for suitable destinations. By the spring of 1988, African nations were "the most likely target for the international trade in hazardous wastes," according to Greenpeace analysts.[6] While many African nations were caught up in relations of structural, economic, and political dependency with the global North similar to those of Haiti or Panama, their reactions to the waste deals differed profoundly. In the greater Caribbean, the opposition to waste imports emerged country by country, often aligning with internal political struggles, and so stood little chance of challenging more powerful actors. Resistance in the African nations, in contrast, became a continental affair.[7]

Waste import deals were familiar to many African countries before the big wave of European and US American traders entering the market in the late 1980s. Earlier deals included Nedlog Technology's proposal to dump several million tons of hazardous waste in Sierra Leone and Diamond Shamrock's shipment of PCBs to South Africa in 1980.[8] The chemical traders Jack Colbert and Charles Colbert sold chemical waste to Zimbabwe for reuse in 1984.[9] And Somalia had imported nuclear waste from Europe in 1985.[10] Each of these deals drew attention throughout the continent but did not evoke a unified response.

But as toxic deals accumulated in 1987, a pan-African resistance movement began to develop. In February 1987 the continent was shaken by its own version of the *Khian Sea* saga. In February 1987, a Maltese ship called the *Lynx* sailed from Italy to Djibouti in East Africa carrying more than eleven thousand drums of chemical waste collected from Italian paint and chemical producers. The deal was handled by a Milan-based disposal company called Jelly Wax. When the *Lynx* arrived in Djibouti, port authorities refused to allow it to dock, suspecting that the ship was carrying not chemical but nuclear waste. The *Lynx* then continued across the Atlantic to Puerto Cabello, Venezuela, where it unloaded its cargo. After six months, the Venezuelan government ordered the removal of the waste. Barrels were leaking, nearby residents had become sick, and the death of a young boy was connected to the waste. A Cypriot ship, the *Makiri*, then took the waste from Venezuela back across the Atlantic to Syria, where a waste disposal company had been paid to dispose of it, but Syrian officials ordered the waste to be removed before disposal could begin. At this point, the owner of the freighter *Zanoobia* stepped in and brought the cargo to Greece, where yet again it was refused. The *Zanoobia* was ocean-bound for another three months before it was allowed to enter an Italian port. By the time the cargo was returned to Italy in May 1988, nine crew members had to be hospitalized, and one of the crewmembers had died en route, possibly from exposure to the chemicals.[11]

As news about the Italian attempts to dispose of chemical waste in Djibouti started to spread across Africa, the *Bark* had just pulled out of Guinea, leaving its cargo of Philadelphia ash on Kassa Island. Guinea's treatment of Bulkhandling, its arrest of the Norwegian honorary consul, Sigmund Strømme, and its demands to have the waste removed from Kassa Island added to the indignation concerning foreign waste deals. At the meeting of the OAU in Addis Ababa in May 1988, delegates from fifty different African countries denounced "colonialist garbage" and "toxic terrorism." They deplored the "outrageous acts" that made Africa "a garbage dumping ground, posing serious health and safety hazards."[12] At the end of the meeting, the OAU passed a "Resolution that Condemns the Dumping of Nuclear and Industrial Waste in Africa as a Crime against Africa and the African People." The Nigeria-sponsored resolution called on all African states to prohibit the import of nuclear and industrial wastes. Additionally, it requested the secretary general of the OAU to collaborate with the relevant international organizations, such as the United Nations Environment Programme (UNEP) and Greenpeace, to help African countries establish relevant control mechanisms.[13]

Yet scarcely had the ink dried on the resolution than Nigeria found itself in the midst of its own toxic-waste scandal. The oil-rich country had started off the 1980s comparatively well. In 1979, with the foundation of the Second Republic, the government had passed from military to civilian rule. This flirtation with democracy lasted until December 1983, when a coup restored military rule. The global fluctuation in oil prices throughout the 1980s hampered Nigeria's economic development and increased the rift between its poor majority and a small, and often corrupt, wealthy elite.[14] Between August 1987 and May 1988, more than ten thousand drums of hazardous waste, consisting mostly of carcinogenic PCBs, had been shipped from Italy to Koko, a small port on the Benin River, which flows into the Gulf of Guinea in the Atlantic. There an unsuspecting farmer had agreed to have the barrels stacked in his yard for a payment of 500 naira (roughly US $100) a month. Exposed to heat and tropical storms, the drums began leaking, probably poisoning a nearby well that supplied drinking water. In the following months, several villagers and the farmer himself fell ill.

In spring 1988 Nigerian students studying in Italy learned about the shipment of waste from Italy, classified as "toxic and radioactive," to Nigeria. They provided the information to the Nigerian press.[15] The country's president, Ibrahim Babangida, had just returned from the OAU meeting in Addis Ababa when he was confronted with the news.[16]

Other stories of toxic waste dumping in Africa also made the news. At a dump near Freetown, Liberia, 625 bags of hazardous waste from the United Kingdom were found. There were rumors about Soviet nuclear waste buried in Benin and Nigeria. West German copper sludge was transported to Namibia. In 1988, virtually every country in Africa was approached by American and European companies seeking cheap disposal sites for foreign waste.[17] In a continent "already besieged by hunger, stifling foreign debts, and economic stagnation," stated a reader of *African Business*, "a new front" had opened that Africa seemed "not in a position to confront."[18] According to Denis Sassou-Nguesso, president of the Republic of the Congo, the industrial nations were "living off [Africa's] wealth, systematically opposing [the continent's] claims for a new international economic order . . . and dumping their trash as if we were their refuse-bin."[19]

All over Africa, people united in an expression of outrage, asserting that Europeans had always considered Africa "a wasteland. And the people who live there, waste beings."[20] In Africa, the violent legacy of colonialism and occupation played a much greater role in this discourse than they had in the Caribbean and Central America. The Nigeria-based magazine *African Concord* provided one of the most important platforms for this opposition, with tens of thousands of readers across the continent and among African expatriates. "From time immemorial," according to a reader of the magazine, "Africa has been used as a footstool and dumping ground for the industrialized nations. . . . In the past, we were being bought as slaves and used as chattels. They looted our riches, colonized and partitioned our land." A "new imperialist warfare against Africa and its people" was being waged as the African continent was yet again "neo-colonized, balkanized, plundered, exploited and poisoned by the same forces."[21] Some readers called for an African revolution. The time had come "for all concerned citizens of Africa to raise hell against such blatant disrespect for a continent."[22]

Anger rose not only against the return of colonial dependencies, violence, and injustice, but also against the African elites facilitating the trade in hazardous waste. "Foreign domination and oppression" would have been "impossible without the permission and congenial concession granted by those in authority in Africa," an angry expatriate wrote to the *African Concord*.[23] In response, African leaders took tough measures against waste traders. Guinea jailed the Norwegian honorary consul. Nigeria detained an Italian freighter docked in Lagos at the time, arrested at least fifty-four people (threatening some of them with the death penalty), and recalled its ambassador from Rome until Italy agreed to remove the barrels of waste at the farm in Koko. In Sierra Leone, police arrested two people, including the wife of a prominent judge, after the discovery of the British waste buried near Freetown. In the Republic of the Congo, authorities arrested five people, including three high-level government officials, in connection with a planned shipment of US and European waste.[24] More and more African heads of state issued declarations condemning or banning the imports of foreign waste.

In May 1988, the president of Benin, Mathieu Kérékou, issued a strict order suspending all activities connected with the import of industrial waste. In July 1988, the Gambia passed a bill establishing large fines for anyone convicted of dumping foreign hazardous waste in the country, and the Ivory Coast passed a law prohibiting the importation of toxic or nuclear waste.[25] The time was ripe for major and sustained change.

The Greenpeace Global Toxics Campaign

While several environmental activist groups expressed concern about the unequal trade in hazardous waste, it was Greenpeace groups that joined forces to organize a global campaign. Making the *Khian Sea* their symbolic target, they alerted politicians, news outlets, and the public to the moral, environmental, and social implications of disposing of hazardous waste in the developing world. Their campaign was successful not only in bringing the matter to the attention of powerful decisionmakers in the global North but also in forging alliances with environmental activist groups and media outlets in the global South.

In the 1980s, Greenpeace was the beacon of the modern environmental counterculture movement. It made environmentalism look cool. With 1.5 million members in 1988, the organization was a leading international player in environmental protection.[26] Still, it was decentralized, with different several Greenpeace groups emerging and operating independently in North America, Europe, Australia, and New Zealand. Greenpeace had grown organically around ideas of high-profile, peaceful, and direct action for environmental protection. The original group, formed in Vancouver in the 1970s, had focused solely on nuclear weapons, but it was a campaign against commercial whaling and sealing that brought Greenpeace its first major global recognition. In addition, North American Greenpeace groups conducted campaigns supporting innovative land-use laws in Oregon and protesting against the Rocky Flats nuclear installation in Colorado and deteriorating water quality in the Great Lakes.[27]

The foundation of Greenpeace International in 1979 gave the group more internal structure and moved away from the grassroots-democracy model that had often made campaign planning and financing a long and complex process. The new organization turned Greenpeace into a European-dominated international organization with a centralized bureaucracy, a hierarchical structure, and headquarters in Amsterdam.[28]

Even so, some Greenpeace campaigns continued to emerge from grassroots initiatives. Its campaign against the global waste economy was a case in point, as Greenpeace groups in Europe and North America simultaneously learned of waste shipments through various media channels, environmental journalists, other environmental action groups, and concerned citizens. For years, Greenpeace groups in the United States had been involved in waste-related issues, opposing ocean incineration in 1983 and incineration in the United States in 1986.

In 1987, the Toxics Campaign, advocating for stricter US toxic-waste laws, put Greenpeace activists on the trail of ships such as the *Khian Sea* and the *Bark*. Coverage by Mark Jaffe of the *Philadelphia Inquirer* and Ramona Smith of the *Philadelphia Daily News*, among others, had already alerted them to waste-disposal problems in Philadelphia.[29] News from Panama had reached them through the Rainforest Action Network and a researcher from the Smithsonian Institution.[30] The environmentalists recognized an emerging pattern of dangerous waste externalization that called for Greenpeace to act.

Early in 1987, Greenpeace USA had hired Pat Costner, a chemist and national expert on waste management and water pollution, as a campaigner for its Toxics Campaign.[31] Costner refocused the campaign on waste-carrying ships leaving US shores for destinations abroad. By September 1987, Costner and her Toxics Campaign team were organizing a high-profile campaign against Bulkhandling's shipment of Philadelphia ash to Panama. They attempted to build awareness in the United States and in Panama, enlisting the support of Panamanian celebrities such as the singer and actor Ruben Blades.[32] The campaign's highlight was the action week against Bulkhandling's shipment in Philadelphia, with climbers unfolding a 40-by-40-foot banner on Philadelphia's City Hall that read "No Envenene Panama."[33] Their information campaign included the publication of a pamphlet called *Burnt Offerings*, which detailed the story of Philadelphia's waste shipment to Panama and the ash's toxicological profile, based on tests that Greenpeace had commissioned. A second edition of *Burnt Offerings*, which also detailed the *Khian Sea*'s journey to Haiti, was published later in English and Spanish.[34]

On February 19, 1988, after the return of members of the Toxic Campaign from Haiti, Costner and Vallette applied to Greenpeace International in Amsterdam for money to continue their campaign against the global transport of incinerator ash from Philadelphia. They recounted how their "investigative team in Haiti" had gathered "powerful documentation of the first known dumping of toxic wastes from the US to the developing world." With the *Bark*'s sudden departure from Philadelphia, they noted, at least two ships were now carrying ash from Philadelphia to "somewhere in the cosmos." While it was impossible to make "definite plans for specific actions," they wanted to begin to prepare for potential action in the Caribbean and Norway, where they expected the *Khian Sea* and the *Bark* to arrive.

They recommended a blockade of the *Khian Sea* somewhere in the Caribbean, since an open-ocean action, by that time a Greenpeace trademark, would not be feasible for under US $35,000. Ideally, Greenpeace would keep the ship at anchor to prevent it from heading out to sea to dump its waste or from docking and unloading its ash on land. Then a Greenpeace action team would board and blockade the ship. Two climbers would hang a banner. Three small Greenpeace boats would surround the ship to prevent it from moving. Ideally, the occupation and blockade would continue until the ship's charterers signed a written agreement to return to Haiti to pick up its abandoned cargo and then offload the ash in Philadelphia. It was important to move forward to "add to the momentum of this great story."[35] Meanwhile, reports from European Greenpeace members about the Italian waste shipments to Koko, Nigeria, underlined the point that this was a global concern.[36]

Amsterdam agreed. By the beginning of 1988, under Costner's leadership, the Greenpeace Global Toxic Trade Campaign began framing the global hazardous-waste trade as a systemic injustice by which environmental regulations and citizen protests in the industrial countries led companies and municipalities to see "the developing nations of the Caribbean, Central and South America as inexpensive dumping grounds for their wastes."[37] They pieced together information about waste shipments and served as an information base for other environmental activists and politicians around the world. Together with Heather Spalding, Vallette edited the Greenpeace *International Trade in Wastes* report. The famous artist Keith Haring drew the image for the report's cover, which Greenpeace also printed on T-shirts for its campaigners and supporters.[38] Meanwhile, members of the campaign testified before government bodies and NGOs throughout the world. Politicians listened to and even relied on data provided by the campaign to assess and understand the dangers and inequities of hazardous waste shipments from developed to developing countries.

By collaborating with local Greenpeace groups and other environmental activist movements, the Global Toxic Trade Campaign was able to act the moment ships arrived or information about upcoming waste deals leaked out. They warned a country's coast guard and environment minister of a ship's impending arrival and the hazards posed by its cargo.[39] The European branch of the campaign followed the voyage of the *Karin B.*, the freighter commissioned to return the leaking Italian hazardous-waste barrels from Koko, Nigeria, to a safe disposal ground in Europe, first around the Mediterranean Sea and then, when Italian ports refused to let the ship anchor, toward Great Britain. Campaigners affiliated with Greenpeace UK and Greenpeace Italy teamed up with Friends of the Earth UK to keep a continuous watch on the ship while launching a series of events that particularly took off in the United Kingdom.[40] They landed stunning and high-profile media images when the Greenpeace ship *Siriun* circled the *Karin B.* in the Mediterranean. British campaigners also scored a surprising coup in September 1988, when Prime Minister Margaret Thatcher gave a major speech identifying the environment as one of the great challenges of the twentieth century.[41]

Meanwhile, however, Costner and Vallette's plan to track down and blockade the *Khian Sea* in the Caribbean turned into a game of cat-and-mouse. After the *Khian Sea* had illegally fled its anchorage at the mouth of the Delaware River in May 1988, it had disappeared. Eventually, Greenpeace toxics campaigners traced its route and its metamorphosis into the *Felicia* and then the *Pelicano,* changing its captain and crew as well. After leaving Philadelphia, the ship attempted to gain permission to unload its cargo in Morocco, Senegal, and Sri Lanka. In August 1988, Greenpeace tracked it down in Yugoslavia, where it had put in for repairs with the name *Felicia*, registered in Honduras. On September 28, 1988, the *Pelicano* passed through the Suez Canal, listing Singapore as its destination.[42]

Early International Governance of Hazardous Wastes

The African nations' outrage and Greenpeace's campaign efforts reinvigorated international efforts to curb the global trade in hazardous waste. In the 1970s, different international organizations had started focusing on the waste issue, driven by the recognition of rising waste levels and in particular the increasing amount of the new and problematic category of hazardous waste. Yet their engagement had never yielded tangible political results.[43]

Concerns about hazardous waste initially focused on the growing quantity of nuclear waste from the medical and military use of radioactive material and the increasing number of nuclear power plants across the industrialized world. Between 1967 and 1982, the European Nuclear Energy Agency of the Organisation for Economic Co-operation and Development (OECD) coordinated a nuclear-waste dumping program in the Atlantic that involved several of its member countries.

In 1967, the World Health Organization (WHO) published a report that noted: "Highly persistent detergents, pesticides, and other toxic wastes are becoming an ever increasing problem in developed countries and in time will present a similar challenge to developing countries."[44] Some years later, the North Atlantic Treaty Organization (NATO) also attempted to address the waste issue. Although NATO was primarily a military alliance, the US president, Richard Nixon, had convinced its members to address environmental issues through its Committee on the Challenges of Modern Society (CCMS).[45] In 1973, the German delegation to CCMS proposed a pilot project on the disposal of hazardous substances. The study was intended to review and test disposal technology and recycling options and, ideally, to create a list of hazardous substances and treatment methods. Between 1974 and 1977, the group met seven times but achieved little. At its final meeting in 1977, the organizers declared that "geographical, climatic and organizational conditions differed so tremendously between the study's participants that no general recommendation for all NATO members could be made."[46]

Discussion of international regulation of the trade in hazardous waste began in the early 1980s. Two international organizations came at the issue from seemingly opposite ends of the story: the OECD and UNEP. Founded in 1972 at the United Nations Conference on the Human Environment, UNEP, with its much broader membership, including most of the countries of the global South, appeared better suited to address environmental injustice. UNEP addressed hazardous wastes through its International Register of Potentially Toxic Chemicals (IRPTC), which was set up in 1974 to "provide a global early warning system of undesirable environmental side effects."[47] In monitoring toxic chemicals, UNEP had detected an unequal trade pattern in chemical products similar to that in hazardous waste a decade later. The chemicals trade tended to follow a one-way path from industrial countries to developing countries, as chemical substances and products banned in industrial countries—such as DDT, aldrin, dieldrin, and leptophos—ended up in developing countries, where their use was still legal.[48]

From tracing potentially hazardous chemical products it was only a small step to tracing hazardous waste. In May 1981 UNEP convened a meeting of senior government officials, all experts in environmental law, to identify subjects for increased global and regional cooperation. In the resulting plan, known as the Montevideo Programme, these experts identified several priorities, including the transport, handling and disposal of toxic and dangerous wastes.[49] The Cairo Guidelines on Environmentally Sound Management of Hazardous Wastes were issued by a UNEP working group in 1985, and UNEP's Governing Council approved them as a nonbinding set of guidelines in 1987.[50]

Although at the time the hazardous-waste trade largely involved transport between two industrial countries—ideally neighboring ones, such as the United States and Canada or West Germany and the Netherlands, to minimize transport costs—UNEP clarified that their particular concern in creating the Cairo Guidelines was the "imbalance" in waste management according to countries' differing states of economic development. It was a situation that "necessitates co-operation . . . especially as regards actual and potential trans-frontier movement."[51] The Cairo Guidelines established three key principles concerning the production, management, and disposal of hazardous waste. First, they called for cleaner manufacturing processes and greater sustainability to reduce the production of hazardous wastes. Second, they recommended that countries establish specific measures to assure the environmentally sound disposal of hazardous wastes within their boundaries. And third, they called for prior informed consent for any international waste shipment.[52]

The concepts of prior informed consent and environmentally sound disposal would underpin all future international regulations concerning the movement of and trade in hazardous waste. Foregrounding these two principles also meant establishing structures that protected individual nations' autonomy and liberal economies at the expense of alternative, non-state-based visions of environmental protection. They also obstructed a legislative pathway toward a complete ban on the unequal trade in hazardous wastes.

While the Cairo Guidelines were addressed to all UNEP members, the second principle—the environmentally sound disposal of hazardous wastes within countries—primarily targeted nations from the global South. Many of these countries, including the Bahamas, Peru, Saint Lucia, and Trinidad and Tobago, lacked any legal definition of hazardous waste, let alone regulations on environmentally sound disposal.[53] Through the Cairo Guidelines, UNEP attempted to create a system in which all trading partners at least recognized hazardous waste as a category, though it left the specific definition up to individual countries. The agency proposed that hazardous waste should mean "waste other than radioactive wastes which, by reason of their chemical reactivity or toxic, explosive, corrosive or other characteristics causing danger or likely to cause danger to health or the environment, whether alone or when coming into contact with other wastes, are legally defined as hazardous in the state they are generated or in which they are disposed of or through which they are transported."[54] It was a weak definition for any international regulatory framework. There were no shared international standards or thresholds, let alone a unified list of hazardous substances.

Like UNEP, the OECD was taking an increasing interest in environmental and transfrontier pollution issues. By the mid-1960s, the organization's work expanded to include a "coherent environmental component."[55] In 1970, the OECD established an Environment Committee to help navigate the relationship between "population, resources, and environment on the one hand and sustainable economic development on the other."[56] In 1973, the OECD created a temporary group focusing on waste disposal, followed in 1974 by the more permanent Waste Management Policy Group. The latter took up its work in 1976 with a focus on waste management, packaging, recycling, product durability, and hazardous waste (a new category) within the OECD's twenty member countries. Many of these countries, including Australia, Denmark, France, and the United States, had adopted or were developing regulatory measures to monitor hazardous waste from cradle to grave.[57] The OECD recognized that their members' national monitoring systems were inadequate for monitoring or controlling transboundary shipments. Pollution issues arising from such shipments could be avoided only through international cooperation that extended beyond the OECD.[58]

Regulation of hazardous waste represented a challenge for the OECD, because its member countries accounted for almost all the global production of hazardous wastes. About 8–10 percent of all hazardous wastes generated within OECD countries—at the time over 2 million tons—were estimated to cross national frontiers within Europe.[59] The OECD recognized that there were "legitimate reasons" to export hazardous waste, such as geographic or geological factors limiting safe disposal sites in the originating country, lack of treatment or disposal capacity, highly specific treatment needs, transportation distances, or the economical use of the waste as raw material in another industry.[60] Yet the organization also recognized the potential ills and injustices that could come with the international shipment of hazardous wastes. In line with the philosophy of free trade, members argued that tighter regulations within OECD countries would raise costs and so encourage trade to centers of least-cost disposal, i.e., the global South.[61] Consequently, the Environment Committee wrote, it was necessary to study the implications of shipments of hazardous wastes to developing countries, the legality of the imposition of export controls by industrialized nations, and methods providing for monitoring and control of transboundary movements of hazardous waste. In the fall of 1982, the OECD Waste Management Policy

Group recommended the development of guidelines for the export and import of hazardous wastes globally.[62]

Like UNEP, also the OECD based its policy recommendations on the principle of prior informed consent and recommended that its members establish authorities to consolidate information on the movement of waste.[63] In 1985 the OECD began to draft a treaty for the control of transboundary movements of hazardous wastes based on prior informed consent, but this provision applied solely to movements between OECD member states.[64] Movements of hazardous wastes to nonmembers should not be allowed without the consent of the importing country, "*unless* the hazardous wastes were directed to adequate treatment and disposal facilities in the importing country."[65]

In 1988, the OECD set out to define the terms *waste, disposal,* and *hazardous waste.* They established a "core list" of wastes to be controlled, which they labeled along the lines of existing regulations on the transport of dangerous goods. Any other wastes defined as hazardous wastes by either the importing or the exporting nation would also be subject to the OECD's framework. Yet once it became evident that the United Nations was moving forward with an international framework for the control of transfrontier movements of hazardous wastes, the OECD paused its work.[66]

In 1984, the European Economic Community (EEC) began to address the issue of waste trade. In December 1984, the EEC passed Directive 84/631 on the supervision and control within the EEC of the transfrontier shipment of hazardous wastes. This directive largely codified the principle of prior informed consent into a form legally binding on EEC member states. A 1986 amendment prescribed prior notification and informed consent for hazardous waste movements involving countries outside the European Economic Community.[67] In August 1988, the European Economic Commission proposed its own definitions of *waste, disposal,* and *hazardous wastes* within the EEC.[68] Toward the end of the 1980s, as news emerged of European waste exports to the former Portuguese colony of Guinea-Bissau, discussion at the European Parliament focused on unequal waste shipments beyond the EEC. African news outlets reported that Guinea-Bissau had signed contracts to receive up to three million tons of waste per year for five years from three European companies for payments of US $150–600 million.[69] Even so, the EEC put its regulatory efforts on hold to wait for the UNEP initiative to be completed.

These early sets of trade regulations all had two common features. First, they relied on the principle of prior informed consent. On a spectrum of possible policy choices, this export policy mantra rested between a ban on the shipment of products deemed unsafe by the exporting nation, and international systems of notice and information exchange, such as the IRPTC.[70] Second, they sought to create a universal definition of hazardous waste. Until the Cairo Guidelines, the lack of any formal definition compounded the problem of determining how and where hazardous waste had been generated around the world, let alone how much. Thus, while UNEP, the OECD, and the EEC all recognized the unequal trade with hazardous wastes as a systemic and global problem, they acknowledged that they had limited means to assess or address it.

The UN Basel Convention

At the time, waste was not the only environmental issue on the international agenda. Environmental problems ranging from acid rain to ozone depletion had ushered in new levels of participation in environmental citizenship around the world. European forests, particularly in Bavaria and the Black Forest, were being damaged from air pollution coming from the United Kingdom. Cross-border pollution problems came sharply into focus with the spread of radioactive fallout across Europe from the Chernobyl nuclear reactor disaster in April 1986.[71] Terms like *greenhouse gases*, *cfc*s, and *global warming* entered general conversation. Environmental activist groups expanded their memberships and scope of operations. Greenpeace opened new offices in Argentina, Ireland, Denmark, Germany, Spain, and Sweden. As a sign of the new political freedom in the Soviet Union, environmental activism was a tolerated political activity.[72]

Governments around the world gave environmental topics new prominence. In the United Kingdom, Margaret Thatcher appeared as a converted environmentalist. France and Italy gave environmental issues unprecedented attention. Even the Soviet Union admitted that it had environmental issues to take care of. On March 2, 1989, the EEC's environment ministers agreed in Brussels to commit the organization's twelve member states to halting the production and consumption of chlorofluorocarbons (CFCs, implicated in the depletion of the Earth's ozone layer) by the year 2000. One week later, 120 nations met in London to address the issue of ozone depletion. A day later, a twenty-four-nation summit convened at The Hague, in the Netherlands, to discuss the establishment of a supranational organization to enforce environmental standards. The Intergovernmental Panel on Climate Change, set up under UN auspices in 1988, established three working groups to review scientific knowledge, assess socioeconomic impacts, and develop response strategies.[73] And a group of 116 nations, lobby groups, and environmental activist groups, along with a range of UN administrators, met in Basel for a discussion about the transboundary nature of hazardous waste. The timing seemed to be ideal for an international agreement on environmental issues and waste.

After the approval of the Cairo Guidelines in 1987, Senegal, Switzerland, and Hungary proposed to start drafting a global convention for governance of hazardous waste disposal. The UN General Assembly ratified the proposal, and UNEP became the organizing agency. Headquartered in Nairobi, UNEP had a proximity to African affairs that helped UN administrators grasp the seriousness of the inequalities involved.[74] Between 1988 and 1989, UNEP organized five working group meetings. At the first meeting in Budapest, Hungary, participants agreed on the format of a framework convention—that is, one that would develop a legally binding treaty establishing broader commitments for the parties but leaving the setting of specific targets to subsequent, more detailed agreements. The convention would also contain provisions for the control of transboundary movements of hazardous wastes, specifying clearly the responsibility of states involved in such movements.[75]

From the start, the convention's delegates were wrestling with a conundrum. On the one hand, they voted to discuss and enforce transnational responsibility and liability. On the other hand, they planned to leave detailed work to the individual member states after the acceptance of a general framework. Ninety-six countries, sixty-six of them from the global South, participated in one or more of the working group meetings. The African nations, in particular, sent large delegations. Although the *Khian Sea*—and with it Greenpeace's global campaign—had started out as a story involving the United States and the Caribbean, the discourse on the ills and effects of the global waste economy was now firmly in the hands of the African nations.[76] The increasingly trying negotiations revealed a substantial rift between countries of the global North and those of the global South.

The Conference of Plenipotentiaries on the Global Convention on the Control of Transboundary Movements of Hazardous Wastes was convened in Basel, Switzerland, in March 1989. It was the final conference in an eighteen-month-long series. Right up to the signing of the Basel Convention on March 22, the delegates were still submitting amendments. The issues at stake were manifold, ranging from the definition of such terms as *territory, area under the national jurisdiction*, and *generator* to the questions of whether radioactive waste should be included and what impact the convention should have on national legislation and existing bilateral agreements.

At the third negotiation meeting in Geneva in November 1988, delegates had agreed to address not only the transboundary movement of waste but also disposal. UNEP's executive director, Mostafa Tolba, had suggested changing the title of the Basel convention to include "management of hazardous wastes." This expanded focus opened up new areas of dispute and led more and more parties to show an interest in the proceedings. At Geneva, twelve strong international NGOs, representing both environmental and industrial interests, were present, each lobbying in a different direction.[77]

By the fourth negotiating meeting in January 1989, a new issue emerged, as the African nations demanded special consideration. After all, most of the highly publicized waste-dumping incidents were happening in their territories. Consequently, they sought not an international regulation of the trade in hazardous waste material but a protocol banning any import of hazardous waste into Africa—a collective action to ensure that no individual African country would accept waste imports. Toward this end the African nations revived the May 1988 resolution of the OAU that condemned the practice of waste exports to Africa as a form of recolonization.

Representatives of industry and the industrial countries were opposed in principle to a ban, as it represented an impediment to free trade. Attempting to find some sort of middle ground, UNEP, in collaboration with representatives from the OAU, proposed an Africa-only meeting. In January 1989, Senegal convened a special meeting in Dakar to which nearly all African states sent delegates at the ministerial level. Several environment ministers from OECD countries also participated. The meeting was tense, as a small group of African representatives stuck to their demand for a ban on hazardous-waste imports that would apply only to their own countries. The meeting in Dakar ended without any clarification of the African position but with a vague will to allow negotiations to continue.[78]

After two more formal and informal meetings, delegates met in Basel in March 1989 to bring negotiations to a conclusion. Several key issues were resolved just before the meeting, such as the United States' concern about the distinction between hazardous and municipal waste (reflecting the US incinerator ash controversy) and the question of how the convention would affect contradictory national legislation or bilateral agreements (such as the United States' agreements with Canada and Mexico). How the African nations would decide as a whole was still a worrisome question. Some of the African delegates had come to Basel with the authority to sign the convention immediately; others were set on opposing it. During the Basel meeting, African delegates frequently broke off into small meetings of their own, during which—as Tolba reported—those opposing the convention "blocked members from signing through shouting and screaming."[79]

In the end Morifing Kone, minister of the environment for Mali—which at the time was the head of the OAU—represented the joint African position. Kone noted that the large presence of African countries in Basel and throughout the entire negotiation process reflected their awareness of the gravity and importance of the problem. He also reminded his audience that they considered the dumping of toxic waste in African countries to be a criminal act. The OAU member countries had jointly concluded that although they appreciated the international effort to address the problem of the trade in hazardous waste materials, they still saw too many open points for discussion. Because of the limited technical capacities of many African countries, Kone said, it would be difficult for them to use the Basel Convention to prevent unscrupulous individuals from illegal dumping. Kone and other African ministers then presented twenty-four different amendments that Tolba and his staff sought to resolve in a ten-hour marathon session. In the end, the OAU countries did not object to the adoption of the Basel Convention, but neither did they sign it.[80]

Various other institutions shared the OAU's view that the legal principle of prior informed consent left too many loopholes, particularly concerning countries that lacked the technical infrastructure to assess waste independently from the information given to them by the exporters. How should they know whether and in which disposal contexts the material was safe? The ACP-EEC Joint Assembly—a cooperative undertaking involving the EEC and the African, Caribbean, and Pacific Group of States (ACP) that had existed since 1957—and the Non-aligned Movement, which represented more than one hundred countries not aligned with any of the Cold War superpowers, had called for a total ban on the international waste trade.[81] Even before the Basel negotiations, the Group of 77, the OAU, and the Rio Group of Latin American countries had similarly demanded that the OECD ban waste exports to non-OECD countries, including semirecyclable wastes.[82]

Among the most vocal proponents of a ban was Greenpeace. Members from the Global Toxic Waste Trade Campaign attended all meetings leading up to the Basel Convention. They favored a ban that covered at least the developing world and criticized the exclusion of radioactive waste from the convention. "While this convention may effectively halt, or at least criminalize, some of the more outrageous waste trade schemes, it will do little but sanction the majority of the waste traffic which is already underway," was the Greenpeace verdict on the

Basel Convention.[83] Only a ban would curb the growth of hazardous waste, since countries would have an incentive to reduce the production of toxic waste only if they were forced to dispose of it within their own borders.[84] The legal mechanisms established by the Basel Convention would not prevent "the despoilment of the global environment"; rather the convention would, "by sanctioning a relatively free trade in wastes, . . . encourage industry to produce more wastes."[85]

On March 22, 1989, the Basel Convention was adopted by the consensus of the 116 nations represented there. In total, 105 nations and the European Economic Community signed the final version, although some, including the United States, took the decision to sign the convention home with them. The main provisions of the Basel Convention were as follows:

1. Every country had the sovereign right to ban the import of hazardous waste.
2. The control system of the Basel Convention would ensure that no hazardous waste was shipped to a country that banned it.
3. Export to and import from countries not party to the Basel Convention were prohibited unless governed by a bilateral, multilateral, or regional agreement, the provisions of which were no less strict than those of the Basel Convention.
4. Every country had the obligation to reduce the production of hazardous wastes and dispose of its wastes as close to the source as possible.
5. Transboundary movements carried out in contravention of the convention would be considered illegal traffic.

The Basel Convention was based on the legal premises of notification and prior informed consent, the obligation of industrial countries to assist developing countries in technical matters related to the management of hazardous waste, and the requirement that the exporting country ensure that hazardous-waste management facilities in the importing country were environmentally sound.[86]

It was not only members of the OAU who were disappointed with the result. The Greenpeace delegate Kevin Stairs pointed out that "the demands of the developing countries for protecting them from the international waste trade have been largely ignored. Industrialized countries had the power to stop waste exports to the Third World; instead they opted to legalize them."[87]

Greenpeace Switzerland demonstration in front of the Palais des Nations in Geneva calling for a worldwide ban on toxic waste exports, March 1989. © Greenpeace/Hans Rupp.

Finding the *Khian Sea* in Southeast Asia

During the negotiations leading up to the Basel Convention, an important protagonist in the story was still missing in action: the *Khian Sea*. News of the whereabouts of the waste ship had been scarce after it had illegally left its anchorage at the mouth of the Delaware River in May 1988.

After its flight, the ship had crossed the Atlantic to West Africa and, following short layovers in Senegal and Sierra Leone, traveled through the Strait of Gibraltar to Yugoslavia. There the ship docked in the port of Bijela for temporary repairs at the end of July 1988.[88] William P. Reilly, vice president of Coastal Carriers and the US representative of the Bahamian company Amalgamated, which was still the time-chartered owner of the *Khian Sea* and its remaining cargo, flew to Yugoslavia to oversee repairs and the sale of the ship and cargo. In July 1988, the *Khian Sea*'s ownership passed from Lily Navigation Inc. to the Romo Shipping Company. Its registration changed from the Liberian to the Honduran flag and its name from *Khian Sea* to *Felicia*. The *Khian Sea*'s captain,

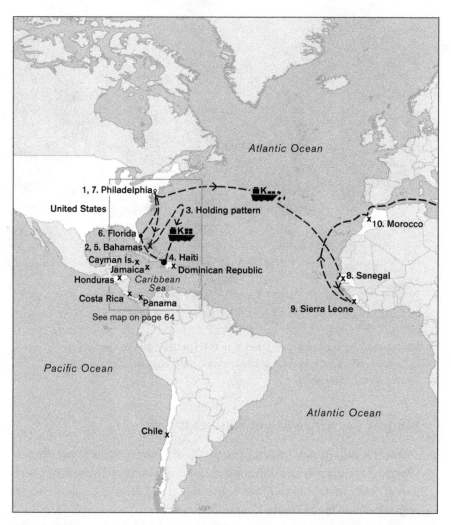

The two-year voyage of the *Khian Sea* between its departure from Delaware Bay and docking in Singapore, as the *Pelicano*, in November 1988. Map by Ben Pease.

Arturo Fuentes Garcia, for the first time expressed a strong desire to leave the ship and go home. Reilly flew in Fuentes's wife and baby from Honduras to placate him for just a little longer.[89]

The sale of the ship, along with the eleven thousand tons of incinerator ash still on board, for a price of ten dollars, was an orchestrated scam that benefited all the companies involved. It released Amalgamated, the time charterer of the

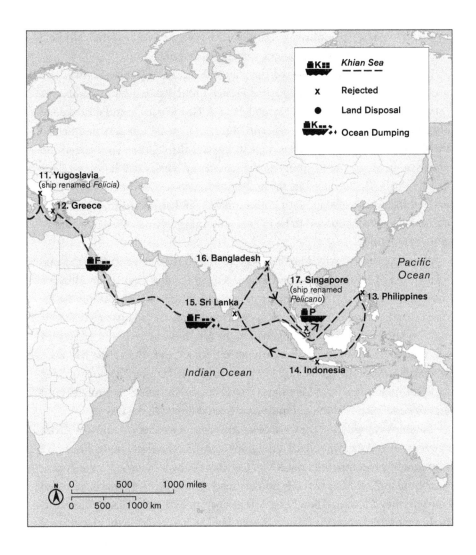

ship, from its contractual obligation to return the *Khian Sea* to Lily Navigation "essentially the same way it had chartered it, and that would have been empty."[90] Both seller and buyer, Lily Navigation and Romo Shipping, were owned by Robert Cordes, who also happened to be the president of Amalgamated. The sale also benefited Coastal Carriers, whose official relationship with the *Khian Sea* ended when it left Yugoslavia and passed through the Suez Canal.[91] The ship was off to new territory, and no one involved in its earlier voyage could be technically held responsible—or so they hoped—for what happened next.

When Greenpeace discovered the ship, the old name *Khian Sea* was still visible under the newly painted name *Felicia*. But the ship disappeared before they could take any action. In November 1988, Greenpeace found it docked in Singapore, now renamed the *Pelicano*. Reilly of Coastal Carriers had helped the ship's new owners, Romo, arrange its passage through the Suez Canal and its arrival in Singapore to complete the temporary repairs that had been done in Yugoslavia. Reilly stayed in the area until sometime in January 1989, when his "unofficial relationship" with Romo ended. John Patrick Dowd, president of Coastal Carriers, happened to be in Singapore, allegedly on different business, at the same time.[92]

When the *Felicia* arrived in Singapore, her holds were empty. When the ship finally docked in Singapore, the captain, Arturo Fuentes Garcia, stood by his statement that the ash had been legally unloaded and disposed of, but he refused to say where, citing his fear of environmentalists.[93] Reilly stated that he had "no knowledge of what happened to the ash that was on board when they left Yugoslavia."[94] When passing through the Suez Canal, the *Felicia* had been several thousand tons lighter, carrying at the time only "3,500 metric tons of scrap material," than when it left Yugoslavia.[95] Greenpeace and other environmentalist groups concluded that the ash must have been dumped in the ocean.

The ship's voyage from the Caribbean and Central America on to West Africa and Southeast Asia symbolized a geographic shift in the waste trade. Just as US waste traders had mirrored the *Khian Sea*'s voyage by moving from the greater Caribbean to West Africa as their primary market, now they followed its eastward course as they discovered Southeast Asia as a new market for US hazardous waste. In the 1990s this region would become the new "final frontier" in the global waste trade. Greenpeace activists found that between 1990 and 1993, Australia, Britain, Canada, Germany, and the United States shipped more than 5.4 million tons of toxic trash to Asia. The primary importing countries were Bangladesh, China, Hong Kong, India, Indonesia, Malaysia, Pakistan, the Philippines, Singapore, South Korea, Sri Lanka, Taiwan, and Thailand.[96]

SEVEN

Return to Sender | *The* Khian Sea's *Voyage Home*

We just don't want it. It's been sitting there in Haiti for years and we really don't know what's in it.

LOUISIANA STATE SENATOR WILLIE MOUNT | cited in Mark Jaffe, "Hopes for Ash Dashed: The Cursed Cargo of the *Khian Sea*," *Philadelphia Inquirer*, May 13, 2000

A page-long telegram arrived at the Greenpeace office in Cambridge, Massachusetts, on June 10, 1988, composed in Haitian Créole by the Komite Tet Ansanm pou Onè Respè Konstitisyon an, the Joint Commission for Honoring the Constitution. Despite its unusual length, the message of the telegram was extremely clear: "Retire fatra pwazon an nan Gonayiv"—remove the poisonous waste from Gonaïves.[1] Soon the Haitian outcry was amplified by a roar from the African continent against garbage imperialism. These voices of global environmental protest had compelled the international community to draft and adopt the Basel Convention in March 1989. Yet twelve years after that Haitian telegram, the ash from Philadelphia's incinerators was still sitting in Gonaïves.

The United States, still the largest producer of hazardous waste materials globally, was caught up in debates over the Basel Convention, liabilities faced by US traders concerning other countries, who should pay for the repatriation of Philadelphia ash, and where it should go. Landfills in Florida, New Jersey, and Ohio refused to take the *Khian Sea*'s "ominous cargo" after it had been "laying around" in Gonaïves for so long.[2]

In January 1988, activists capture the *Khian Sea* docking at Sedren Wharf in Gonaïves, Haiti. © Michèle Montas/Radio Haiti.

The United States' Wrestle with Basel

When the US delegation returned from Basel in 1989, they arrived in Washington, DC, to face a conundrum. Although legislators generally favored participating in the Basel Convention, stark controversies erupted over the premises of regulating the international trade in wastes (prior informed consent versus an export ban) and whether national waste reform should precede the ratification of the convention or vice versa. The political discussion in the United States was complicated by the desire to maintain existing waste-export agreements with Canada and Mexico that were based on prior informed consent.[3] Additionally, US politicians faced the problem of a waste-export program that had shown itself inadequate for controlling US exports, with or without Basel.[4] Many issues would have to be resolved before the United States could even consider joining the Basel Convention.

The political wrangling was further complicated by the complex relationship between states and the federal government, and the division between Republicans and Democrats. In the United States, the ratification of an international treaty or convention requires a two-thirds vote in the US Senate as well as the approval of the president. When the Basel Convention was up for debate, there was a Republican president (George H. W. Bush), while the Democrats controlled both the House of Representatives and the Senate.[5] In addition, the president and Senate were generally reluctant to exercise a treaty power that would override the laws of the fifty states.[6]

Moreover, in 1989, US national hazardous-waste legislation was incompatible with the Basel Convention because of the differing definitions of waste. Legislators needed to decide whether they should first change national laws to be consistent with Basel and then ratify the convention, or whether they should ratify the convention and then accept all the changes to national legislation that Basel would require. While the first approach allowed greater freedom in enacting national waste legislation, the second demonstrated a stronger commitment by the United States to international environmental governance.[7] Since the Basel Convention was not yet in force, US politicians could take their time to decide whether it was in the "national interest" to sign it at all.[8] It took a year before President Bush endorsed the agreement and referred it to the US Senate for ratification in March 1990.[9]

Even then, the issue of when and how to reform US waste legislation for conformity with Basel remained unresolved.[10] The Basel Convention defined waste more broadly than the United States for both disposal and recycling purposes.[11] Additionally, Basel provided no exemptions for wastes remaining as residues—such as incinerator ash—and many items, such as car batteries, were considered hazardous waste in other nations but not in the United States. Another contentious issue was the extent of the jurisdiction of the Environmental Protection Agency.[12] The Basel Convention's inclusion of household waste and incinerator ash in the scope of the notification and consent scheme would require the EPA to seek expanded authority. The United States would have to strengthen its regulations on hazardous wastes in order to comply with the convention.[13] In January 1990 John Conyers—who had been one of the leading spokespersons in the debate on the *Khian Sea* in 1988—submitted a bipartisan bill that would replace the EPA with a cabinet-level Department of Environmental Protection.[14] The bill died, as would many others following it.

In February 1992, Australia became the twentieth United Nations member state to ratify the Basel Convention, starting the ninety-day countdown to its implementation.[15] US administrators from the EPA and the State Department impressed on Congress that the clock was ticking. On May 5, 1992, the Basel Convention would enter into force, and a first meeting of its signatory states would be convened—possibly without the United States. Members would then decide on details of the convention, among them the definition of environmentally sound management and questions of international liability.[16] As it stood in 1992, the text of the Basel Convention was a result of highly successful US intervention. During the negotiations, the US delegation had managed to strike language bringing waste-trade notifications into the public domain, to prevent the key term *environmentally sound management* from being defined, and to oppose a ban on waste exports to countries with less environmentally sound management systems.[17] Without signing the convention, the United States would no longer be able to protect these interests.

At the time, the political discussion on the Basel Convention in the US centered on three proposed bills: first, the Waste Export and Import Prohibition Act, H.R. 2580, introduced in June 1991 by Representative Edolphus Towns (D-NY), which sought to ban the export and import of waste from and to the United States; second, the Waste Export Control Act, H.R. 2358, introduced by Representatives Mike Synar and Howard Wolpe on May 15, 1991, which sought to regulate, rather than prevent, the international export of US waste, allowing for export to facilities that conformed to US waste disposal standards; and third, the Hazardous and Additional Waste Export and Import Act, H.R. 2398, prepared by the Bush administration and introduced on May 20, 1991, which provided the absolute minimum regulation necessary to implement the Basel Convention. Proposing a general ban on waste exports, it required the US government to enter into an agreement with any other government in order to enable waste trade between the two. The agreements required prior informed consent and demanded the environmentally sound management of wastes. The bill neither specified environmentally sound standards nor explained how facilities would be evaluated.[18]

In all three bills, the key issues were the ban, bilateral agreements, and the technical specifications of "environmentally sound management." The proposals of Towns and the Bush administration were almost diametrically opposed in these respects. While Towns promoted a ban with only minor exceptions—such as "small quantities of personal household waste carried by individuals traveling abroad"[19]—the president's bill called for only a nominal ban, exempting all other arrangements with bilateral agreements. Mike Synar raged that the effect of such exemptions would be a bill that had "no impact whatsoever."[20] Synar and

Wolpe's bill proposed the continuation of the international waste trade, given that sometimes export might be an "environmentally preferred solution," but with stringent restrictions. The United States had to ensure that when waste was disposed of in foreign nations, citizens there received "the same degree of protection that we demand for our own citizens."[21]

The bilateral agreements with Canada and Mexico, signed in 1986, were the hot potatoes. These agreements regulated exports on the principle of prior informed consent.[22] If the US joined the Basel Convention, they would require modification to broaden their definitions of hazardous wastes: they would have to include, for example, the thousands of US car batteries exported to Mexico for recycling. Additionally, the United States would have to establish control mechanisms for enforcement of its laws beyond US borders. Some representatives saw this as a breach of a foreign country's sovereignty.[23] Once again, as in 1988, turning the discussion of waste exports into a matter of national sovereignty diverted attention from issues of liability that US businesses might face when their actions negatively affected foreign countries.

Although representatives did not reach a consensus, they decided that it would be beneficial for the United States to join the Basel Convention, and the Senate agreed to ratify it in August 1992.[24] The decision had no practical implications, as the legislation necessary for the president to act on the Senate decision was never put in place. None of the bills on the US waste trade were passed.

The political process stalled over two issues: agreement between the Senate and the president, and changes to national waste legislation to prevent the Basel Convention from overriding existing US laws. After 1992, hopes were briefly raised that the Clinton administration would act. Vice President Al Gore was a vocal environmentalist and supporter of the ban on waste exports. But after the Republicans took control of Congress in 1994, the Clinton administration could not follow through on its declared intentions. Instead, the secretary-general of the United Nations Environment Programme (UNEP) received a note that the United States would "deposit its instrument of ratification of the Basel Convention."[25] To this day, the United States is not a member of the Basel Convention.[26]

Adjustments to and beyond the Basel Convention

As of May 5, 1992, Argentina, Australia, China, Czechoslovakia, El Salvador, Finland, France, Hungary, Jordan, Liechtenstein, Mexico, Nigeria, Norway, Panama, Romania, Saudi Arabia, Sweden, Switzerland, Syria, and Uruguay had ratified the Basel Convention, and so the UN's framework for regulating the (unequal) global trade with hazardous wastes entered into force. It was a weak framework, lacking the participation of many of the major industrial countries—most notably the United States, the European Economic Community (except for France), and Japan—that together produced about 90 percent of the world's hazardous waste, as well as many of the African, Caribbean, and Latin American countries most often targeted to receive it.[27] The convention was also highly criticized by Greenpeace activists, who argued that the UN's framework established only a "global toxic waste trade notification system" that allowed the unequal trade to continue based on an unverifiable "prior consent" and an undefined notion of "environmentally sound disposal."[28] At the first meeting of the convention's members in Uruguay in December 1992, even UNEP's executive director, Mostafa Tolba, complained that the Basel Convention was "limping" into effect.[29]

Tolba worried that the situation would give rise to alternative global governance frameworks, making Basel even less attractive for UN members to join. A number of nations had already begun to take precautionary measures to control the wastes coming their way. In 1986, Guatemala had been the first nation to enshrine a ban on waste imports in its constitution, followed by Haiti in 1987 and Nigeria, Benin, the Gambia, and Togo in 1988.[30] Such initiatives had been encouraged by Greenpeace, whose activists worried that the slow process of negotiating an international framework convention failed to address the urgency of the situation. Then, as the ratification of the Basel Convention continued at a similarly slow pace, other countries instituted their own waste bans. Between 1988 and 1994, the number of countries banning the trade in hazardous waste rose from 6 to 103. Most of these countries were in the global South, though Italy and Norway had both passed a waste-trade ban after the scandals concerning the *Bark* and the *Karin B*.[31]

The inconsistencies between bans instituted by individual nations made it easy for traders to find legal loopholes. Additionally, these bans placed the burden of identifying waste imports as hazardous on the importing countries. As the story of the *Khian Sea* had illustrated, these countries often did not have the financial and technical resources to monitor imported wastes or the political will (or stability) to enforce their bans.[32]

Seeking to pool resources through an international governance framework while implementing their individual bans, many countries from the global South did just as Tolba feared: they used or created alternative platforms to that of the United Nations. Directly following the negotiations in Basel in 1989, the African,

Caribbean, and Pacific Group of States (ACP), founded in 1975 and representing seventy-nine countries, insisted that the European Economic Community (EEC) impose a ban on exports of hazardous wastes to their regions. This ban would become part of the Lomé IV Convention, the fourth installment of an aid and trade agreement between the EEC and the ACP. The EEC first suggested continuing to allow exports as long as disposal technologies were exported with them, but it backed down after the ACP refused to deviate from its demand for a ban. In a compromise, the ACP countries agreed not to accept any hazardous wastes from any other countries, such as the United States, in return for an export ban on hazardous wastes to their region through the EEC. The Lomé IV agreement came into force in 1991 and was valid until 2000.[33]

Many of the African nations had left Basel with the intention of setting up an alternative governance framework for hazardous waste through the Organisation of African Unity (OAU) and the OAU resolution from May 1988 in Addis Ababa, where they had deplored the industrial countries' "toxic terrorism." In January 1991, at an OAU ministerial meeting in Bamako, Mali, its members adopted the Bamako Convention on the Ban of the Import into Africa and the Control of Transboundary Movement and Management of Hazardous Wastes within Africa.[34]

The Bamako Convention banned the import of hazardous wastes, including radioactive wastes, into African countries. Additionally, it addressed ocean dumping, imposed strict liability (which made generators legally responsible for harms resulting from hazardous waste even in the absence of fault or criminal intent), and forbade the import of banned or canceled substances or products. These provisions illustrated that the OAU wanted to address the structures that allowed for global environmental inequality rather than singular cases of it. Finally, the convention called for the transfer of pollution-management technologies to Africa. By March 1996, the Bamako Convention had gained the necessary ratifications from ten member nations and came into force.[35]

Other regions soon followed the African example. In 1992, six presidents of Central American nations signed the Central American Agreement on the Transboundary Movement of Hazardous Wastes. The convention was similar to the Bamako Convention in calling for a ban not only on waste trading but also on the transportation, ocean dumping, and ocean incineration of hazardous wastes. In 1993, nineteen countries in the Mediterranean region agreed to negotiate a protocol banning the waste trade within the framework of the existing Barcelona Convention for the Protection of the Mediterranean Sea against Pollution

(1975). The resulting Izmir Protocol, which was adopted in 1996, called for the protection of the Mediterranean Sea by banning the trade and transit of hazardous wastes and their disposal between industrial and developing countries in the region. It went into force in 2008. In late 1993, the South Pacific Forum began negotiations on a regional convention known as the Waigani Convention. Adopted in September 1996, implemented in 2001, and still in effect, it bans the import of hazardous and radioactive wastes from outside the convention area to developing countries in the convention area, and prohibits New Zealand and Australia from exporting hazardous or radioactive wastes to developing countries in the convention area.[36]

Greenpeace played a pivotal role in all of these regional conventions. One of the organization's key criticisms of the Basel Convention was that it had merely transformed the trade from disposal, which it restricted, to recycling, which it did not. Exporters increasingly relabeled their waste as commodities that were bound for recovery options. According to Greenpeace data, some 90 percent of the hazardous waste trade had shifted from disposal to recycling operations.[37] Through defining their activities as recycling, waste traders could also circumvent many of the regional bans on waste imports.

In response, a new alliance between environmental activists and governments, primarily from countries in the global South, was formed to revisit the UN framework of the Basel Convention, theoretically the most powerful global governance structure, and the idea of a ban. At the conferences of the parties (COPs) to the Basel Convention, which were growing in membership over the 1990s, they revived the campaign to include a ban in the Basel Convention. The COP 2 meeting in 1994 favored a ban, but this decision lacked legal force. Only in 1995 was the ban adopted as an amendment to the Basel Convention.[38] Any amendment to a UN convention, however, needs to undergo a ratification process similar to that of a convention, and the accompanying discussions again led to renegotiations, reinterpretations, and delay—in this case, a very long delay. The ban did not come into force until September 2019, when Croatia became the ninety-seventh country to ratify it.[39]

The *Khian Sea* in Court

As the international community wrestled over the Basel Convention and possible alternative frameworks, the *Khian Sea* for once remained in the spotlight. At the height of the drama, almost everyone involved in its story had agreed that *someone* should be held responsible. In a convoluted set of court cases in the early 1990s, the US legal system attempted to figure who that should be.

The legal process of assigning liability began in May 1988. Paolino & Sons, the original waste contractors with the city of Philadelphia, had filed suits against other companies involved. Although they had outsourced the disposal of the ash to Amalgamated, they worried that the city would hold them responsible if the ship and cargo went missing. In response, a United States District Court issued a preliminary injunction preventing Coastal Carriers and Amalgamated from offloading the incinerator ash without first providing Paolino with at least three days' written notice of the proposed place, manner, and method of disposal. The defendants in the Paolino suit whom the US court focused on were Henry Dowd, his son, J. Patrick Dowd, and William P. Reilly, representing Coastal Carriers, the *Khian Sea*'s US agent; and Amalgamated, the Bahamian charterer of the *Khian Sea* and the contractual partner of Paolino & Sons.[40]

On December 15, 1988, after the *Khian Sea* had reappeared as the *Felicia* in Singapore with her holds empty, the district court held a hearing to determine whether the defendants had violated the injunction. Reilly was asked under oath if he had "any knowledge as to what happened to the incinerator residue." Reilly denied any knowledge.[41] US officials took their chance of finding out where the ash had gone in October 1989, when a ship called the *San Antonio* turned up at the Port of Houston. It flew under the Honduran flag, not the Liberian one, but during a routine checkup by the coast guard, the number on the hull—6930180— revealed that it was indeed the *Khian Sea*. The ship's empty hulls were the first confirmation in the United States that the ash had indeed been unloaded. The coast guard also found a broken depth finder, which they used as a reason to detain the ship until US $50,000 in fines could be paid. Some days later they returned with a subpoena from the US attorney's office in eastern Texas, demanding the ship's logbooks. According to speculation, these were gone, as was the ship just days later. Somebody had paid the fine, and the coast guards had had to let the *Khian Sea* go. As the *San Antonio*, the ship continued to Egypt, loaded with bags of white flour. A member of the coast guard commented that he was unsure if the ship's hulls had ever been cleaned. Still, Reilly's answer from a year earlier that he knew nothing about the ash stirred up a legal maelstrom as authorities attempted to pin down responsibility for the disappearance of the *Khian Sea*'s cargo.[42]

In January 1990, the Environmental Crime Section at the US Department of Justice took up the investigation, which was led by the attorney Howard Stewart and brought before a grand jury for the District of Delaware that was investigating potential ocean dumping violations in connection with the voyage of the *Khian Sea* between September 1986 and December 1988.[43] Stewart meticulously reconstructed the vessel's journey after it had left Haiti in February 1988. According to both, Reilly and Dowd, who appeared before the same grand jury a month later, in February 1990, the *Khian Sea* had sailed straight from Haiti back to Philadelphia, where it arrived in March 1988. A large fire at the pier of Paolino & Sons only days prior to the *Khian Sea*'s arrival had prevented the discharge of its cargo and led to its month-long stay at the mouth of the Delaware River.[44] While some took the fire as mere coincidence, Reilly described it to the federal grand jury as an act of ecoterrorism, most likely by Greenpeace, whose activists had allegedly "threatened to blow the ship up if she came up the Delaware River."

Reilly, who had plenty of reason to hold a grudge against the activists, professed memory gaps. He did not remember the names of members of the coast guard who had conveyed this message to him, nor the name of the Greenpeace activist who had uttered the threat.[45] Portraying Greenpeace as ecoterrorists and potential arsonists supported Reilly's strategy of representing himself and J. Patrick Dowd as the victims of environmentalists who had lost their grip on reality.

Reilly also forgot to mention that Paolino had not been keen on the return of the *Khian Sea*. Paolino had refused payment to Amalgamated on the grounds of breach of contract (since the ash had not been disposed of as agreed), and the two companies had been involved in legal proceedings since March 1987.[46] Spreading the blame wider, Reilly attributed the illegal departure of the *Khian Sea* in May 1988 to its captain, Arturo Fuentes Garcia. Given the "daily harassment in the form of the news media or overflying helicopters" and "the complete torching" of Paolino's pier, which was shown on TV, Reilly suggested that the *Khian Sea*'s captain and crew panicked and fled.[47] Importantly, although pressed by the attorney, Howard Stewart, Reilly could not remember having met with the Dowds the day before the *Khian Sea*'s departure to discuss the vessel's fate.[48]

The most important part of Reilly's testimony, backed by Dowd's testimony a month later, concerned the *Khian Sea*'s voyage of roughly five thousand nautical miles from Yugoslavia, where the ship had put in for repairs and changed ownership, flag, and name, through the Suez Canal to Singapore. Somewhere on that trip the *Khian Sea*'s highly contested cargo had disappeared. At the time, Fuentes had told reporters that they had unloaded the ash in port but refused to say in what country.[49] Because the ship's contractor, Amalgamated, had won a contract to dispose of the Khian Sea's ash in addition to another fifty million tons of waste from several US cities, Fuentes claimed that revealing the name of the country might "jeopardize the contract."[50] Appearing before the grand jury in January 1990, Reilly supported Fuentes's version of events.[51] Greenpeace contested that no such contract had materialized. They maintained that the crew had dumped the cargo illegally in the Indian Ocean before reaching Singaporean territorial waters. The US Department of Justice also suspected that the *Khian Sea*'s cargo had ended up in international waters, violating the London Dumping Convention of 1972, but they could not bring proof of this at the hearing. Both Reilly and J. Patrick Dowd went unscathed.

Dowd and Reilly were not the only waste traders to come under US government scrutiny. With the prospect of the United States ratifying the Basel Convention, law officials started focusing on the illegal export of hazardous wastes, which they predicted would become "the international crime of the 1990s—a problem as big as arms or drugs trafficking."[52] Surveillance increased, with a particular emphasis on the US-Mexico border, along which many Mexican production facilities (maquiladoras) were located. According to a 1983 agreement, US companies manufacturing goods in Mexico had to bring their wastes back to the United States. Since the 1986 bilateral waste agreement, US waste could be exported to Mexico only for recovery. Experts now feared that rising costs of hazardous-waste treatment in the United States would lead companies to dump waste illegally in Mexico.[53] California, along with other states, set up a waste-trade task force. On May 9, 1990, shortly after President Bush had stated his support for the Basel Convention, the California task force indicted two waste traders, Raymond Franco and David Torres, on felony charges of international waste smuggling. This was the first case in which individuals were charged and convicted for violation of the Resource Conservation and Recovery Act. The RCRA at the time forbade knowingly transporting hazardous waste to an unlicensed facility, as well as disposing of the material without a permit.[54]

In the same year, two other convicted waste traders, Charles Colbert and Jack Colbert, featured in a national TV documentary. Following the news about the *Khian Sea*, the California-based Center for Investigative Research had started digging into America's trade in waste. In collaboration with the PBS television network, they produced *Global Dumping Ground*. The Colbert brothers, from New York City, had been successful for decades in what they called the "surplus chemicals business." They bought all sorts of chemicals and chemical products—ranging from oxidizers, alkalis, and pesticides to slightly contaminated toothpastes—recycled some of them into more or less usable chemicals, and disposed of the rest. In particular, they traded in chemicals banned from sale in the United States. In 1986, the US District Court for the Southern District of New York convicted the two brothers—not for trading in hazardous waste but for defrauding a US government agency. One of their business partners in Zimbabwe had paid for what turned out to be defunct chemicals using funds from USAID.[55] To those familiar with the global waste trade, the Colberts' scheme involving banned chemicals was a familiar one. Their conviction drew attention to the environmental impacts of USAID in countries it was intended to assist.

In 1992, just after the Basel Convention had been ratified, the US District Court for the District of Delaware revisited the narrative on the *Khian Sea*. This time their key witness was the ship's former captain, Arturo Fuentes Garcia, whose testimony radically contradicted the story Reilly and Dowd had told of the hapless but harmless voyage of the *Khian Sea*. Fuentes revealed that Reilly, who had served as his contact with Amalgamated and Coastal Carriers, had ordered him not to sail straight back to Philadelphia from Haiti but to dock at the Bahamas to pick up a small bulldozer with which to dump the ash overboard in the Atlantic. Reilly had then met the *Khian Sea* in Florida, where he promised the ship's officers and crew additional compensation for carrying out the illegal act of ocean dumping. Before they could start, however, the ship received orders to "suspend operations" and sail to Philadelphia. Presumably the Americans had hopes of discharging the cargo legally in Philadelphia—which were dashed by the fire at Paolino's pier.[56]

The plan for ocean dumping was revived after the ship's illegal departure from its anchorage at the mouth of the Delaware. Again Fuentes testified that his orders to take the *Khian Sea* across the Atlantic came from Reilly. A few days after the departure from Delaware, the crew began discharging the *Khian Sea*'s cargo into the Atlantic. Two weeks into the task, the dumping equipment broke down. In July 1988 the *Khian Sea* docked at Bijela, Yugoslavia, for repairs. Reilly, on behalf of Amalgamated, arrived in Yugoslavia to oversee the sale of the ship and its cargo from Lily Navigation to Romo Shipping Corporation (both owned by Robert Cordes) for US $10.[57]

In Yugoslavia, Reilly gave Fuentes further instructions. As of now, they would no longer refer to the ship's cargo, but rather to its "ballast," and Fuentes would receive instructions as to when to get rid of that "ballast." Reilly left Fuentes with instructions to sail toward Colombo, Sri Lanka.[58] Attempts were made to find a dumping ground for the ash in Greece, the Philippines, Indonesia, and Singapore. In Bangladesh, according to Greenpeace, heavy rain foiled a dumping attempt.[59]

Some days after the *Khian Sea*'s departure from Yugoslavia, a radiotelegram instructed Fuentes to arrive in Sri Lanka with only five hundred tons of "ballast" on board. The crew dumped all the rest in the Indian Ocean and, after yet another change of plan, proceeded toward Singapore. In November 1988 the *Khian Sea* reached Singapore with empty holds. According to Fuentes, J. Patrick Dowd boarded the ship in Singapore, removed all gear connected to the ocean dumping operation, and told Fuentes to replace the logbook with a falsified one. Any inquisitive journalists should be told that the ash had been dumped in a country that could not be named.[60]

Fuentes's testimony proved that Reilly and Dowd not only knew about the illegal ocean dumping but had ordered it. Indictments against both men followed in 1992 and 1993. In 1993 Reilly was convicted of two counts of making false declarations before a grand jury and one count of ocean dumping. Dowd was convicted of one count of making a false declaration.[61]

At first sight, the convictions of these traders seemed to demonstrate the Bush administration's tough new stance on the unequal international trade in wastes. On closer inspection it became obvious that US law could not target unequal trade deals as such but only other aspects of the transactions. The Colbert brothers were indicted for misappropriating federal money, Reilly for lying to a US grand jury. Only Franco and Torres had been convicted for illegal waste disposal. In any event, successful prosecutions would not allow legislators to put a stop to shady recycling. Between 1989 and 1992, about 590 million tons of hazardous waste legally crossed US borders.[62]

Return to Sender

Despite the attention paid in the media and the courts to the voyage of the *Khian Sea*, the incinerator ash the ship had offloaded in Haiti continued to sit on the beach at Gonaïves, almost exactly where the *Khian Sea* had left it: in an open concrete-block depot, exposed to wind and water.[63] A first attempt to have the ash returned to Philadelphia came shortly after the *Khian Sea*'s departure from Haiti. During the protests at Gonaïves on March 25, 1988, the opposition leader in Haiti's National Assembly, Jean-Robert Lalane, called on the masses "to stand up to require Manigat's government to remove the poisonous waste from the face of the people."[64] It was the intransigence of the American actors involved in the transaction, rather than the Haitian government, that turned the repatriation attempts into a decade-long battle.

On their return from their investigation in Haiti in February 1988, Greenpeace activists brought back samples of the ash, primarily for scientific testing but also as a "small gift" for Philadelphia's mayor, Wilson Goode. A Philadelphia grassroots initiative supported Greenpeace in protesting ash-handling operations at the Paolino pier.[65] Goode agreed to meet with members of Greenpeace and the Washington Office on Haiti, a human rights group that monitored Haiti's political and economic development. Fritz Longchamp, a representative of the Washington Office on Haiti, delivered a petition with 850 signatures of Gonaïves residents asking Philadelphia to remove the ash.[66] The city government ducked and assigned responsibility to the waste traders, asserting that Paolino still had a valid contract.[67] Tensions grew when the government of Haiti threatened a lawsuit against Philadelphia. As Longchamp explained, for an African American mayor to send Philadelphia's waste to Haiti was "a big blow to the people of Haiti and the Haitian community in the US, who look at the black leadership in the US as family."[68]

US State Department officials refused to get involved in the dispute, as no laws had been broken when the ash was unloaded as topsoil fertilizer.[69] In the end, the EPA and the United Nations Development Program sent representatives to Gonaïves to investigate the site. They recommended the construction of a permanent containment facility for the ash. Haitian authorities later removed the waste and sealed it in concrete on a hillside only a few miles from the original dump site at Sedren Wharf.[70]

Throughout the 1990s, political and activist groups in Haiti, Canada, and the United States continued to rally for the repatriation of the ash. In May 1991 Evans Paul, mayor of Port-au-Prince and a close adviser to President Jean-Bertrand Aristide, traveled to Washington, DC, to seek congressional and public support for the removal of the ash. He also met with Edolphus Towns, chair of the US Congressional Black Caucus and the sponsor of the bill to ban all US waste exports, with the intention of striking an Afro-Caribbean–African American alliance. Both Towns and Paul believed that only a ban could protect countries with weak environmental laws. Paul also argued that the US had the moral responsibility for the incinerator ash in Gonaïves. "People who put it there, should remove it."[71]

Another initiative was prompted by the Haiti Communications Project, a Boston-based organization of Haitian Americans. Its director, Earl Lafontant, led fact-finding missions to Gonaïves in 1991 and 1992 to investigate the state of the environment after the ash had been sitting there for about three years. They returned with five hundred envelopes filled with samples of the incinerator ash. Half of them were addressed to Philadelphia's mayor, Wilson Goode, and the other half to William K. Reilly, then chief administrator of the EPA. Each envelope was inscribed, "Contains Philadelphia Waste. Return to Sender. Delivered three years ago. Mislabeled as fertilizer."[72]

Radical political changes in Haiti abruptly terminated both initiatives. In September 1991 the Haitian military removed the progressive President Aristide, elected only eight months earlier in Haiti's first democratic elections. After the coup, the military targeted pro-Aristide officials, rural-development and peasant organizations, neighborhood and community associations, and trade unions. They destroyed food stores, killed livestock, and shut down independent radio stations. Civilians were killed and arrested en masse. A huge exodus resulted: as of February 4, 1992, fourteen thousand Haitian "boat people" had arrived at Guantanamo, Cuba, where the US Navy had set up a tent camp.[73] In response, the Bush administration suspended all humanitarian aid to Haiti, instituted embargoes, froze Haitian government assets in the United States, stopped arms shipments, and suspended most American business activity in Haiti.[74] These developments made it more difficult to campaign for the cleanup and removal of the ash.

The indictment of William P. Reilly and J. Patrick Dowd in 1992 and the Bush administration's posturing against waste traders gave activists an opportunity to reframe their campaign for the repatriation of the ash. It ended in an unsuccessful attempt to draw connections between the waste trade and the Bush administration's anti-immigration policy toward Haitian boat people, placing both in the framework of ongoing colonialism. "What kind of president ignores international law by turning away political refugees while violating Haitian law and allowing US waste to poison our beaches?" asked Lafontant from the Haitian Communications Project, to no avail.[75]

Initiatives to repatriate the ash were grounded in observations of environmental degradation and health problems in Gonaïves that locals saw as linked to the ash. After the cargo of the *Khian Sea* was unloaded in January 1988, about one thousand tons of the material had been used as fill in the dock area to provide a road base for heavy equipment used in the offloading. The remainder of the discharged cargo, about three thousand tons, was brought to an area just behind Sedren Wharf. Some of it may have been hauled away by local farmers for use on their fields.[76] In a first attempt to clean up the area in June 1988, Haiti's Manigat government had ordered the ash to be moved to Morne Lapierre, a small mountain about seven kilometers north of Gonaïves, and placed in sealed metal containers.[77] Yet in 1992, American activists reported that most of the ash still lay in piles completely exposed to sun, air, and wind in an open roadside pit with no fencing or warning signs, easily accessible to grazing cattle and to people.[78]

The toxic substances in the ash—including lead, cadmium, carcinogenic dioxins, and benzene—contaminated the soil and water.[79] Meanwhile, local residents continued to use the water nearby for swimming, cleaning, or cooking, "unaware of the harmful effects and dangers, and also out of necessity, because of the lack of piped water." By 1988 residents noted that their cattle were dying for no identifiable reason.[80] In 1995, the International Liaison Office of Haitian President Jean-Bertrand Aristide (who returned to power in 1994) claimed that the ash's chemicals had "killed fish and other marine life . . . goats and other animals which graze on the soil, and adversely affected the health of the 5,000 people living near the site. Local residents were forbidden from using salt drying beds nearby, and could no longer depend on fishing for food or income."[81] The Collectif Haïtien pour la Protection de l'Environnement et un Développement Alternatif, (COHPEDA), a Haitian environmental group, claimed that people living near Morne Lapierre had died. Haitian officials told international journalists that several workers who had helped unload the *Khian Sea*'s cargo in 1988 had since died. Other workers reportedly suffered from skin lesions and vision problems.[82] Proof was difficult to establish, however, because there was no medical follow-up in the area and no autopsies were carried out on the animals, and the reports did not galvanize the support necessary for repatriating the ash.

New opportunities to negotiate the return of the ash arose when Bill Clinton became president of the United States in 1992. During the election campaign, Clinton had pledged that he would reverse the Bush administration's policies on Haitian refugees and support Aristide's return to power. In 1994, Clinton was persuaded to act on this promise and to intervene in Haiti on behalf of Aristide, backed by strong Senate approval for the military operation Uphold Democracy.[83] Greenpeace immediately sent a request to the US Army to take samples of the ash in Gonaïves and bring it back after completing their mission.[84] The US military did go to Gonaïves to investigate the disposal site, but they left the material as they found it after concluding that the ash contained no toxic materials in excess of US thresholds.[85]

Haitian activists took advantage of the Clinton administration's growing need to portray Haiti as a democratic and foreign policy success. When Clinton visited Haiti in 1995, he was greeted by activists carrying a petition for the removal of the waste at Gonaïves, signed by forty-five Haitian organizations.[86] Similarly, activists targeted Vice President Al Gore. In his 1992 book *Earth in the Balance*, Al Gore had decried the global waste economy as "disquieting" and "unthinkable."[87] Now activists called on citizens all around the world to write to Gore and urge him to follow through on his message.[88] Clinton's secretary of state, Madeleine Albright, also drew the attention of activists during her visits to Haiti in 1997 and 1998 to resolve the political problems resulting from the 1997 Haitian election. In an open letter, COHPEDA requested Albright to provide US $200,000 for the return of the waste to Philadelphia.[89]

In the end, it was Paolino that provided activists with the best chance of repatriating the ash. Paolino had continued its waste-hauling operations almost undisturbed after the scandal of the *Khian Sea*. No member of the company was ever prosecuted for involvement in the affair. Yet in 1996 the ship came back to haunt them. That year, New York City had created the Trade Waste Commission, intended to purge the city's waste-hauling industry of corrupt officials and the influence of organized crime. The city received an application from Eastern Environmental Services, a New Jersey–based garbage-hauling company, for a permit to collect and dump waste from businesses in New York City. During its routine background check of the company, the city uncovered connections to the *Khian Sea*: Louis Paolino, an executive of Eastern Environmental Services, had formerly managed Paolino & Sons.

The commission recommended to Eastern Environmental Services that it would help their application for a license if they first cleaned up the ash in Haiti.[90] Under an unusual deal, Eastern Environmental Services agreed to remove the ash and dispose of it in a private landfill in Chambersburg, Pennsylvania. The company agreed to pay $100,000 toward the removal and disposal, estimated to cost $150,000 in total.[91] This commitment was a small one considering the revenues Eastern Environmental Services expected to gain from a waste-hauling permit for New York City. By the terms of the deal, if the balance of the funds was not secured by May 1998—within roughly two years—the company would be relieved of this obligation and allowed to secure the waste hauling permit without it.[92]

The announcement of the deal sparked the interest of Greenpeace and other environmental activist groups in the United States and Haiti, and they revived the Return to Sender campaign in 1997. As Greenpeace had by then redirected many of its resources toward other campaigns, Essential Action, a Washington DC–based organization, became the center of the initiative. The activists first attempted to pressure the City of Philadelphia into paying the remaining costs of the removal of the ash—initially estimated at $50,000, but soon swelling to $200,000.[93] The activists' strategy was based on generating international publicity for the story of the *Khian Sea* and the remaining ash on Haiti's beach, portraying it as an ethical and environmental crime. They organized letter-writing campaigns and sent samples of the ash in envelopes to US officials.[94] On Valentine's Day 1998, they sent two hundred Valentines with pink hearts to Philadelphia's mayor, Ed Rendell, that read "Have a Heart. This Valentine's Day, help bring Philly's waste home from Haiti." During another action, activists plastered the area near City Hall with signs featuring photographs of Philadelphia's mayor over the phrase "WANTED for Environmental Racism."[95]

Haiti was the poorest nation in the world, with a GDP of about US $2.4 billion and an average annual per-capita income of US $380 in 1998. The City of Philadelphia had a budget of $2.6 billion and per capita income of $2,510. In comparison to Haiti, activists argued, Philadelphia was "fabulously wealthy."[96] Back in 1988, Philadelphia had never paid for the disposal of the ash on board the *Khian Sea*: it had refused payment to Paolino after the company failed to provide proof that the ash had been legally disposed of. According to Greenpeace, this had saved the city some $600,000. Activists also pointed to the $130 million budget surplus that Philadelphia had supposedly had in 1997. The cost of returning the ash, they argued, would be a small price to pay to remove "this threat from Haiti and win a victory for international environmental justice."[97] Rendell, however, said that the city could not afford the cost.[98]

On the Haitian side, COHPEDA had become the lead actor for the campaign, acting increasingly independently from Western environmental institutions. COHPEDA representatives participated in the intersectoral meetings organized by the Haitian foreign minister, involving a number of different Haitian ministries and the Port Authority, to work on the repatriation of the waste. A "chrono-gramme" of activities was developed by which the return of the ash was planned for March 1998.[99] Then, coinciding with US secretary of state Albright's visit to Haiti, a group of US and Canadian activists with the Return to Sender campaign traveled to Port-au-Prince to meet with partner organizations. They held a number of joint protest actions in front of the US Embassy to emphasize the United States' moral obligation to aid in the repatriation of the ash.[100] Their window of opportunity would close in May 1998, when Eastern Environmental Services' obligation to solve the issue of the ash in Gonaïves would expire. Yet officials at the US Embassy stated that they had no plans to respond to the demonstration.

In their view, the ash was a matter between the Haitian government and a private company.[101] Events received another push when the brothers Alexandre Paul and Antonio Paul were arrested in early April 1998 for having violated Article 258 of the 1987 Haitian constitution, which prohibited the introduction of foreign waste into the country. Both were proprietors of Éleveurs de l'Ouest, the company that in 1987 had imported Philadelphia incinerator ash as "fertilizer." To COHPEDA, the arrest of the two brothers was an encouraging sign.[102]

Meanwhile, the Return to Sender campaign increased the pressure on the City of Philadelphia, whose officials reiterated that the removal of the ash was not their responsibility and refused to contribute to the cost.[103] Global Response, a US-based transnational network that seeks to force action by flooding officials with letters, now became a key player in the story. Within days, hundreds, if not thousands, of letters flooded Mayor Rendell's office.[104] The mayor's office answered all the letter writers, politely restating that the city had "no legal obligation" to help in the matter since the ash had been discharged in Gonaïves without "the permission or the knowledge of the City." Although they were certainly willing to offer support for the removal of the ash from Haiti, that support did not extend to providing financial assistance.[105]

The City of Philadelphia was facing pressure over waste disposal for other reasons as well. Initially, the city's waste problems had appeared to be resolved when Philadelphia signed a deal with Waste Management in 1988 for the disposal of about 2.1 million tons of waste, roughly 80 percent of its annual municipal solid waste, at two landfills in Bucks County.[106] By 1990, this arrangement was proving inadequate, and Rendell signed a multiyear contract to send one hundred thousand tons of Philadelphia's trash to an incinerator in Chester, a small industrial town on the Delaware waterfront southwest of Philadelphia. The choice of Chester again linked Philadelphia with environmental racism. As a result of deindustrialization, Chester, once a thriving town, was now one of the poorest communities in Delaware County. Its predominantly African American and low-income population battled with high crime and poverty rates. It housed not only the fourth-largest waste incinerator in the US, but also the largest medical-waste autoclave, a sewage treatment facility, and a sludge incinerator, among other polluting industries.[107]

By 1992, citizens of Chester had started organizing against the waste facilities that had promised jobs but brought only noise, dust, and pollution to the town. Under the leadership of Zulene Mayfield, a group of citizens formed Chester Residents Concerned for Quality Living (CRCQL) to take on Pennsylvania's

Department of Environmental Protection (DEP) and a number of corrupt businesspeople who had benefited from deals that sited waste management and treatment facilities in Chester. Supported by the Philadelphia public interest lawyer Jerome Balter, they fought the building of a sterilization plant for infectious medical waste all the way to the Pennsylvania Supreme Court. They also challenged the granting of a permit to the Cherokee Environmental Group to burn contaminated soil at Chester. The campaigns had mixed success.[108] In 1996 CRCQL sued the State of Pennsylvania, accusing the DEP of discrimination for concentrating the city's waste-processing sites in Chester. In January 1998 a federal court ruled that residents had a "private right of action" to challenge the distribution of waste treatment and management facilities in Chester on grounds of racial discrimination.[109]

CRCQL subsequently charged the City of Philadelphia with environmental racism, using the analogy with Haiti to argue that racist aggression had a long legacy. The notion of environmental racism had gained recognition and boosted the work of environmental justice groups across the US since 1994, when President Clinton had signed an executive order on environmental justice. In response to Clinton's executive order, the EPA conducted a six-month cumulative risk assessment in Chester. Their data, released in 1995, found that the pollution in Chester was associated with unacceptable risks of cancer and other diseases, such as kidney and liver diseases and respiratory problems. Children in Chester had alarmingly high blood lead levels, higher than any other community in Pennsylvania, and residents' lung cancer rates were 60 percent higher than the national average.[110]

In October 1998, Haiti's Ministry of the Environment announced that the ash from the *Khian Sea* would finally be removed and transported to a suitable site in Virginia under a contract between the US company Caribbean Dredging and Excavation, Inc., and the Haitian Ministry of the Environment. The removal, described in a ministry press release as the "fruit of long and delicate negotiations," was a concerted effort by many actors, including Haitian and US public authorities, local authorities in Gonaïves, international organizations (including UNDP, WHO, and USAID), and civil-society organizations and NGOs from both countries.[111] Of the estimated cost, approximately US $450,000, the Haitian government would pay $272,000, Eastern Environmental Services US $225,000 ($100,000 in cash and the rest in in-kind services), and the City of Philadelphia—although it never admitted any responsibility—$50,000.[112] The proposal called for the ash to be removed beginning October 8, 1998, to arrive in Virginia October 25, 1998, and to be disposed of in a landfill five days later.[113]

In the event, Caribbean Dredging and Excavation notified the Haitian government that the ship would arrive on November 13, 1998, and the government issued a press release. Workers in Gonaïves collected the material and transported it from the open-air pit at Morne Lapierre to Sedren Wharf. The deputy mayor of Gonaïves, a representative of the Haitian Ministry of the Environment, and representatives of local and national environmental organizations were on hand to celebrate the removal of the ash.[114] But the ship never arrived.

The Toxic Homecoming of Philadelphia's Ash

The events of November 1998 had a strangely familiar ring. The ship had reached Port-au-Prince, but the final destination of the ash remained an unresolved matter. Without a proper import destination, Caribbean Dredging and Excavation could not get the necessary papers to allow the cargo to enter US waters.[115]

Initially the Haitian actors maintained an optimistic attitude. News outlets recounted that only" administrative formalities" were keeping the boat in Port-au-Prince.[116] But the days turned into weeks, and weeks into months. Caribbean Dredging and Excavation suspended its work, and, having failed to find a destination for the ash in the United States, "packed up its bags" and left.[117] By December 1998, the people of Gonaïves were angry. Yet again a US company had left waste sitting on their wharf. Workers had dumped the ash on the ground and covered it only with carpet, as it was due to be picked up within days. Now the ash lay exposed and uncontained. If it rained, it would be "catastrophic for the population of Gonaïves."[118] The Commission of Justice and Peace from Gonaïves, a small civil-society organization, began a campaign protesting the second abandonment of the ash, putting up signs and distributing T-shirts with the slogan "Retour Philadelphie."[119]

COHPEDA urged the Haitian Ministry of Foreign Affairs, the Ministry of the Environment, and US state officials to intervene.[120] Yet Haitian officials could do little to intervene in a conflict involving US domestic laws, and the US government did nothing to help. COHPEDA reported that according to an anonymous source, the US Embassy in Port-au-Prince had asked Caribbean Dredging and Excavation to suspend the provisional work of getting the ash ready for transport while the import license was pending.[121] As a sign of goodwill, the US Embassy in Haiti held a press conference "saluting the efforts made by the Haitian government and civil society organizations to bring a definitive solution to the Gonaïves toxic waste file." They continued to applaud Haitian efforts from the sidelines. When asked about US government support in the search for a US disposal site, the US press attaché only noted that this issue was not "within his competence."[122]

Unwilling to give up, activists in Haiti and the United States mobilized for what they hoped would be their final battle. In actions jointly organized by the Penn Environmental Group and the Penn Human Rights Group, students at the University of Pennsylvania strongly criticized Philadelphia's inaction.[123] Together with Greenpeace, the student groups demanded that the city create a dumping ground for the ash from Gonaïves if need be.[124] In an act of international solidarity, more than seventy activists from different organizations based in Haiti, the United States, and Puerto Rico met in Haiti in June 1999 and helped organize a demonstration involving tens of thousands of Haitians to protest the delayed removal of the ash. Protesters dressed in white carried placards and shouldered symbolic coffins while chanting, "Gonaïves is not a garbage can!"[125]

For close to two years, the return of the ash seemed to be an unresolvable dilemma. Haiti's Ministry of the Environment fell silent on both the possible return of the ash and measures to prevent contamination from the material at its unprotected site at Sedren Wharf.[126] Then the issue almost seemed to resolve itself. In spring 2000, the Haitian Office of the President, the Haitian Ministry of the Environment, the US Department of Agriculture, and the New York City Trade Waste Commission negotiated an agreement for removing the ash.[127]

Underpinning this agreement was another deal concerning a New York City waste-hauling permit and the company Waste Management, Inc. In August 1998, Waste Management had purchased Eastern Environmental Services and thereby become the world's largest waste-management company. With the acquisition of Eastern Environmental Services, however, it also inherited the controversy over Philadelphia's incinerator ash.[128] The company's decision to tackle the repatriation was based in part on its ambition to obtain a waste-hauling permit with New York City: the city's Waste Trade Commission made the granting of the permit contingent on the removal of the Philadelphia incinerator ash.[129] In addition, Waste Management probably saw a public relations advantage in bringing the *Khian Sea*'s ash home. Since the 1970s, the company had been the target of environmentalists, the media, and the public over issues including the 1980s waste crisis, incineration, and toxic waste management. In early 1983, the *New York Times* had run a front-page story about Waste Management's "toxic empire."[130]

The company had worked hard to change its tarnished image. On April 5, 2000, the *Santa Lucia*, a Greek cargo ship, left Gonaïves carrying Philadelphia ash back from Haiti after more than twelve years.[131]

Even so, it was an uncertain homecoming. Waste Management had not specified a US destination for the ash on board the *Santa Lucia* when leaving Haiti. It had announced only that it planned to dispose of the cargo in one of its landfills in the southern United States. Yet, in contrast to the case of Caribbean Dredging and Excavation, US officials were ready to believe that the biggest player on the US waste disposal market, one that ran its own landfills and recycling facilities, would find a place for the ash, and so they let it enter US territorial waters. When the ship arrived in Stuart, Florida, it unloaded its cargo onto five barges at the port and departed for operations elsewhere.[132] What happened next should come as no surprise: no community was willing to provide a dumping ground for the material, regardless of whether Waste Management ran their local landfill.

Before the ash reentered the United States, the US Department of Agriculture had demanded that it be fumigated to ensure that no living organisms were carried back with it. Upon its arrival in Florida, several US agencies—among them the US Department of Agriculture, the US EPA, the Florida Department of Environment Protection, the City of Philadelphia, and US Biosystems—independently conducted tests. They all returned with the same results. The ash was not toxic: according to US waste regulations, it constituted nonhazardous waste. It contained traces of heavy metals, but not enough to make it hazardous.[133] In fact, the ash that had returned from Haiti was very similar to other incinerator ash that had been dumped in US landfills.

Despite this scientific assessment, multiple waste disposal facilities refused to accept the cargo. Georgia rejected it because Haiti had had an outbreak of hog cholera. Louisiana was suspicious because Philadelphia did not want to accept it. Florida, the state that had initially agreed to dispose of the cargo at its Pompano Beach facility, rescinded the offer six days later.[134] Waste Management then attempted to convince the Cherokee Nation in Oklahoma to take the waste, again targeting a vulnerable community, but without success.[135]

The ash sat on the five barges at port in Stuart for another two years. History has no sense of justice, but sometimes it has a sense of irony. After all other options had fallen through, it was the Pennsylvania DEP that eventually agreed to dispose of the waste. Florida's Department of Environmental Protection, meanwhile, would pay $600,000 to move it. Beginning in June 2002, 128 truckloads of incinerator ash arrived in Pennsylvania. Environmental activists and members of the local Green Party staged a mock "welcome home" party, serving, among other things, ash cake. Its final resting place was the Mountain View Reclamation Center landfill in Franklin County, about 120 miles outside Philadelphia.[136]

At what appeared to be the end of the story of the *Khian Sea*, all involved counted their gains and losses. A decade earlier, Greenpeace had scored one of its biggest successes by helping to bring the Basel Convention into being, but in all the intervening years, it had failed to get the Philadelphia ash home. Additionally, the Basel Convention had become a sore point for environmentalists all around the globe. Neither the United States nor Haiti would join, and Basel Convention members would not ratify a ban on the trade between industrial and developing countries until 2019. Haitian environmentalists could proudly claim that their perseverance had been key in sending the ash home, and COHPEDA had become a key player in Haitian civil society. Yet those responsible had gotten off lightly. J. Patrick Dowd and William P. Reilly had not been charged for violating Haitian laws by disposing of foreign trash but only for dumping part of the *Khian Sea*'s cargo in the ocean. Alexandre Paul and Antonio Paul, the original Haitian importers, had been arrested by Haitian law enforcement, but they were never tried or indicted on charges of environmental crime. The City of Philadelphia never quite came to terms with its ash story. While it contributed US $50,000 to the repatriation of the ash, it never admitted any legal responsibility.

The incinerator ash left traces all around the globe—in Philadelphia, on Haiti, on Kassa Island in Guinea, in the depths of the Atlantic and Indian Oceans, and in a landfill in rural Pennsylvania. It had breached attempts to contain it and mixed with natural elements and living bodies, leaving an uncertain legacy of potential harms, especially for the people on Gonaïves. There is "no happy ending to the story," said Lisa Finaldi, national coordinator of the toxics campaign at Greenpeace, but hopefully, "there was a lesson learned from this, and we can do better at managing . . . waste."[137]

CONCLUSION
Living with the Toxic Commons

Squeezing between multitudes of spider webs, I peered down into the "hold" and couldn't believe my eyes. Australian pines were everywhere, some as tall as 10 feet. There were dandelions, weeds with small blue-and-yellow blossoms, patches of seemingly manicured grass, and tall brown weeds resting in layers across grayish piles punctuated by pure-white chunks of who-knows-what. And there was a hibiscus plant with pretty pink blooms.

GLENN HENDERSON | journalist for the *Palm Beach Post*, inspecting Philadelphia incinerator ash from the *Khian Sea* in 2002

In 2002, the ash from the *Khian Sea*, which was returned from Haiti to Florida aboard the *Santa Lucia*, did not resemble a postapocalyptic wasteland. As the journalist Glenn Henderson noted when inspecting it on the two-year anniversary of the arrival of the globe-trotting incinerator ash in Martin County, Florida, plant life had taken over.[1] Carried on board by wind or on the boots of dock workers, seeds of the Australian pine, dandelions, grass, and other plants had sprouted in the mixture of ash and soil. Ants and earthworms were active beneath the surface. Above the ash, bees hummed, and butterflies hovered. There, "growing from 3,000 tons of the world's most famous piles of garbage-turned-ash, a forest was in the making." Little did the sight of this ecosystem signal the presence of dioxins or heavy metal contamination.[2]

Incinerator ash contains not only hazardous substances but also plant nutrients, such as phosphorus, potassium, and calcium. The scheme to sell Philadelphia incinerator ash as topsoil fertilizer was not entirely spurious, and when Glenn Henderson related his discovery of "healthy flora flourishing on top of ash deemed 'toxic'" to Carol C. Bailey, Martin County's agricultural extension director, she expressed little surprise: "There is water to support it, plenty of nutrients, and nobody is bothering it," she said.[3] In recent years, some waste engineers have proposed using incinerator ash not as fill material in road construction or as raw material for cement and concrete (both proposed as uses for the ash aboard the *Khian Sea* and the *Bark*) but as a component in growing media for plants that could eventually replace commercial fertilizers. Although the use of incinerator ash as fertilizer is prohibited in nearly all industrial countries because of its high concentrations of heavy metals, these scholars argue that it could easily be used in landfill sites and remediation projects in closed industrial areas, where maximum concentration limits often do not apply.[4] Some plants and animals thrive in environments that humans categorize as polluted, toxic, or harmful. Famous examples include the soybean, blueberries, and flax growing near the site of the Chernobyl nuclear reactor, which exploded in 1986 (the same year the *Khian Sea* left Philadelphia).[5] More than 330 wildlife species roam the territory of Rocky Mountain Arsenal, near Denver, Colorado, a former US Army weapons manufacturing facility. One of the United States' worst toxic waste sites, it is now a designated US wildlife refuge. Although hunting is allowed on the refuge to manage wildlife numbers, eating fish or game from the refuge is forbidden because of high levels of radioactive contamination.[6]

When disaster strikes a place, plants cannot leave, like humans or animals. They either die or survive. If they survive, they provide new breeding grounds for invertebrates, mammals, birds, amphibians, reptiles, and fish. Some of these species appear to thrive on poisoned lands. Toxic chemicals do not necessarily prohibit life: they alter it.[7] Sometimes, they do so in ways that allow for the unexpected. "I've been trying hard to grow a hibiscus in my backyard," Henderson observed, "and despite all efforts, it was impossible to keep it alive." But here it thrived on Philadelphia's incinerator ash. "If this stuff is really deadly, someone forgot to tell Mother Nature," Henderson concluded.[8]

Blooming dandelions and a blossoming hibiscus are more than hopeful expressions to end an otherwise gruesome story. They also represent the myriad ambiguities and paradoxes that fundamentally shaped the story of the *Khian Sea* in particular, and that of the global waste trade more generally.

The global waste trade is a complex system of historically shaped structures, ideologies, and personal narratives that have defined and enabled but also limited the choices of societies and individuals to participate in or oppose it. From the onset of the trade, disputes over the unequal trade in hazardous waste arose from ambivalent, and often conflicting, actions, norms, and philosophies. For some actors, the export of hazardous waste constituted "toxic colonialism." For others, it was a system of "voluntary exchange" that allowed actors to choose the most economical (i.e., cheapest or closest) disposal facility, or to prioritize economic growth, even if it meant endangering human health and the environment. For still others, often those living near the toxic material, it represented simultaneously a form of exploitation and endangerment and of economic opportunity.

The Toxic Ship has focused on these tensions and sought to tease out the complexities that, in the end, make the study of the global waste trade, but also the perusal of this book, a practice in bearing contradictions. After all, given the intricate connectedness of the ash with legacies of colonial exploitation and patterns of environmental racism, a blooming dandelion does not represent a happy ending.

Mutability and Mobility

A peculiar and insoluble link between mutability and mobility enabled this story of ambiguities to unfold. Over the decades, the unequal trade in hazardous wastes has gone through three main phases, all involving territorial differences and different evaluations of what constitutes hazardous waste. In the 1970s, the mobility of waste was intimately tied to the campaign against the indiscriminate use of pesticides spurred by Rachel Carson and other environmental activists. A number of synthetic chemicals and subsequently also consumer products—ranging from pesticides to children's sleepwear and baby pacifiers—were banned in many industrial countries, tipping off an almost cyclical pattern of de- and recommodifying them.[9] Substances and goods newly classified as unusable, nonsalable, or hazardous in industrial countries were exported to countries in the global South, where they were still considered commodities. Waste traders exploited opportunities created through the political instabilities and economic dependencies that resulted from decolonization, regime changes, and Western policies of economic development.

The trade in these products created massive and continuing problems for the recipient countries. In addition to inadvertently poisoning people, livestock, and environments on multiple occasions, for instance, the massive quantity of pesticides shipped from industrial countries has created the new problem of pesticide obsolescence. Through international aid programs, donors from the global North sent more pesticides than developing countries could ever use. UN agencies and environmental activists have warned of the hazards posed by aging stockpiles of these synthetic chemicals, often stored in corroding containers and unprotected from the weather, in countries that lack appropriate disposal facilities. The Food and Agriculture Organization of the United Nations estimated that at the beginning of the millennium, there were more than one hundred thousand tons of obsolete pesticides in Africa and Eastern Europe. Often such stockpiles are difficult to repatriate, as the manufacturers and traders responsible for transporting them have long since gone out of business. The questions of who will pay for the cleanup and where contaminated soil will be disposed of remain unanswered.[10]

In the 1980s, a new waste trade pattern emerged: the sale of postconsumption waste, ranging from sewage sludge and municipal incinerator ash to industrial chemical byproducts. Again this form of waste mobility resulted from new regulatory practices in the industrial countries, specifically the introduction of the category of hazardous waste. The United Kingdom's Deposit of Poisonous Waste Act and Germany's Abfallbeseitigungsgesetz (waste disposal legislation), both passed in 1972, were among the first pieces of legislation governing hazardous wastes.[11] The United States defined hazardous wastes as part of the Resource Conservation and Recovery Act (RCRA) of 1976, which became law in 1980. Norway's Pollution Control Act took effect in 1981, and many other industrial countries passed similar legislation.[12] Heralded as timely environmental and health protection measures, these laws came with a catch similar to the consumer safety regulations of the 1970s. They made waste disposal within the respective countries an extremely costly and politically unpopular practice. Exporting hazardous materials to countries with less strict rules thus became an economically viable solution. Between 1989 (when this trade became measurable for the first time) and 1994, member nations of the Organisation for Economic Cooperation and Development (OECD) alone shipped an estimated 2.6 million metric tons of hazardous waste to poorer, non-OECD countries.[13]

While structurally similar, the practices of trading consumer products that new governance had technically turned into waste, such as banned pesticides, and postconsumption waste, such as incinerator ash, represent two separate regulatory categories. In the United States, this split was created in 1980 by President Jimmy Carter's Inter-agency Working Group. With the implementation of the Basel Convention in 1992 and subsequently the Rotterdam Convention, covering the trade of hazardous chemicals, and the Stockholm Convention, restricting the production and use of persistent organic pollutants, both in 2004, this distinction found its way into international governance agreements. Since then, it has been seen as an impediment by administrators and activists, who argue that the externalization of all such hazards—that is, the export or relocation from countries with effective environmental and health protection and labor laws to countries with weaker legislation—is triggered by the same structural deficiencies and requires the same regulatory responses. Both discussions are concerned with the multiple externalization processes that happen throughout the commodity chain without a parallel liability and responsibility system in place. They begin with the extraction of resources and the outsourcing of dirty production and extend to the export of outdated consumer products and schemes to reuse and recycle postconsumption waste.[14]

By the 1990s, with the Basel Convention and the Bamako Convention, the trade in postconsumption waste slowed down markedly. This decrease resulted in part from an increasing number of schemes that focused on defining waste as material for recycling.[15] This shift brought under scrutiny the rapidly and massively growing trade in electronic waste (e-waste) and plastics. Of an estimated fifty million tons of e-waste produced in Europe and the United States, the majority is shipped to countries in Asia and Africa for recycling.[16] In January 2018, China, until then the largest importer of plastics, banned these imports. As with the regional shifts of the waste trade from the greater Caribbean to West Africa, this ban did not necessarily alter practices of waste disposal in the exporting countries: it just changed their destination from China to Vietnam, Malaysia, or another country down the line.[17] The structural patterns that link waste's global mobility on mutable waste governance systems is still in place.

Why Philadelphia?

In a story of two ships' ocean voyages, I have dwelt long on their home port, Philadelphia. The voyages of the *Khian Sea*, the *Bark*, and their cargoes is a global story of wasting and wanting, and its starting point could have been almost any US city in the 1980s. US environmental activists reported on similar schemes in Baltimore, Detroit, New York, and Los Angeles. Their European counterparts dug up stories from Frankfurt, Germany, and Milan, Italy. Yet it is worth asking why Philadelphia, in particular, ended up shipping its waste to the global South.

Prior to an international trade scheme, waste from US cities like Philadelphia was traded locally, dumped in rivers or at sea, or shipped out of state. Philadelphia's waste was shipped primarily to New Jersey. International waste disposal became attractive for Philadelphia only when these more local options fell through. The decision to export to the greater Caribbean was driven by multiple forces: necessity, pressure, and opportunity.

The need for Philadelphia to find an alternative to local waste disposal arose from national environmental legislation, such as the US Water Pollution Control Act of 1948 and the Resource Conservation and Recovery Act of 1976; deindustrialization and municipal impoverishment; white flight; and NIMBY (not in my backyard) activism against hazardous waste disposal sites. Pressure to reform municipal disposal systems came from all sides: the national and federal governments, cities' overflowing landfills, and citizens concerned about environmental and human health. In the United States, these pressures were exacerbated by the rapidly rising quantity of waste (the result of increasing mass consumption) and its changing composition (a greater proportion of plastics, packaging, and synthetic chemicals).[18] Cities lacked the financial means to implement substantive waste reforms, while waste disposal costs skyrocketed. In Philadelphia, a city of 1.5 million residents, disposal costs soared from less than $20 million in 1980 to nearly $50 million in 1988.[19]

The opportunities for waste disposal outside the United States arose from weaker (or nonexistent) environmental and waste management legislation in other countries, in concert with political instability, economic downturn, and development policies welcoming foreign investment. This made it easy to designate the *Khian Sea*'s cargo of municipal incinerator ash, or any other hazardous waste from the United States, as material to be repurposed, often under the pretext of contributing to economic development.[20] Philadelphia's ash was represented as material for building roads that would spur the growth of industry and subsequently of jobs, health care, and education. In addition, many importing agents and governments considered land reclamation through ash disposal as a valid practice and saw mangrove forests as wastelands rather than important wetlands.

The irony that Philadelphia, a city with a large African American population, ended up attempting to dump on structurally and ethnically similar places in the Caribbean and West Africa received little attention. Some activists from the greater Caribbean attempted to establish an ethnic alliance by appealing to Representative John Conyers, cofounder of the Congressional Black Caucus and one of a small group of African American intellectuals who saw environmental degradation as an issue of civil rights and racial justice. Others, primarily those concerned with waste imports to African nations, played up the issue of waste imperialism and a recolonization of the world through trash. Philadelphia's ethnic and economic status complicated the issue, torpedoing a neat narrative of white perpetrators and black victims. The example of Philadelphia illustrates the complexities of waste disposal. It is an additional irony that when Philadelphia incinerator ash from the *Khian Sea* was repatriated from Haiti, it had to be exported out of the city yet again to a Pennsylvania landfill.

THE PARADOXES OF MODERN ENVIRONMENTALISM

Philadelphia's decision to export waste was based not only on a mixture of necessity, pressure, and opportunity, but also on a lack of reflection on alternatives. In the 1970s and 1980s, the new category of hazardous wastes in industrial countries triggered a wave of disgust, fear, and suspicion. NIMBYism became the dominant principle for action. People of New Jersey barred Philadelphia's waste from their landfills. "Haïti n'est pas la poubelle de l'extérieur!" clamored Radio Haiti-Inter, and delegates from fifty African countries raged that former colonial powers were attempting to make Africa "a garbage dumping ground."[21] No community in this story wanted to function as waste disposal site, particularly not for someone else's waste.

Largely missing from this outcry was any discussion on where else these toxic materials should go, how else they could be disposed of, or whether the root of the problem might be the production of these materials rather than their disposal. This lack of reflection was particularly conspicuous in the industrial countries that produced the bulk of the world's hazardous waste. In the United States, responses tended to reflect a faith in the ability of technology to fix the problem. Recycling programs received much less attention than technological solutions.[22]

What allowed Americans—and citizens of other industrial nations—to transport their waste elsewhere instead of altering their consumption and discarding practices was the patchwork nature of the international regulation of waste disposal. While delegates discussed a globally applicable definition of hazardous waste at the first UN Conference on the Human Environment in Stockholm in 1972, it took the United Nations Environment Program (UNEP until 1985 to suggest a working definition and another decade to implement it.[23] Although regulatory frameworks were developed in the industrial countries, many of the countries that the *Khian Sea* approached—such as the Bahamas, Panama, Saint Lucia, Trinidad and Tobago, the Dominican Republic, and Colombia—had no definition of hazardous waste until well into the 1990s. Other countries had a definition but no legislation governing its management, trade, or disposal.[24]

This patchwork approach illustrates the limitations of a philosophy of international governance that saw the environment as compartmentalized by political boundaries, instead of as a congruent and interdependent planetary ecosystem.

In the United States, early twentieth-century regulators debated and enacted laws governing air and water pollution, for instance, without considering what to do with waste materials once producers stopped discharging them into the air or water.[25] Similarly, the US Ocean Dumping Act of 1972 was implemented without considering the additional pressure the legislation would place on land disposal facilities. Throughout the 1970s, the EPA and the US Consumer Safety Commission banned chemical substances and products without considering the range of problems US bans would create abroad.

This compartmentalizing mindset played a role in US foreign policy when the nation revisited its hazardous-substances export policy under President Jimmy Carter. Spurred by the tris sleepwear scandal, US policymakers debated whether national environmental protection laws should also apply to the rest of the world. In 1979, they concluded that such a move would not protect foreign users from potential harm, as it would neither stop US companies from manufacturing US-banned substances abroad nor prevent foreign users from purchasing such substances from a third-country source.[26] Even the Natural Resources Defense Council concluded that US environmental and health standards should not be forced on other nations.[27]

A similar debate occurred a decade later over the export of postconsumption waste. The US Environmental Protection Agency declined to tell other countries what to do with US waste. Hiding behind an equally paternalistic interpretation of postcolonial rhetoric, EPA officials claimed that "some developing countries . . . just don't like to be talked down to by big brother Uncle Sam."[28] Waste traders supported this view on the grounds that deregulated neoliberal markets—and economic growth—thrived on international differences. The Colbert brothers, two waste traders from New Jersey, demanded to know why one should come out and say that "our EPA knows better than 165 other countries in the world."[29]

Hiding behind such expressed reluctance to infringe on other countries' sovereignty stood powerful economic interests. This rhetoric also revealed the environmental privilege of powerful nations, centering on the idea that some places on this planet could function as sanctuaries from contamination and pollution. Seen from this perspective, the global waste trade manifested and reproduced existing inequities in the valuation of human life and environments produced through centuries of colonialism and Western exploitation.

Living with Toxic Legacies

Today, in the age of the Wasteocene—a term more fitting in the context of this book than *Anthropocene*—notions of an ultimate sink (that is, a disposal place or technology with no environmental or social side effects), environmental privilege, and sanctuaries from pollution have lost their credibility.[30] Similarly, seeing residents of the global North as mere bystanders to an unfolding global environmental catastrophe, who do not need to alter their practices of consumption and disposal or mobility and travel has become less and less convincing. Environmental problems such as climatic changes, biodiversity loss, and deforestation affect the entire planet and all its denizens. Toxic chemicals and hazardous waste have left their imprint everywhere. This book shows how they have woven a global network connecting people and ecosystems in the United States, the Caribbean, Central America, Western Africa, Europe and Southeast Asia.[31]

As toxic legacies, their sites and practices have massively expanded, particularly since the 1970s. Both the World Health Organization and UNEP have identified a "toxic pandemic" as one of the greatest global health concerns of the twenty-first century.[32] As *The Toxic Ship* has illustrated, this pandemic comes with the technical challenges of site remediation and cleanup, the scientific challenge of (globally) defining hazards and harm, and the political challenge of dealing with legacies that are often sidelined because they are too hard to address. Today the dominant forms of mainstream environmentalism focus on stopping (new) pollution at its source. Meanwhile, there are numerous sites of previous contamination where it is difficult to clearly assign responsibility, where the polluters are states or companies that no longer exist, where it is difficult to individualize responsibility to consumers, and where remediation has failed to reconstruct pristine nature but has fostered a practice of willful forgetting. In these instances, such as the Haitian port of Gonaïves, affected communities may spent decades living next to toxic waste sites.

While I do not want to understate the importance of these challenges (for future research), one question that kept bothering me while I was writing *The Toxic Ship* was how to live in the alter(ed)-life. The increasing contamination of our planet, camouflaged in the appearance of grasslands, swamps, rocky desert, or forests; of urban wastelands with assemblages of concrete plants, warehouses, and parking lots; and of Australian pines, dandelions, and hibiscus plants with pretty pink blooms, is a reality to reckon with.[33] In my eyes, this reality holds out the challenge not only of learning to bear contradictions while not giving up on environmental justice, but also of seeking alter-futures that offer ways to live with a permanently polluted planet in ways that go beyond remediation and cleanup while being mindful of social and economic inequalities. *The Toxic Ship* is no manual for survival, but I hope it gives inspiration to explore such new pathways.

Notes

INTRODUCTION

1. "Bay Forecast: Delaware Bay," *Morning News* (Wilmington, DE), March 4, 6, 9, 10, 13, 15, 20, 22, 25, 29, 31, 1988; "Bay Forecast: Delaware Bay," *News Journal* (Wilmington, DE), March 1, 11, 16, 17, 22, 24, 1988.

2. Testimony of Captain Edward K. Roe, US Coast Guard, cited in House Government Operations Environment, Energy, and Natural Resources Subcommittee, *International Export of US Waste*, 241.

3. Testimony of Arturo Fuentes Garcia, Wilmington May 24, 1993, United States District Court Delaware, Criminal Case Files, Records of District Courts of the United States, US National Archives, Philadelphia, 1345–47, 1359–61, 1367; WPVI, "WPVI_NY_ Khian Sea," February 1988, WPVI News Footage and Logs.

4. United States of America v. William P. Reilly. Argued May 2, 1994, United States Court of Appeals for the Third Circuit Collection, Records of the United States Courts of Appeals, US National Archives, Philadelphia, 1–2.

5. Cited in Mark Jaffe, "Hopes for Ash Dashed: The Cursed Cargo of the *Khian Sea*," *Philadelphia Inquirer*, May 13, 2000.

6. United States of America v. William P. Reilly, 2–4.

7. United States of America v. William P. Reilly, 2–4.

8. The terms *global North* and *global South* are used to denote the division between the richest and the poorest countries on this planet. *Global South* is thus a term less pejorative than *least developed* or *developing countries*, both historical terms from the 1980s, and more concrete than *majority of the world*.

9. United States of America v. William P. Reilly, 2–4.

10. On the intellectual divides on the concept of the global environment, see Corona, "What Is Global Environmental History?"; Warde, Robin, and Sörlin, *The Environment*; Burke and Pomeranz, *The Environment and World History*.

11. Clapp, *Toxic Exports*; Asante-Duah and Nagy, *International Trade in Hazardous Wastes*; Hilz, *An Investigation*; O'Neill, *Waste*.

12. Key activist groups document their work on their websites and in interviews, publications, photographs, and videos, among them Greenpeace, the Basel Action Network (BAN), Essential Action, and *Rachel's Hazardous Waste News*. For a scholarly perspective see Pellow, *Resisting Global Toxics*. On environmental justice see Bullard, *Dumping in Dixie*; McGurty, *Transforming Environmentalism*; Sze, *Environmental Justice*.

13. Kummer, *International Management of Hazardous Wastes*; Krueger, *International Trade and the Basel Convention*; Andrews, "Beyond the Ban."

14. Brownell, "Negotiating the New Economic Order of Waste"; Satz, *Why Some Things Should Not Be for Sale*; Gwam, *Toxic Waste and Human Rights*; Müller, "Rettet die Erde vor den Ökonomen."

15. On global environmental justice, see Carmin and Agyeman, *Environmental Inequalities;* Faber, *Capitalizing on Environmental Injustice*.

16. Lessenich, *Living Well at Others' Expense*; Moore, *Capitalism in the Web of Life*.

17. Milanović, *Global Inequality*; Nützenadel and Chassé, "Global Inequality and Development after 1945."

18. Bergquist, "Business and Sustainability"; Jones, *Profits and Sustainability*.

19. Douglas, *Purity and Danger*; Gille, *From the Cult of Waste*, 14; Müller, "The Life of Waste"; Liboiron, *Pollution Is Colonialism*.

20. Goldstein, "Waste," 329; Strasser, *Waste and Want*.

21. McCarthy, *Auto Mania*, 66–72; Goldstein, "Waste," 335. Waste is a vast field of historical research. For an introduction, see Melosi, *Fresh Kills*; Köster, *Hausmüll*; Stokes, Köster, and Sambrook, *Business of Waste*; Gille, *From the Cult of Waste*. See also Krebs and Weber, *The Persistence of Technology*, 2021.On recycling see Zimring, *Cash for Your Trash*; Jørgensen, *Recycling*.

22. Goldstein, "Waste," 336; United States Environmental Protection Agency, *National Overview: Facts and Figures on Materials, Wastes and Recycling*, www.epa.gov/facts-and-figures-about-materials-waste-and-recycling/national-overview-facts-and-figures-materials#Trends1960-Today, accessed July 16, 2020.

23. Reith, *Umweltgeschichte der Frühen Neuzeit*; Jarrige and Le Roux, *The Contamination of the Earth*.

24. US EPA definition cited in Rosenfeld and Feng, *Risks of Hazardous Wastes*, 1.

25. Epstein, Brown, and Pope, *Hazardous Waste in America*, 9–11.

26. Langston, "New Chemical Bodies," 260, 270–72.

27. On nuclear wastes see Walker, *The Road to Yucca Mountain*; Hamblin, *Poison in the Well*.

28. See Zachmann and Ehlers, *Wissen und Begründen*; Murphy, *Sick Building Syndrome*; Jasanoff, "Science, Politics, and the Renegotiation of Expertise at EPA."

29. Adam, *Timescapes of Modernity*; Müller and Nielsen, *Toxic Timescapes*; Hecht, "Interscalar Vehicles."

30. Scherr, "Hazardous Exports."

31. Joshua Karliner, "Backyard Dumping: Toxic Waste Export to the Third World," n.d., Delaware Valley Toxic Coalition Records.

32. Clapp, *Toxic Exports*, 22, 47; Borowy, "Hazardous Waste."

33. The US EPA began compiling statistics on US exports in 1986 but did not keep those records longer than five years. Letter from EPA to the author, "Freedom of Information Act Request EPA-HQ-2018–009879," August 8, 2018; letter from EPA to the author, "Freedom of Information Act Requests EPA-HQ-2018–009883," August 8, 2018.

34. Vallette and Spalding, *The International Trade in Wastes*.

35. Interview with Mark Jaffe, Philadelphia, July 20, 2018.

36. Testimony of William P. Reilly, January 9, 1990, United States District Court Delaware, Criminal Case Files, Records of District Courts of the United States, US National Archives, Philadelphia, 40, 51.

37. Cited in WPVI, "WPVI_NY_Khian Sea," February 1988, WPVI News Footage and Logs.

38. Warner, "If All the World Were Philadelphia."

39. Melosi, *Garbage in the Cities*.

40. Armiero, *Wasteocene*; Liboiron, Tironi, and Calvillo, "Toxic Politics."

ONE | "A Classic Situation"

1. Julia M. Klein, "Trash Cleanup at Mid-point, End Near," *Philadelphia Inquirer*, July 21, 1986.

2. Cynthia Burton, "Plenty of Rubbish and Plenty of Questions," *Philadelphia Daily News*, July 18, 1986; Tony Locv, "Crisis too Close to Home," *Philadelphia Daily News*, July 18, 1986.

3. For instance, Barbara Edney of North Philadelphia, cited in Lesly Scism, "Dump Site Park No Picnic for Neighbors," *Philadelphia Daily News*, July 18, 1986.

4. Scism, "Dump Site Park No Picnic"; Michael E. Ruane and Dale Ruzzacappe, "Trash Workers Shout a Defiant No!" *Philadelphia Inquirer*, July 18, 1986.

5. Arnesen and Arnesen, *Encyclopedia of U.S. Labor and Working-Class History*, 864–65; Melosi, "Down in the Dumps"; Blumberg and Gottlieb, *War on Waste*.

6. John L Moore, "Garbage, Sewage Solutions," *Pocono Record* (Stroudsburg, PA), September 5, 1973.

7. On Philadelphia history, see Warner, *The Private City*; Conn, *Metropolitan Philadelphia*.

8. Geffen, "Industrial Development and Social Crisis, 1841–1854," 308; McDaniel, "Immigration and Migration (Colonial Era)."

9. Geffen, "Industrial Development and Social Crisis," 308; Conn, *Metropolitan Philadelphia*, 121; On Chicago, see Cronon, *Nature's Metropolis*.

10. Sicotte, *From Workshop to Waste Magnet*, 72.

11. Ross and Amter, *The Polluters*, 17–27; John K. Smith, "Chemical Industry."

12. EPA data cited in Sierra Club, "The Hazards of Waste"; McCarthy, *Auto Mania*, 66–72.

13. Sicotte, *From Workshop to Waste Magnet*, 79.

14. John Fuchs, "Williams Wants Trash Dumps Eliminated," *Courier Post* (Camden, NJ), October 23, 1974.

15. Cindy Schraeger, "Statement of the Pennsylvania Environmental Council before the Legislative Oversight Committee City Council, City of Philadelphia," February 6, 1987, Delaware Valley Toxics Coalition Records, Urban Archives, Temple University, Philadelphia.

16. Ross and Amter, *The Polluters*, 2010.

17. Melosi, *Garbage in the Cities*, 177; Cross and Brohman, *Project Leadership*, 17.

18. Philadelphia Bureau of Surveys, *Report on the Collection and Treatment of the Sewage of the City of Philadelphia* , 872.

19. Guarino, Nelson, and Almeida, "Ocean Dispersal as an Ultimate Disposal Method."

20. Guarino, Nelson, and S. Townsend, "Philadelphia Sludge Disposal in Coastal Waters," 737.

21. Cook-Thajudeen, "Landfills."

22. Sicotte, *From Workshop to Waste Magnet*, 80, 97, 106; Cook-Thajudeen, "Landfills."

23. Schraeger, "Statement of the Pennsylvania Environmental Council"; Mark Jaffe, "Picking up Pieces of City Trash Plan," *Philadelphia Inquirer*, March 11, 1984; Cook-Thajudeen, "Landfills."

24. Beth Gillin, "As the Garbage Turns into Trash," *Philadelphia Inquirer*, August 22, 1982.

25. Sicotte, *From Workshop to Waste Magnet*, 79.

26. Melosi, *The Sanitary City*, 87.

27. Sicotte, *From Workshop to Waste Magnet*, 98; Cook-Thajudeen, "Landfills"; Robert Reilly, "You vs. Your Trash: Where Will It All End?," *Philadelphia Inquirer*, February 20, 1972.

28. Larry Eichel, "City's Dilemma: Taking the Waste out of Waste Pickup to Cut Costs," *Philadelphia Inquirer*, January 25, 1975.

29. Sicotte, *From Workshop to Waste Magnet*, 79.

30. Melosi, *Fresh Kills*.

31. Soderlund, *Lenape Country*, 149.

32. Conn, *Metropolitan Philadelphia*, 184; Sicotte, *From Workshop to Waste Magnet*, 76.

33. Conn, *Metropolitan Philadelphia*, 184, 190.

34. Sykes, *Past and Present*, 1–2, 12, 18–20.

35. De Sylva, Kalber, and Shuster, *Fishes and Ecological Conditions*, 2.

36. Sykes, *Past and Present*, 21; Encyclopedia Britannica, "Delaware River"; Rupert, "The Delaware River Basin Commission."

37. Kraft, "U.S. Environmental Policy and Politics," 22; Andrews, *Managing the Environment, Managing Ourselves*, 203–5.

38. Sykes, *Past and Present*, 21; Encyclopedia Britannica, "Delaware River."

39. Susan Q. Stranahan, "EPA Orders Toxic Waste Cleaned before Disposal in Sewer System," *Bulletin*, June 21, 1978; Kramek and Loh, "The History of Philadelphia's Water Supply," 9–10.

40. Ferguson, *The Shock of the Global*.

41. McKee, *The Problem of Jobs*, 22.

42. Sicotte, *From Workshop to Waste Magnet*, 119.

43. Boehm and Corey, *America's Urban History*, 291.

44. Davis, *The Global 1980s*, 25–27.

45. Weiler, *Philadelphia*, 56.

46. J. A. Livingstone, "Philadelphia's Fiscal Woe," *Clarion-Ledger* (Jackson, MS), May 16, 1976.

47. Jack Roberts, "Fiscal Foibles," *Philadelphia Daily News*, November 6, 1986; Hackworth, *The Neoliberal City*.

48. Simon, *Philadelphia*, 93.

49. George Wilson, "What to Do for Those Who Can't Pay Heating?" *Philadelphia Inquirer*, January 13, 1984.

50. Boehm and Corey, *America's Urban History*, 290.

51. Mires and Hepp, "Railroad Suburbs."

52. Mason, "Metropolitan Philadelphia," 191; Conn, *Metropolitan Philadelphia*, 248; Sicotte, *From Workshop to Waste Magnet*, 100.

53. Conn, *Metropolitan Philadelphia*, 20; Sicotte, *From Workshop to Waste Magnet*, 65; Amsterdam and Vitiello, "Immigration"; Wolfinger, "African American Migration."

54. Sicotte, *From Workshop to Waste Magnet*, 102.

55. Conn, *Metropolitan Philadelphia*, 8.

56. Eggert-Crowe and Knowles, "Bicentennial (1976)," 289.

57. Knowles, *Imagining Philadelphia*, 78.

58. Rome, "'Give Earth a Chance.'"

59. Rome, *The Genius of Earth Day*; Al Haal, "That Was the Week," *Philadelphia Inquirer*, April 19, 1973.

60. Rome, *The Genius of Earth Day*, 14.

61. "TV Covers Earth Day Events," *San Bernadino County Sun* (CA), April 22, 1970; "30,000 Mark Earth Day at Fairmount Park Rally," *Philadelphia Inquirer*, April 23, 1970.

62. "Earth Day Events Focus against Pollution," *Daily News* (Lebanon, PA), April 22, 1970.

63. Turner and Isenberg, *The Republican Reversal*, 35; Kirkpatrick, *The Green Revolution*; Kraft, "U.S. Environmental Policy and Politics"; Flippen, *Nixon and the Environment*.

64. "EPA appoints Regional Chief," *Philadelphia Inquirer*, September 23, 1971.

65. Turner and Isenberg, *The Republican Reversal*, 207, 256.

66. Pomper, "Recycling Philadelphia v. New Jersey," 1311; Sicotte, *From Workshop to Waste Magnet*, 84.

67. Müller, "Cut Holes and Sink 'Em," 263–84.

68. Mary Walton, "Shore Towns Oppose Philadelphia's Dumping," *Philadelphia Inquirer*, April 17, 1973.

69. Eugene J. Zawoiski, letter to the editor, *Philadelphia Inquirer*, September 24, 1969.

70. "DuPont, Phila. Sued on Ocean Dumping," *Philadelphia Inquirer*, July 19, 1971.

71. Müller and Stradling, "Water as the Ultimate Sink," 35–36; "Ocean Pollution Controls Sought," *Gazette and Daily* (York, PA), October 8, 1970.

72. Council on Environmental Quality, *Report of the Council on Environmental Quality*, 11.

73. Vig and Kraft, *Environmental Policy*, 9–10.

74. Feliciano, "Bringing about an End to Ocean Dumping," 276.

75. Vig and Kraft, *Environmental Policy*, 19; Guarino, Nelson, and Townsend, "Philadelphia Sludge Disposal," 742–4.

76. Guarino, Nelson, and Townsend, "Philadelphia Sludge Disposal," 742–43.

77. Weinstein-Bacal, "The Ocean Dumping Dilemma," 901; Guarino, Nelson, and Townsend, "Philadelphia Sludge Disposal," 743.

78. Sze, *Noxious New York*, 61.

79. Stranahan, "EPA Orders Toxic Waste Cleaned."

80. Cited in Walton, "Shore Towns Oppose Philadelphia's Dumping."

81. Weinstein-Bacal, "The Ocean Dumping Dilemma," 886.

82. Bob Dragin, "Toxic Waste: Everybody Hates It, but It's Got to Be Put Somewhere," *Philadelphia Inquirer*, December 12, 1982.

83. Louis, "A Historical Context," 316; Jones, *Profits and Sustainability*, 147; Hickman, *American Alchemy*, 50–56.

84. McCarthy and Reisch, *Hazardous Waste Fact Book*, 5.

85. Rosenfeld and Feng, *Risks of Hazardous Wastes*, 1.

86. Environmental Protection Agency, *EPA's Program to Control Exports of Hazardous Wastes*, 8; Louis, "A Historical Context" 317; Hickman, *American Alchemy*, 70–73.

87. Randel, "Hazardous Waste in Philadelphia." Delaware Valley Toxics Coalition Records.

88. Bob Drogin, "Toxic Waste: Everybody Hates It, but It's Got to Be Put Somewhere," *Philadelphia Inquirer*, December 12, 1982; Randel, "Hazardous Waste in Philadelphia," 22–23.

89. Davis and Lester, "Hazardous Waste Politics," 2–3; Rod Nordland and Josh Friedman, "Poison at Our Doorsteps: Where Perilous Chemical Lay in Large Quantities," *Philadelphia Inquirer*, September 23, 1979.

90. Davis and Lester, "Hazardous Waste Politics, 2–3.

91. Andrew Maykuth, "These Days, Hazardous-Waste Disposal Is Risky Business," *Times Leader*, July 10, 1988.

92. Louis, "A Historical Context of Municipal Solid Waste Management," 317.

93. Roger Cohn, "Toxic Waste Sites: Outcasts across the Region," *Bulletin*, July 24, 1981.

94. Rod Nordland, "In New Jersey the Trash Piles Runneth," *Philadelphia Inquirer*, August 19, 1973; City of Philadelphia, City of Philadelphia Trash Contracts, June 23, 1987, Delaware Valley Toxics Coalition Records.

95. "Dumping Chemical Waste," *Bulletin*, December 6, 1979.

96. "Landfill Operator sees Crisis in Solid-Waste Disposal," *Bulletin*, April 15, 1973.

97. "Landfill Operator sees Crisis in Solid-Waste Disposal"; Nordland and Friedman, "Poison at Our Doorsteps."

98. Nordland and Friedman, "Poison at Our Doorsteps."

99. "We Deserve Clean Water," *Bulletin*, August 19, 1979.

100. Vernon Loeb and Phillip Dixon, "Penna. Proposes Toxic-Waste Reform," *Bulletin*, October 5, 1979.

101. "Residue of Poison Brings Mob Cash," *Bulletin*, December 17, 1980.

102. "Defunct Disposer Indicted in Bribes," *Bulletin*, August 2, 1980; "Where Perilous Chemical Lay in Large Quantities."

103. A. W. Geiselman, "Suit Names 15 Firms in Illegal Dumping," *Bulletin*, March 6, 1981.

104. Susan Stranahan, "Warnings on Wastes Ignored," *Bulletin*, February 14, 1979.

105. Environmental Protection Agency, *Valley of the Drums*.

106. Karan and Suganuma, *Local Environmental Movements*, 25; Newman, *Love Canal*.

107. Sicotte, "Saving Ourselves," 232.

108. Nordland and Friedman, "Poison at Our Doorsteps."

109. Rome, *The Bulldozer in the Countryside*, 181–85; McHarg, *Design with Nature*.

110. Mark Jaffe, "Group Marks 20 Years of Fighting for Clean Air," *Philadelphia Inquirer*, October 20, 1987.

111. Roger Cohn, "Bill Seeks Disclosure of Poisons," *Philadelphia Inquirer*, June 27, 1980.

112. Public Interest Law Center, "50 Years of Fighting for Environmental Justice."

113. Robert Cohn, "Right to Know about Toxic Matter, Yes, but Phila. Bill Is Yet to Be Tested," *Philadelphia Inquirer*, February 1, 1981.

114. McCarthy and Reisch, *Hazardous Waste Fact Book*, 34.

115. Fran Scullion, "Letter to Ms. Dougherty, EPA," July 21, 1983, Delaware Valley Toxics Coalition Records.

116. Laura Quinn, "Barred from Kinsley, Independents Cut Service," *Philadelphia Inquirer*, November 30, 1984.

117. Ace Service Corporation, "Application for TSDF Facility," November 24, 1982, Delaware Valley Toxics Coalition Records.

118. Terry Siman, cited in Mark Jaffe, "City Moves to Stop Toxic Waste Center," *Philadelphia Inquirer*, May 18, 1984.

119. Fran Scullion, cited in Gardner Cox, "Ace Services Inc. and Public Meeting Put on 1/12/83 by the Pennsport Civic Association," January 13, 1983, Delaware Valley Toxics Coalition Records.

120. Cox, "Ace Services Inc. and Public Meeting."

121. Vince Fumo, cited in Cox, "Ace Services Inc. and Public Meeting."

122. Pennsport Civic Association, "Meeting Notice. Hazardous Waste Task Force," February 4, 1983, Delaware Valley Toxics Coalition Records; Albert Einstein Medical Center, "Community Breakfast Meeting," March 16, 1984, Delaware Valley Toxics Coalition Records; Pennsport Civic Association, "Letter to Legislature and Community," March 19, 1984, Delaware Valley Toxics Coalition Records.

123. Bob Warner, "It's Round 2 for Rizzo in Toxic Waste Battle," *Philadelphia Daily News*, December 15, 1982.

124. Valeria M. Russ, "City Wants Toxic Stash out of Site," *Philadelphia Daily News*, May 19, 1984; Pennsport Civic Association, "All South Philadelphia Residents," May 1984, Delaware Valley Toxics Coalition Records.

125. Leo A. Brooks, "Letter to Connie McHugh," June 1, 1984, Delaware Valley Toxics Coalition Records; Stuart H. Shapiro, City of Philadelphia, "Letter to Lawrence H. Lunsk, DEP," May 15, 1984, Delaware Valley Toxics Coalition Records.

126. Cox, "Ace Services Inc. and Public Meeting."

127. Letter from Harold S. Levin, board of directors, Washington Square West Project Area Committee and Civic Association, to Stuart Shapiro, April 6, 1984, Delaware Valley Toxics Coalition Records.

128. William Eels, president of Ace Services, Inc., cited in Warner, "It's Round 2 for

Rizzo"; letter from Greg Schirm, Delaware Valley Toxics Coalition Educational Fund, to Connie McHugh, May 3, 1984, Delaware Valley Toxics Coalition Records; letter from Robert J. Blaszciak to Mary Ware, Pennsport Civic Association, June 1, 1984, Delaware Valley Toxics Coalition Records.

129. Letter from Mary Anne Rushlau to Senator John Heinz," October 4, 1983, Delaware Valley Toxics Coalition Records.

130. See diverse articles compiled by Mutual Press Clipping Services, Inc., "Tyson Dump," 1983, Delaware Valley Toxics Coalition Records.

131. Alexander Reid, "Landfill Dumped on 'Ideal' Setup," *Philadelphia Daily News*, August 10, 1984.

132. Mason, "Metropolitan Philadelphia," 191.

133. Sicotte, *From Workshop to Waste Magnet*, 67–69; Milroy, "Pro Bono Publico."

134. Oberholtzer, *Philadelphia*.

135. Sicotte, *From Workshop to Waste Magnet*, 66.

136. Cited in Nordland, "In New Jersey the Trash Piles Runneth."

137. Eileen McGurty, "Solid Waste Management," 30–31.

138. Alewitz, "Garbage," 300.

139. Joey Williams, "Stadium, Yes! Fresh Air? Too Expensive," *Philadelphia Inquirer*, February 7, 1970.

140. Scott Heimer, "Lids Clamp Shut on All of Philly's Trash Cans," *Philadelphia Daily News*, November 27, 1973.

141. Heimer, "Lids Clamp Shut"; Cook-Thajudeen, "Landfills."

142. Cook-Thajudeen, "Landfills"; "New Jersey Bans Out-of-State Garbage," *News-Item* (Shamokin, PA), October 24, 1973.

143. Cook-Thajudeen, "Landfills."

144. City of Philadelphia et al., Appellants, v. State of New Jersey, et al., 437 U.S. 617 (1978).

TWO | "Send It on a Caribbean Cruise"

1. Shimizu, *Japanese Firms*, 49; Ship Spotting, "Khian Sea—IMO 6930180," www.shipspotting.com/gallery/photo.php?lid=2979699, accessed June 4, 2020; Shipnostalgia, "Khian Sea," www.shipsnostalgia.com/gallery/showphoto.php/photo/237515/title/khian-sea/cat/510, accessed June 4, 2020.

2. Joel Spivak, "Girard Point Grain Elevator," *Workshop of the World*, May 2007, www.workshopoftheworld.com/south_phila/girard_point.html.

3. "Joseph Paolino, 88; Led Contracting Firm," *Philadelphia Inquirer*, December 21, 1984.

4. Vernon Loeb, "Contractor Ordered to Repay Phila. for Using Too Few Minority Firms," *Philadelphia Inquirer*, July 13, 1985.

5. Robert J. Terry and Michael E. Ruane, "Fire Damages Girard Point Pier, Destination of Ash Ship *Khian Sea*," *Philadelphia Inquirer*, March 2, 1988.

6. William Robbins, "Election of Black Mayor in Philadelphia Reflects a Decade of Change in the City," *New York Times*, November 10, 1983.

7. "When I'm Mayor . . . ," *Philadelphia Daily News*, August 2, 1983.

8. Walsh, Warland, and Smith, *Don't Burn It Here*, 162.

9. Annie Eberhart, "Too Much Trash," *Public Citizen*, May–June 1988, 10.

10. City of Philadelphia, press release, March 19, 1987, Delaware Valley Toxics Coalition Records; Walsh, Warland, and Smith, *Don't Burn It Here*, 166.

11. Pat Costner, "Letter to Ruben Blades," August 21, 1987, Jim Vallette private archive; Arty Zulawski, "Real Villains of the Piece Lost in the Kinsley Uproar," *Courier-Post* (Camden, NJ) December 9, 1984.

12. William K. Stevens, "Philadelphia Trash: Too Much and Nowhere to Go," *New York Times*, March 9, 1986.

13. Joseph Paolino & Sons Inc., Appellant, v. City of Philadelphia, Appellee, 429 Pa. Super. 191 (1993).

14. Mathew Paust, "Landfill Owner Appeals to Have Injunction Lifted," *Daily Press* (Newport News, VA), February 6, 1986; Robin Clark, "For Trash Residue, a Long Road with an Unknown End," *Philadelphia Inquirer*, February 26, 1986; Matthew Paus, "Phila. Ash barred by Va. Judge," *Philadelphia Daily News*, January 29, 1986.

15. Robin Clark, "Waste Hauler Agrees to Clean Up Site," *Philadelphia Inquirer*, January 23, 1986.

16. Clark, "For Trash Residue"; City of Philadelphia v. State of New Jersey and New Jersey Department of Environmental Protection,73 N.J. 562 (1977), 376 A.2d 888; City of Philadelphia et al., Appellants, v. State of New Jersey, 437 U.S. 617 (1978).

17. Cited in Brownell, "Negotiating the New Economic Order of Waste," 276.

18. Robin Clark, "Ohio Landfill to Stop Taking City Ash," *Philadelphia Inquirer*, March 6, 1986.

19. "S.C. Governor Seeks to End Phila Trash Dumping," *Morning Call* (Allentown, PA), April 20, 1986.

20. Ramona Smith, "States Gives Company 30 Days to Make Ash Disa-Pier" *Philadelphia Daily News*, March 17, 1988.

21. Agreement Paolino & Sons and Amalgamated Inc., June 1986, Records of the United States Court of Appeals, National Archives, Philadelphia.

22. United States of America v. William P. Reilly and John Patrick Dowd, filed July 24, 1994, United States Court of Appeals for the Third Circuit Collection, Records of the United States Courts of Appeals, US National Archives, Philadelphia.

23. IBP USA, *Global Privatization Laws and Regulations Handbook*, 48; Nevins, Barlas, and Yong, *Bahamas*, 62, 66.

24. "Disposal Firm Suit Could Force EPA to Close Loopholes," *Environmental Policy Alert*, December 14, 1988.

25. "Philadelphia Ash Ship Is Still Trying to Unload Cargo," *Asbury Park (NJ) Press*, August 19, 1987; Richard G. Andrews (state attorney), memorandum in support of the response of the United States to appellant's motion to stay execution of sentence pending appeal, October 22, 1993, United States Court of Appeals for the Third Circuit Collection, Records of the United States Courts of Appeals, US National Archives, Philadelphia, 4.

26. Agreement Paolino & Sons and Amalgamated Inc.

27. Belenky, "Cradle to Border," 118; Asante-Duah and Nagy, *International Trade in Hazardous Wastes*, 80.

28. John Hay, "Toxic Garbage Dump," *Ottawa Citizen*, December 29, 1988; Vera-Morales, "Dumping in the International Backyard."

29. Canada-US Agreement Concerning the Transboundary Movement of Hazardous Waste, Ottawa, November 8, 1986. Consolidated text available at www.canada.ca/en/environment-climate-change/services/managing-reducing-waste/international-commitments/canada-united-states-agreement/transboundary-movement.html.

30. "Federal Officials Try to Halt African Waste Dumping Plan," *Times-News* (Twin Falls, ID), January 28, 1980; Richter, "Giftmüllexporte nach Afrika."

31. Cathy Trost, "New Export from U.S.?" *Detroit Free Press*, July 11, 1982.

32. Andrew Frowman, "Sewage Treatment Wastes Would Fertilize Research Farms in the Dominican Republic," *Fort Lauderdale News*, October 5, 1982.

33. Frowman, "Sewage Treatment Wastes"; Sandy Banisky, "Sludge Decision Delayed," *Baltimore Sun*, December 9, 1982; Richard Berke, "City Officials Are Told Sludge Is Simply 'Too Good to Waste,'" *Baltimore Evening Sun*, December 9, 1982, 60.

34. Juan O. Tomayo, "Forgery Is Suspected in Waste Export Deal," *Miami Herald*, July 2, 1983.

35. Higman, *A Concise History of the Caribbean*, 280.

36. Krenn, *The Impact of Race on U.S. Foreign Policy*, 250; see also Colby, *The Business of Empire*, 4.

37. Braveboy-Wagner, "Introduction," 12.

38. Higman, *A Concise History of the Caribbean*, 290–301.

39. Grugel, "The Historical Evolution of the Caribbean Basin," 29.

40. Faber, *Environment under Fire*, 4, 16; Rhett A. Buttler, "The Rainforest," in Mongabay, https://rainforests.mongabay.com/20carib.htm, accessed June 7, 2020.

41. Braveboy-Wagner, "Introduction," 1; Higman, *A Concise History of the Caribbean*, 259.

42. Tucker, *Insatiable Appetite*, 4; Colby, *The Business of Empire*.

43. Cassá, "The Economic Development of the Caribbean," 9.

44. Roett, "The Debt Crisis and Development in Latin America," 133.

45. Galanes, "History of Caribbean Economies"; Higman, *A Concise History of the Caribbean*, 286.

46. Higman, *A Concise History of the Caribbean*, 285–86; Craton and Saunders, *Islanders in the Stream*, 402, 404, 418, 422–23.

47. Harris and Nef, *Capital, Power, and Inequality*, 83–84; Middlebrook and Rico, *The United States and Latin America in the 1980s*, 3.

48. Galanes, "History of Caribbean Economies."

49. Braveboy-Wagner, "Introduction," 12.

50. Sutter, "Nature's Agents or Agents of Empire?" 725.

51. Braveboy-Wagner, "Introduction," 1; Higman, *A Concise History of the Caribbean*, 286; Faber, *Environment under Fire*, 5; O'Brien and Johnson, *Making the Americas*, 272.

52. Faber, *Environment under Fire*, 6.

53. Voyles, *Wastelanding*.

54. Eckholm and Scherr, "Double Standards and the Pesticide Trade," 442.

55. Faber, *Environment under Fire*, 100–101.

56. Faber, *Environment under Fire*, 3–4.

57. Weir and Mark Schapiro, *Circle of Poison*, 69.

58. Nading, "Central America."

59. "Largest Countries and Territories in the Caribbean, by Total Area," Statistica, April 2019, www.statista.com/statistics/992416/largest-countries-territories-area-caribbean.

60. Faber, *Environment under Fire*, 3; Higman, *A Concise History of the Caribbean*, 5.

61. Craton and Saunders, *Islanders in the Stream*, 402–23; Meditz and Hanratty, *Caribbean Islands*.

62. Organization of American States, *Bahamas National Report,* 7; Bahamas Ministry of Tourism, "History of Tourism," www.tourismtoday.com/about-us/tourism-history, accessed September 6, 2022.

63. "Philadelphia Ash Ship Is Still Trying to Unload Cargo."

64. "Bahamas Refuses Refuse," Associated Press, May 7, 1987; Higman, *A Concise History of the Caribbean*, 299–300.

65. Testimony of William P. Reilly, January 9, 1990, United States District Court Delaware, Criminal Case Files, Records of District Courts of the United States, US National Archives, Philadelphia, 23; Bruce Gledhill, Philadelphia streets commissioner, cited in Committee on Government Operations, *International Export of US Waste*, 41.

66. "Bahamas Refuses Refuse."

67. Melosi, *Fresh Kills*, 35.

68. United Nations Food and Agriculture Organization, *The World's Mangroves*, 4, 67.

69. Organization of Eastern Caribbean States, *Biodiversity of the Caribbean*, 7–8.

70. Testimony of William P. Reilly, 23–26.

71. Testimony of Arturo Fuentes Garcia, Captain of the *Khian Sea*, May 24, 1993, United States District Court Delaware, Criminal Case Files, Records of District Courts of the United States, US National Archives, Philadelphia.

72. Engineering and Mining Journal, *E & MJ International Directory of Mining*, 83.

73. Translation of letter from Ideal Dominicana to director of mining, Dominican Republic, sent from Henry Dowd to William P. Reilly, January 1987, in Committee on Government Operations, *International Export of US Waste*.

74. IBP USA, *Dominican Republic Mineral and Mining Sector*, 200.

75. Translation of letter from Ideal Dominicana to director of mining, Dominican Republic.

76. Fred W. Cohrs, minutes of meeting in Santo Domingo and Cabo Rojo, February 6, 1987, in Committee on Government Operations, *International Export of US Waste*.

77. Letter from Coastal Carriers Inc., J. Neumann, Chile, February 20, 1987, in Committee on Government Operations, *International Export of US Waste*.

78. Testimony of William P. Reilly, 104.

79. Frenkel, "Jungle Stories," 323–24; Adas, *Dominance by Design*.

80. Testimony of William P. Reilly, 83.

81. Translation of letter from Edgardo A. Pascall to Jorge I. Craniotis, National Port Authorities Honduras, in Committee on Government Operations, *International Export of US Waste*.

82. UNESCO, *Convention on Wetlands*; Tripp and Dudek, "The Swampbuster Provisions of the Food Security Act."

83. "Philadelphia Ash Ship Is Still Trying to Unload Cargo."

84. Anita Huslin, "Panama Rejects Phila Ash; Barge Continues Year-long Voyage," *Daily Item* (Sunbury, PA), September 12, 1987.

85. Cited in Clark, "For Trash Residue."

86. Mark Jaffe, "Environmentalists Cheer Plan to Close Incinerators," *Philadelphia Inquirer*, March 25, 1988.

87. Jaffe, "Environmentalists Cheer Plan."

88. Ramona Smith, "Incinerators Stop: Trash Pick-up Next?" *Philadelphia Daily News*, August 11, 1987.

THREE | "We Exist for the Good of Others"

1. United Nations Food and Agriculture Organization, *The World's Mangroves*.

2. Spalding, *World Atlas of Mangroves*, 206.

3. Spalding, *World Atlas of Mangroves*, 206; Guzman et al., "A Site Description."

4. Keeley, *Marvelous Mangroves*.

5. Thampi, "Indigenous Contestations," 49.

6. Thampi, "Indigenous Contestations," 53.

7. Agreement City of Philadelphia and Bulkhandling Inc., December 19, 1986, Jim Vallette private archive.

8. Kolltveit, "Torvald Klaveness."

9. Agreement City of Philadelphia and Bulkhandling Inc.

10. Robin Clark, "City's Ash to Be Sent to Panama," *Philadelphia Inquirer*, January 4, 1987.

11. Bill Hall and Joshua Karliner, "Eco-crisis in America's Backyard," unpublished manuscript, Jim Vallette private archive; parts later published in Hall, Karliner, and Whitney, "Garbage Imperialism," 10–11.

12. Zimbalist and Weeks, *Panama at the Crossroads*, 23–27, 37–38; Lindsay-Poland et al., *Emperors in the Jungle*, 2–4.

13. Cited in Betegon, "An Exploration: Panama Environmental Law History," 8.

14. Brañes Ballesteros, *El desarrollo del derecho ambiental latinoamericano*, 12, 23.

15. Linowes and Hupert, "The Tropical Waste Dilemma," 105.

16. Brañes Ballesteros, *El desarrollo del derecho ambiental latinoamericano*, 18.

17. John C. Martin, EPA inspector general, cited in "Philadelphia Tries to Ship Toxic Ash to the Third World," *Rachel's Hazardous Waste News*, November 22, 1987.

18. Committee on Government Operations, *International Export of US Waste*, 37.

19. United Press International, "LA Bids to Ship 350 Tons of Sludge Each Day to Guatemala for Fertilizer," *Arizona Republic* (Phoenix), August 26, 1987, 21.

20. Letter from Jerome Balter to David Cohen, January 7, 1987, Delaware Valley Toxics Coalition Records.

21. Robin Clark, "City's Ash to be Sent to Panama," *Philadelphia Inquirer*, January 4, 1987.

22. Jerome Balter to David Cohen, January 7, 1987.

23. Juan Gonzales, "Get Your Ash out of Here, Panama Tells City," *Philadelphia Daily News*, September 11, 1987.

24. "Gobierno no aceptara la basura contaminada," *La Critica*, May 12, 1987; "No es toxica la basura para relleno," *La Estrella de Panama*, May 12, 1987.

25. "Basura contaminado perjudicará a Bocas del toro, dicen ecólogos," *La Prensa*, May 17, 1987, my translation.

26. Hall and Karliner, "Eco-crisis in America's Backyard," 10–11.

27. Letter from Michael Marshall to Greenpeace Southeast, May 12, 1987, Jim Vallette private archive.

28. Letter from Wills Flowers to Denise Voelker, Rainforest Action Network, May 27, 1987, Jim Vallette private archive.

29. Letter from Jenny Stannard, Greenpeace, to Bruno Regno, Greenpeace, May 20, 1987, Jim Vallette private archive.

30. Dooley and MacGowan, "Long Island's Infamous Garbage Barge," *Newsday*, March 22, 2017.

31. Zelko, *Make It a Green Peace!* 4.

32. "The World," *Arizona Republic*, August 25, 1987.

33. "Poll Says Americans Favor Burning Trash," *Palm Beach (FL) Post*, June 3, 1987.

34. "Plea for Prevention," *American Statesman* (Austin, TX), August 6, 1987.

35. Letter from Pat Costner, to Ruben Blades, August 21, 1987, Jim Vallette private archive.

36. Stannard to Regno.

37. Costner to Blades; Gonzales, "Get Your Ash out of Here."

38. Greenpeace, *Offers of Poison/Ofrendas envenenadas*. February 15, 1988, Jim Vallette private archive.

39. "La oposición nos quiere convertir en el basurero de los Estados Unidos," *La Republica*, September 4, 1987.

40. "The Spidermen of Greenpeace," *Philadelphia Inquirer*, September 9, 1987; "Protesters Climb Tower," *Standard-Speaker* (Hazleton, PA), September 9, 1987.

41. Gonzales, "Get Your Ash out of Here"; Paul Baker and Joe O'Dowd, "2 Environmental Protesters Show Towering Rage," *Philadelphia Daily News*, September 8, 1987.

42. Gonzales, "Get Your Ash out of Here."

43. "US Freezes Aid to Pressure Panama," *Florida Today*, July 24, 1987; Meade, *A History of Modern Latin America*, 301.

44. Greenpeace, *Offers of Poison*.

45. John C. Martin, *Flash Report: Philadelphia Incinerator Ash Exports for Panamanian Road Project; Potential Environmental Damage in the Making*, US Environmental Protection Agency, October 5, 1987, Jim Vallette private archive; "Philadelphia Tries to Ship Toxic Ash to the Third World, but Plan Is Sunk by Suppressed EPA Data," *Rachel's Hazardous Waste News*, November 23, 1987.

46. Gonzales, "Get Your Ash out of Here."

47. Gonzales, "Get Your Ash out of Here."

48. Ramona Smith, "Incinerators Stop: Trash Pick-up Next?" *Philadelphia Daily News*, August 11, 1987.

49. Gonzales, "Get Your Ash out of Here."

50. Radio Haiti, "Déchets toxiques," March 22, 1988, Radio Haiti Papers.

51. Testimony of William P. Reilly, January 9, 1990, United States District Court

Delaware, Criminal Case Files, Records of District Courts of the United States, US National Archives, Philadelphia, 30–31.

52. On Haitian exceptionalism, see Trouillot, "The Odd and the Ordinary."

53. Dubois, *Avengers of the New World*, 3–4.

54. Dubois, *Avengers of the New World*, 3–4.

55. Higman, *A Concise History of the Caribbean*, 262.

56. Girard, *Haiti*, 105; Plummer, *Haiti and the United States*, 193–209.

57. Farmer, *AIDS and Accusation*.

58. Plummer, *Haiti and the United States*, 198–206; Farmer, *AIDS and Accusation*, 2.

59. Plummer, *Haiti and the United States*, 207.

60. Plummer, *Haiti and the United States*, 217–23; Higman, *A Concise History of the Caribbean*, 264.

61. Margot Hornblower, "Haitian Lawlessness on Upswing following Fall of Duvalier Regime," *Alabama Journal*, December 18, 1986.

62. Brañes Ballesteros, *El desarrollo del derecho ambiental latinoamericano*, 12.

63. Letter from Mareille Durocher-Bartin to Jean Polycard, director general, National Port Authority, Haiti, application for import permit, December 3, 1987, Jim Vallette private archive.

64. Testimony of William P. Reilly, 33; Bureau des Mines et de l'Énergie, "Report final du Khian Sea," January 25, 1988, Radio Haiti Papers.

65. Radio Haiti, "Déchets toxiques."

66. Bellegarde-Smith, "Dynastic Dictatorship," 278; Clammer, *Haiti*, 26; On literacy rates, see UNESCO Institute for Statistics, "Haiti," http://uis.unesco.org/en/country/ht.

67. Smarth, "Popular Organizations," 102–5.

68. Federation of the Friends of Nature (FAN)/Greenpeace Media, "Toxic Ash in Haiti," video, February 20, 1988, https://media.greenpeace.org, unique identifier GP04G2L.

69. Andrew Maykuth, "Haitians Thank God and Gonaives," *Philadelphia Inquirer*, February 12, 1986.

70. Smarth, "Popular Organizations," 102–5.

71. Alfonson Chardy, "Youths: We Were Seeds of Haiti Revolt," *Miami Herald*, February 15, 1986,

72. Trzyna, Margold, and Osborn, *World Directory of Environmental Organizations*, 164.

73. Mark Jaffe, "Haiti Is the Latest to Reject Ash," *Philadelphia Inquirer*, February 2, 1988; "Haiti Officials Reject Cargo of Philadelphia Waste Ash," *Sioux City Journal*, February 3, 1988.

74. WPVI, "WPVI_NY_Khian Sea," February 1988, WPVI news footage and logs, minute 1:30 to 2:09; see also Bloc Unitaire Patriotique, "Ayiti Pa Poubel," February 2, 1988, Radio Haiti Papers.

75. Haitian interviewee, in FAN/ Greenpeace Media, "Toxic Ash in Haiti."

76. Hornblower, "Haitian Lawlessness on Upswing"; Bell and Danticat, *Fault Lines*, 127–30; Don Bohning, "Cheap Smuggled Rice Hurts Haitian Farmers," *Miami Herald*, February 16, 1987.

77. Letter from Robert Boack, executive vice president, First City Development of Haiti SA, to Elliot Abrams, assistant secretary for inter-American Affairs, Department of State, February 18, 1988, Jim Vallette private archive

78. Victor Fiorillo and Liz Spikol, "Ashes to Ashes, Dust to Dust," *Philadelphia Weekly*, January 17, 2001; Jaffe, "Haiti Is the Latest to Reject Ash."

79. Ministère de la Justice, Haiti, "Déchets toxiques," February 4, 1988, Radio Haiti Papers.

80. Radio Haiti, "Report," February 3, 1988, Radio Haiti Papers.

81. Testimony of Arturo Fuentes Garcia, May 24, 1993, United States District Court Delaware, Criminal Case Files, Records of District Courts of the United States, US National Archives, Philadelphia, 1323.

82. Radio Haiti, "Report," February 5, 1988, Radio Haiti Papers.

83. WPVI, "WPVI_NY_Khian Sea"; Letter from Commission Gonaïves to ministre de la santé publique, February 26, 1988, Radio Haiti Papers.

84. Pamela Constable, "Coastal Town Has Kept Heat on Haiti's Governments," *Boston Globe*, November 11, 1986.

85. Bloc Unitaire Patriotique, "Ayiti Pa Poubel."

86. Louis Dejoie II, president of PAIN, "Communiqué," February 4, 1988, Radio Haiti Papers.

87. Parti Politique MDN, "Le MDN se prononce sur l'affaire des déchets toxiques," February 20, 1988, Radio Haiti Papers.

88. Asanble Popile Nasyonal, "Not pou la près," March 24, 1988, Radio Haiti Papers; Centrale Autonome des Travailleurs Haitiens, "Kominike pou la près," March 23, 1988, Radio Haiti Papers.

89. Parti Démocrate Chrétien Haitien, "Note de presse," February 2, 1988, Radio Haiti Papers.

90. Commission Gonaïves to ministre de la santé publique.

91. Centrale Autonome des Travailleurs Haitiens, "Déchets toxiques," January 29, 1988, Radio Haiti Papers.

92. Radio Haiti, "Bark," February 26, 1988; Mouvement pour l'Instauration de la Démocratie en Haiti, "Note de presse," March 1988; Gonaïves Youth, "Note de presse," March 18, 1988; Comité Féminin pour la Libération d'Haiti, "Not pou la pres," March 23, 1988, all in Radio Haiti Papers.

93. See for instance, Komite Tet Ansanm pou Onè Respè Konstitisyon an, "Pep Gonayv," March 24, 1988, Radio Haiti Papers.

94. Mouvement pour l'Instauration de la Démocratie en Haiti, "Note de presse."

95. Parti Démocrate Chrétien Haitien, "Kominike pou la pres," March 24, 1988, Radio Haiti Papers.

96. "Dépendence," *Kiskeya* 2, no. 3 (April 1988); Gaden Serge, "Évêché des Gonaïves," September 29, 1988, Jim Vallette private archive; Subcommittee on Transport and Hazardous Materials, *Waste Export Control*, 163.

97. President Leslie Manigat, cited in Jim Vallette, "Greenpeace Testimony," in Subcommittee on Transportation and Hazardous Materials, *Waste Export Control*, 164.

98. Serge, "Évêché des Gonaïves."

99. Girard, *Haiti*, 105; Plummer, *Haiti and the United States*, 263.

FOUR | "The Most Tested Ash on This Planet"

1. WPVI, "WPVI_NY_Khian Sea," February 1988, WPVI News Footage and Logs.

2. WPVI, "WPVI_NY_Khian Sea."

3. Cited in WPVI, "WPVI_NY_Khian Sea."

4. Collins, *Toxic Loopholes*, 105.

5. Barry Commoner, cited in Committee on Environment and Public Works, *Resource Conservation and Recovery Act—Oversight*, 11.

6. Mayor's Office of Communication, press release, June 23, 1987, Delaware Valley Toxics Coalition Records; letter from W. Wilson Goode to Joseph E. Coleman, president, City Council, June 23, 1987, Delaware Valley Toxics Coalition Records.

7. Delaware Valley Toxics Coalition, "The Trash Nexus," 1987, Delaware Valley Toxics Coalition Records.

8. Diane Sicotte, *From Workshop to Waste Magnet*, 113; Curlee, *Waste-to-Energy in the United States*.

9. Oppelt and Oppelt, "Incineration of Hazardous Waste," 574; Mukherjee, Debnath, and Ghosh, "A Review on Technologies," 529; Wittich, *Biodegradation of Dioxins and Furans*, 75; Langston, "New Chemical Bodies," 271.

10. Zierler, *The Invention of Ecocide*.

11. Collins, *Toxic Loopholes*, 90–96.

12. "Emissions," *Tampa Bay Times* (St. Petersburg, FL), January 28, 1985.

13. Strasser, *Waste and Want*, 267–68.

14. Hamra, "Municipal Incinerator Ash," 110.

15. Hamra, "Municipal Incinerator Ash," 35–36.

16. Schiller, "Courts, Deregulation, and Conservatives," 281–82.

17. Walsh, Warland, and Smith, *Don't Burn It Here*, 8, 17–18; "Emissions."

18. Oppelt and Oppelt, "Incineration of Hazardous Waste," 574.

19. Walsh, Warland, and Smith, *Don't Burn It Here*, 8, 11, 20; "Emissions."

20. Sicotte, *From Workshop to Waste Magnet*, 113, 141.

21. Sicotte, *From Workshop to Waste Magnet*, 143.

22. Walsh, Warland, and Smith, *Don't Burn It Here*, 174.

23. Walsh, Warland, and Smith, *Don't Burn It Here*, 24.

24. Walsh, Warland, and Smith, *Don't Burn It Here*, 168.

25. Turner and Isenberg, *The Republican Reversal*, 102–11.

26. Mintz, *Enforcement at the EPA*, 58; Dunlap and Mertig, *American Environmentalism*, 81.

27. Turner and Isenberg, *The Republican Reversal*, 110–11.

28. Jasanoff, "Science, Politics, and the Renegotiation of Expertise at EPA," 198–99.

29. Jasanoff, "Science, Politics, and the Renegotiation of Expertise at EPA," 199–200.

30. Walsh, Warland, and Smith, *Don't Burn It Here*, 113.

31. Environmental Protection Agency, "Region III Tests Philadelphia Incinerator," September 1986, Delaware Valley Toxics Coalition Records.

32. Ellen O'Brian and Mark Jaffe, "N.J. Bans Phila. Ash Bearing Dioxin," *Philadelphia Inquirer*, October 13, 1984.

33. Letter from John Daniel and Concerned Citizens to Greenpeace, February 6, 1987, Jim Vallette private archive; Joyce Gemperlein, "Incinerator Ash Is Called No Threat," *Philadelphia Inquirer*, January 3, 1985.

34. John C. Martin, *Flash Report: Philadelphia Incinerator Ash Exports for Panamanian Road Project; Potential Environmental Damage in the Making,* US Environmental Protection Agency, October 5, 1987, Jim Vallette private archive; EPA, Office of Solid Waste, "Responses to Questions and Answers Re: Exportation of Ash to Haiti," revised draft, March 17, 1988, Jim Vallette private archive; Mark Jaffe, "City's Standoff with Panama Illustrates Debate over Ash," *Philadelphia Inquirer*, September 13, 1987.

35. Environmental Protection Agency, "Region III Tests Philadelphia Incinerator," September 1986, Delaware Valley Toxics Coalition Records.

36. Gemperlein, "Incinerator Ash Is Called No Threat"; Environmental Protection Agency, "Region III Tests Philadelphia Incinerator," September 1986.

37. Mark Jaffe, "Panama Officially Rejects Shipment of Incinerator Ash," *Philadelphia Inquirer*, September 17, 1987.

38. Pat Costner, on behalf of Greenpeace Toxics Campaign, "Attention to All Greenpeace Activists," September 8, 1987, Delaware Valley Toxics Coalition Records; Pat Costner, Greenpeace, "Greenpeace Protests Export of Philadelphia Incinerator Ash," press release, September 8, 1987, Jim Vallette private archive.

39. Jaffe, "Panama Officially Rejects Shipment of Incinerator Ash"; Costner, "Attention to All Greenpeace Activists."

40. Peter Montague, "Philadelphia Tries to Ship Toxic Ash to the Third World, but Plan Is Sunk by Suppressed EPA Data," *Rachel's Hazardous Waste News,* November 23, 1987.

41. Letter from Michael A. Callahan, EPA Exposure Assessment Group, Office of Health and Environmental Assessments, to Gordon Milbourn, EPA Special Audit Unit, September 18, 1987; letter from Thomas Duke, EPA research coordinator, to John L. Schaum, EPA Office of Health and Environmental Assessment, September 18, 1987, Radio Haiti Papers; letter from Agency of Toxic Substances and Disease Registry to Gordon C. Milbourn, EPA Office of the Inspector General, September 28, 1987, Radio Haiti Papers.

42. John C. Martin, *Flash Report. Philadelphia Incinerator Ash Exports for Panamanian Road Project; Potential Environmental Damage in the Making,* US Environmental Protection Agency, October 5, 1987.

43. Letter from Agency of Toxic Substances and Disease Registry to Gordon C. Milbourn, EPA Office of the Inspector General, September 28, 1987, Radio Haiti Papers.

44. Environmental Protection Agency, "Environmental News: EPA responds to Inspector General," November 10, 1987, Delaware Valley Toxics Coalition Records.

45. A. James Barnes, Environmental Protection Agency deputy administrator, memorandum to John C. Martin, inspector general, "Response to Inspector General's Flash Report on Philadelphia Incinerator Ash Exports for Panama Road Project," November 10, 1987, Delaware Valley Toxics Coalition Records.

46. Action Center, "The Basics of a Landfill," March 26, 2003, www.ejnet.org/landfills.

47. Agency of Toxic Substances and Disease Registry to Milbourn.

48. Panamanian officials cited in Jaffe, "City's Standoff with Panama."

49. Davis, *Banned*, xi, 153–55.

50. Higman, *A Concise History of the Caribbean*, 257, 285, 306.

51. Translation of letter from Edgardo A. Pascall to Jorge I. Craniotis, National Port Authorities Honduras, n.d. (ca. late 1986 or early 1987), in Committee on Government Operations, House of Representatives, *International Export of US Waste.*

52. Agreement Paolino & Sons and Amalgamated Shipping, June 1986, United States Court of Appeals for the Third Circuit Collection, Records of the United States Courts of Appeals, US National Archives, Philadelphia, Section 9.

53. Pascall to Craniotis.

54. Agreement Paolino & Sons and Amalgamated Shipping, section 9.

55. Bill Hall and Joshua Karliner, "Eco-crisis in America's Backyard," unpublished manuscript, Jim Vallette private archive; Hall, Karliner, and Penelope, "Garbage Imperialism," 10–11.

56. Greenpeace, press release, September 11, 1987, Radio Haiti Papers.

57. Philadelphia streets commissioner, cited in Jaffe, "City's Standoff with Panama."

58. Jaffe, "City's Standoff with Panama."

59. Gina Boubion, "Residents Tell EPA to Haul Ash," *Philadelphia Daily News,* November 11, 1987.

60. Pete Bentley, EPA Region III, "Salient Issue on Philadelphia Incinerator Ash," internal memo, November 2, 1988, Jim Vallette private archive.

61. Bevington, *The Rebirth of Environmentalism*, 20.

62. Blumberg, *War on Waste*, 109–11; Iver Peterson, "Critics Assail Safety of Nation's 111 Garbage Incinerators," *New York Times*, November 21, 1987.

63. Testimony of William P. Reilly, January 9, 1990, United States District Court Delaware, Criminal Case Files, Records of District Courts of the United States, US National Archives, Philadelphia, 28–29.

64. Environmental Protection Agency, *Federal Register: Hazardous Waste Management System*, 20603; Bureau des Mines et de l'Énergie, "Rapport de mission effectué aux Gonaïves," January 25, 1988, Radio Haiti Papers.

65. "Gonaives consacrée ville de déchets toxiques," *Le Matin* (Port-au-Prince), January 26, 1988, Radio Haiti Papers; Nathaniel Sheppard, "Haiti Fears U.S. Wants to Use It As a Dump," *Chicago Tribune*, February 2, 1988.

66. Memorandum from Bureau des Mines and de l'Énergie, Haiti, to ministre du commerce, January 21, 1988, Radio Haiti Papers.

67. Ministère du Commerce et de l'Industrie, communiqué, January 21, 1988, Radio Haiti Papers.

68. Ministère du Commerce et de l'Industrie, "Note de Presse," January 27, 1988, Radio Haiti Papers.

69. "Gonaives consacrée ville de déchets toxiques."

70. Pierre David, "Introduction: Triage de déchets solides en Haiti; Proposition Jonathan M. Murphy. Memorandum à Ministre du Commerce, Mario Celestin," December 18, 1987, Radio Haiti Papers.

71. Mark Jaffe, "Haiti Is the Latest to Reject Ash," *Philadelphia Inquirer*, February 2, 1988; "Haiti Officials Reject Cargo of Philadelphia Waste Ash," *Sioux City Journal*, February 3, 1988.

72. Cited in Jaffe, "Haiti Is the Latest to Reject Ash."

73. Federation of the Friends of Nature (FAN)/Greenpeace Media, "Toxic Ash in Haiti," video, February 20, 1988, https://media.greenpeace.org, unique identifier GP04G2L.

74. Testimony of Captain Arturo Fuentes Garcia, May 24, 1993, United States District Court Delaware, Criminal Case Files, Records of District Courts of the United States, US National Archives, Philadelphia, 1321.

75. Radio Haiti, "Déchets toxiques," February 1, 1988, Radio Haiti Papers.

76. FAN/Greenpeace Media, "Toxic Ash in Haiti"; Loomis, *Out of Sight*; Jerry Schwartz, "Ship Can't Find Port in Environmental Storm," *Press and Sun Bulletin* (Binghamton, NY), September 3, 2000.

77. Hill, *Understanding Environmental Pollution*.

78. Jasanoff, "Science, Politics, and the Renegotiation of Expertise at EPA," 199.

79. WPVI, "WPVI_NY_Khian Sea."

80. FAN/Greenpeace Media, "Toxic Ash in Haiti."

81. Mayor of Gonaïves, quoted in FAN/Greenpeace Media, "Toxic Ash in Haiti."

82. WPVI, "WPVI_NY_Khian Sea."

83. Gaden Serge, "Évêché des Gonaives," September 29, 1988, Jim Vallette private archive.

84. FAN/Greenpeace Media, "Toxic Ash in Haiti."

85. Interview with Kenny Bruno, Greenpeace global toxics campaigner, August 8, 2018.

86. The Court of Common Pleas, First Judicial District of Pennsylvania Civil Trial Division, consent order, August 1987, Delaware Valley Toxics Coalition Records.

87. Jim Vallette and Pat Costner, Greenpeace, to ambassador of Guinea to the United States, May 2, 1988, Jim Vallette private archive.

88. Richter, "Giftmüllexporte nach Afrika," 339; Vallette and Costner to ambassador of Guinea; Bruce Diamond, EPA Regional Council, to Wendy Grieder, EPA Office of International Activities, "Conversation with Attorney for Bulkhandling Inc. Concerning the Vessel Bark," February 18, 1988, Jim Vallette private archive; Mark Jaffe, "Phila Ash Leaves Trail of Confusion," *Philadelphia Inquirer*, February 22, 1988.

89. Ramona Smith, "Bark Unloads Ash Cargo in Guinea," *Philadelphia Daily News*, March 17, 1988.

90. Harbo, H, "Nordmenn under Streng Bevoktning: Guinea Reagerer," *Aftenposten* (Oslo), June 25, 1988; Adresseavisen/NTB-Reuter, "Norge Fjerner Avfallet," *Adresseavisen* (Trondheim), June 16, 1988; Smith, "Bark Unloads Ash Cargo"; "US waste Threatens African Island," UPI International News Wire, May 18, 1988.

91. Vallette and Costner to ambassador of Guinea.

92. Ramona Smith, "It's Back Again: Banya Returns to Unload Ash," *Philadelphia Daily News*, July 22, 1988; Mark Jaffe, "3d Ship with Phila Incinerator Ash Scheduled to Sail the Seas," *Philadelphia Inquirer*, June 27, 1988.

93. UNEP, "INFOTERRA Helps Guinea Solve Controversial Ash Problem," *INFOTERRA Bulletin*, 1989.

94. UNEP, "INFOTERRA Helps Guinea"; Smith, "It's Back Again"; Jaffe, "3d Ship with Phila Incinerator Ash."

95. Vallette and Costner to ambassador of Guinea.

96. US Agency for Toxic Substances Disease Registry (ATSDR), "Health Consultation," cited in Vallette and Costner to ambassador of Guinea.

97. Vincent Fournier, *Jeune Afrique*, photograph reprinted in *Newsweek*, November 7, 1988.

98. Ankomah, "African Wasteland," 36.

99. Lansana Conté, cited in Associated Press, "Guinea Worried by Philadelphia

Waste," *Philadelphia Daily News*, July 12, 1988; Ramona Smith, "Guinea Wants Phila Ash out of Africa," *Philadelphia Daily News*, May 3, 1988.

100. United Nations, *Report of the United Nations Conference on the Human Environment*, 24.

101. Heid, "UN Sets Up Global Monitoring Program," 1846; Martyn, *Report on the Evaluation of INFOTERRA*, 4.

102. Mongillo and Zierdt-Warshaw. *Encyclopedia of Environmental Science*, 174.

103. "US Waste Threatens African Island."

104. UNEP, "INFOTERRA Helps Guinea."

105. Smith, "Guinea Wants Phila Ash out of Africa."

106. Sheldon Meyers, acting associate administrator EPA, "Philadelphia Ash in Guinea," memorandum, June 14, 1988, Jim Vallette private archive.

107. "Arrestert for gift-dumping," *Dagbladet* (Norway), June 10, 1988; "More Officials Held in Guinea Waste Scandal," *Reuters*, June 16, 1988.

108. Sheldon Meyers, Acting Associate Administrator, EPA, "Philadelphia Ash in Guinea," memorandum, June 14, 1988, Jim Vallette private archive.

109. Dagningen/NTB-Reuter, "Avfallet fjernet frå Guinea: Vil ikke bruke betong med gift," *Dagningen* (Lillehammer), June 29, 1988.

110. H. Hegtun, "Arrestert konsul i fin form," *Aftenposten*, June 13, 1988.

111. "Omstridt avfall i Guinea: Asken losses på ukjent sted," *Aftenposten*, July 6, 1988.

112. Letter from Roland W. Schrecongost, EPA Hazardous Waste Management Division, to Mary Gade, EPA Waste Management Division, May 25, 1988, Jim Vallette private archive.

113. Environmental Protection Agency, "EPA and DER to Oversee Sampling of Philadelphia Ash Returning from Guinea," *EPA Environmental News*, July 12, 1988.

114. WPVI, "WPVI_NY_Khian Sea."

115. Environmental Protection Agency, "DER and EPA Announce Banya Sampling Results," *EPA Environmental News*, July 22, 1988.

116. Letter from Edward I. Merrigan, lawyer for Bulkhandling, to Sheldon Meyers, EPA, October 6, 1988, Jim Vallette private archive.

117. Testimony of William P. Reilly, 40, 82.

118. Testimony of William P. Reilly, 97, 101, 103.

119. Testimony of William P. Reilly, 111.

FIVE | American Rules in a Global Environment

1. Committee on Government Operations, *International Export of US Waste*, 35.

2. US House of Representatives, "Committee on Government Reform: Background/History," May 20, 2006.

3. John Conyers, cited in Committee on Government Operations, *International Export of US Waste*, 6.

4. Flynn, "Bush, Dukakis Target Environment."

5. Waste Export Prohibition Act, H.R. 5018, 100th Congress (1988).

6. Merchant, *American Environmental History*, 193.

7. Carson, *Silent Spring*.

8. For a history that goes beyond *Silent Spring*, see Montrie, *The Myth of* Silent Spring.

9. Merchant, *American Environmental History*, 187.

10. Environmental Protection Agency, "DDT Ban Takes Effect: EPA Press Release," December 31, 1972; Davis, *Banned*.

11. Walter, "Economic Repercussion of Environmental Policy," 36.

12. Müller, "Hidden Externalities."

13. Cullather, *The Hungry World*; Kinkela, *DDT and the American Century*; Shiva, *The Violence of the Green Revolution*.

14. Mart, *Pesticides, a Love Story*, 83–84.

15. Kinkela, *DDT and the American Century*, 175.

16. Atkeson et al., "International Regulation of Toxic Substances," 77, 81.

17. Almeida et al., "Regulatory Toxicology."

18. United States General Accounting Office, *Better Regulation of Pesticide Exports*; Committee on Foreign Affairs, *Export of Hazardous Products*, 2.

19. Robert Harris, cited in Committee on Foreign Affairs, *Export of Hazardous Products*, 50.

20. Azevedo, "Trade in Hazardous Substance,"136.

21. Street, "U.S. Exports Banned for Domestic Use."

22. World Health Organization, *Safe Use of Pesticides*.

23. Azevedo, "Trade in Hazardous Substances"; Graham, *Environment and Trade*, 147.

24. Waldo, "A Review of US and International Restrictions," 17.

25. World Health Organization, *Occupational Health Programme*.

26. Environmental Defense Fund, Inc., v. USAID, 6 ELR 20121 (DDC 1975).

27. Atkeson et al., "International Regulation of Toxic Substances," 83; Macekura, *Of Limits and Growth*, 185.

28. Meyer, "How the U.S. Protects the Environment."

29. Gold, Blum, and Ames, "Another Flame Retardant."

30. Mehri, "Prior Informed Consent," 370.

31. Dowie, "The Corporate Crime of the Century."

32. Azevedo, "Trade in Hazardous Substances"; Graham, *Environment and Trade*, 143.

33. Committee on Foreign Affairs, *Export of Hazardous Products*, 46.

34. Hiscox, "The Magic Bullet?"

35. Eckes, *Opening America's Market*, chapter 6.

36. Michael D. Barnes, cited in Committee on Foreign Affairs, *Export of Hazardous Products*, 4.

37. Abd-el Monsef, Smith, and Darwish, "Impacts of the Aswan High Dam."

38. Charles Warren, cited in Yost, "American Governmental Responsibility," 533.

39. Abd-el Monsef, Smith, and Darwish, "Impacts of the Aswan High Dam," 1877; Barakat, "Epidemiology of Schistosomiasis in Egypt."

40. Rubin, "A Predominantly Commercial Policy Perspective."

41. Peter Kilborn, "U.S. Trade Deficit Set Record in 1984," *New York Times*, January 31, 1985.

42. Committee on Government Operations, *U.S. Export of Banned Products*, 5.

43. Jacob Scherr, cited in Committee on Government Operations, *U.S. Export of Banned Products*, 34.

44. Julius Kiano, cited in Committee on Government Operations, *U.S. Export of Banned Products*, 35.

45. Committee on Foreign Affairs, *Export of Hazardous Products*, 46; UNEP Governing Council, cited in Committee on Government Operations, *U.S. Export of Banned Products*, 35.

46. Committee on Foreign Affairs, *Hazardous Product Exports*, 6.

47. Azevedo, "Trade in Hazardous Substances"; Graham, *Environment and Trade*, 142, 146; Committee on Government Operations, *U.S. Export of Banned Products*, 2.

48. Ives, *The Export of Hazard*.

49. Azevedo, "Trade in Hazardous Substances"; Graham, *Environment and Trade*, 145.

50. Jacob Scherr, in Committee on Government Operations, *U.S. Export of Banned Products*. See also Azevedo, "Trade in Hazardous Substances"; Graham, *Environment and Trade*, 145.

51. Turner and Isenberg, *The Republican Reversal*, 48–49.

52. Mehri, "Prior Informed Consent," 370.

53. Lewis A. Engman, cited in Ives, *The Export of Hazard*.

54. Greenwood, "Restrictions on the Exportation of Hazardous Products," 138; Lori Onstenk, "Mixed News on Dumping," *Mother Jones*, January 1981, 8.

55. Barnes, cited in Committee on Foreign Affairs, *Export of Hazardous Products*, 3.

56. Esther Peterson, cited in Committee on Foreign Affairs, *Export of Hazardous Products*, 14.

57. Blum, *Love Canal Revisited*; Newman, *Love Canal*.

58. Cathy Trost, "New Export from U.S.?" *Detroit Free Press*, July 11, 1982.

59. "Federal Officials Try to Halt African Waste Dumping Plan," *Times-News* (Twin Falls, ID), January 28, 1980.

60. William Anston Hayne, State Department, cited in Committee on Foreign Affairs, *Export of Hazardous Products*, 72.

61. "Federal Officials Try to Halt African Waste Dumping Plan."

62. Leon Dash, "Sierra Leone Bristles with Economic Discontent," *Washington Post*, July 14, 1980.

63. "Federal Officials Try to Halt African Waste Dumping Plan."

64. Telegram from State Department, cited in Committee on Foreign Affairs, *Export of Hazardous Products*, 11; Christopher McLeod, "Winning Hearts and Minds with Hazardous Wastes," *Minneapolis Star Tribune,* August 20, 1980.

65. "Sierra Leone," *Facts on File World News Digest,* February 29, 1980.

66. McLeod, "Winning Hearts and Minds," 7; "Federal Officials Try to Halt African Waste Dumping Plan"; "Sierra Leone"; Committee on Foreign Affairs, *Export of Hazardous Products,* 12.

67. McLeod, "Winning Hearts and Minds," 7.

68. McLeod, "Winning Hearts and Minds," 7.

69. Edward Flattau, "Will Hazardous Waste Be Buried across the Border? *Ithaca (NY) Journal* , February 29, 1980.

70. Environmental Protection Agency, "Hazardous Waste Management System," 8744; Environmental Protection Agency, *EPA's Program to Control Exports of Hazardous Wastes*, 9.

71. John C. Martin, cited in Committee on Government Operations, *International Export of US Waste*, 12.

72. Environmental Protection Agency, "Hazardous Waste Management System," 8744; Environmental Protection Agency, *EPA's Program to Control Exports of Hazardous Wastes*, 9; Environmental Protection Agency, "Hazardous Waste Management System," 8744.

73. Trost, "New Export from U.S.?"

74. Richard Golob, cited in James Simon, "A Warning on Exporting Waste," *Boston Globe*, May 11, 1981; interview with Richard Golob, August 29, 2018.

75. Martin, cited in Committee on Government Operations, *International Export of US Waste*, 12; Environmental Protection Agency, "Hazardous Waste Management System," 8744.

76. Committee on Government Operations, *International Export of US Waste*, 13.

77. Committee on Government Operations, *International Export of US Waste*, 13, 14, 23.

78. Mike Synar, cited in in Committee on Government Operations, *International Export of US Waste*, 256.

79. "Congress Tightens Hazardous Waste Controls."

80. Philip Shabekoff, "Environmentalists Say Either Bush or Dukakis Will Be an Improvement," *New York Times*, September 1, 1988.

81. Conyers, cited in Committee on Government Operations, *International Export of US Waste*, 4.

82. Theoharis, *The Rebellious Life of Mrs. Rosa Park*; B. Aptheker, *The Morning Breaks*; Racial Justice Act, H.R. 4442, 100th Congress (1988).

83. Shabecoff, *A Fierce Green Fire*, 233; Pollack, Coling and Grozuczak, *Reagan, Toxics and Minorities*.

84. Conyers, "Preface," ii.

85. Bullard, *Dumping in Dixie*, 14, 36.

86. Committee on Government Operations, *International Export of US Waste*, 6.

87. Bellegarde-Smith, "Dynastic Dictatorship," 280.

88. Kosmerick, "Synar, Michael Lynn"; Richard Pearson, "Oklahoma's Mike Synar Dies at 45," *Washington Post*, January 10, 1996.

89. Chris Casteel, "Maverick Ex-Congressman Synar Succumbs to Cancer," *Oklahoman*, January 10, 1996.

90. "Handling of Toxic Waste by Pentagon Criticized," *Washington Post*, August 16, 1983.

91. Michael Weisskopf, "Liquid Pesticide Recalled by EPA Remains Threat as Stockpiles Leak," *Washington Post*, November 12, 1986.

92. Michael Weisskopf, "Firm Allegedly Dumped PCBs," *Washington Post*, April 7, 1987.

93. Richard Willing, "U.S. Firm Seeking Right to Dump in Africa," *News Journal* (Wilmington, DE), June 19, 1988; "Africans Oppose Hazardous Waste Proposal," *Detroit Free Press*, June 20, 1988.

94. Committee on Government Operations, *International Export of US Waste*, 7.

95. Waste Export Prohibition Act, H.R. 5018, 100th Congress (1988).

96. Waste Export Control Act, S. 2598, 100th Congress (1988).

97. Kapur, Lewis, and Webb, *The World Bank*, 664.

98. Waste Export Control Act, S. 2598.

99. Committee on Government Operations, *International Export of US Waste*, 254.

100. William Clinger, cited in Committee on Government Operations, *International Export of US Waste*, 4.

101. Synar, cited in Committee on Government Operations, *International Export of US Waste*, 2.

102. Committee on Government Operations, *International Export of US Waste*, 11.

103. Committee on Government Operations, *International Export of US Waste*, 283.

104. William Nitze, cited in Committee on Government Operations, *International Export of US Waste*, 305.

105. Sheldon Meyers, cited in Committee on Government Operations, *International Export of US Waste*, 302.

106. Conyers, cited in Committee on Government Operations, *International Export of US Waste*.

107. Synar, cited in Committee on Government Operations, *International Export of US Waste*.

108. Moyers and Bergman, "Global Dumping Ground."

109. McLeod, "Winning Hearts and Minds," 7.

110. Committee on Government Operations, *International Export of US Waste*, 516.

111. Tom Friend, "Redskins, William Will Talk," Joan Reinthaler, "Summer Chorus at the Cathedral," and weather forecast, *Washington Post*, July 14, 1988.

SIX | Stop "Garbage Imperialism"

1. Vallette and Spalding, *The International Trade in Wastes*.

2. Letter from Andreas Bernstorff to Uta Bellion, Greenpeace International, June 3, 1988, Jim Vallette private archive.

3. Letter from Jim Vallette to Pat Costner and Dave Rappaport, "Proposal for a Global Waste Patrol Campaign," March 8, 1988, Jim Vallette private archive.

4. David Morris, "Garbage Imperialism: Let's Force Cities to Keep Wastes in Their Own Backyard," *Los Angeles Times*, May 18, 1987.

5. On the globalization of environmental justice, see Pellow, *Resisting Global Toxics*.

6. Jim Puckett, *Toxic Waste: Resisting the Southerly Path*, report prepared for the United Nations Centre for Transnational Corporations, West African Workshop on Hazardous Waste, Monrovia, Liberia, May 8, 1989, Jim Vallette private archive.

7. J. Davis, *The Global 1980s*, 54–59.

8. "Federal Officials Try to Halt African Waste Dumping Plan," *Times-News* (Twin Falls, ID), January 28, 1980; Vallette and Spalding, *The International Trade in Wastes*, 40.

9. Müller, "Hidden Externalities."

10. Cited in Richter, "Giftmüllexporte nach Afrika," 341.

11. Greenpeace USA, *International Trade in Toxic Wastes*, 120; Allen, *Waste Not Want Not*, 181–82.

12. OAU resolution, cited in Philis Williams, "New African Disputes over 'Colonialist Garbage' and 'Toxic Terrorism,'" UPI Spot Weekender, June 6, 1988.

13. Tolba and Rummel-Bulska, *Global Environmental Diplomacy*, 113.

14. J. Davis, *The Global 1980s*, 64.

15. Ladapo, "The Contribution of Cartoonists to Environmental Debates"; Akingbade, *Nigeria*, 7.

16. Allen, *Waste Not Want Not*, 179; Williams, "New African Disputes"; Dotun Akintomide, "Koko Toxic Waste: 30 Evacuation Workers Die of Strange Ailments," *Nigerian*

News Direct, December 19, 2016, http://nigeriannewsdirect.com/koko-toxic-waste-30
-evacuation-workers-die-of-strange-ailments, accessed August 8, 2020.

17. James Brooke, "Waste Dumpers Turning to West Africa," *New York Times*, July 17, 1988; Tunde, *Nigeria*, 9.

18. Abdulhamid A. Elmi, "Dumping Waste in Africa," letter to the editor, *African Business*, July 1988.

19. "Africa Will Not Be the World's Rubbish Dump," Reuters, June 16, 1988.

20. Cited in Brooke, "Waste Dumpers Turning to West Africa."

21. "An African Revolution," letter to the editor, *African Concord*, July 26, 1988.

22. Pierre Osei-Owusu, "Africa's Black Sheep," *West Africa*, July 18, 1988. See also Akanji Fakorede, "Africa Must Not Become a Dumping Ground," *West Africa*, July 4, 1988.

23. "An African Revolution."

24. Kjersti Sortland, "Africa as Dumping Ground," *Bergens Tidende*, June 23, 1988; Greenpeace USA, *International Trade in Toxic Wastes*, 7; Jim Vallette, testimony of Greenpeace before Committee of Foreign Relations, US Senate, March 12, 1992, 2, Jim Vallette private archive; Steven Greenhouse, "Toxic Waste Boomerang: Ciao Italy!" *New York Times*, September 3, 1988.

25. Vallette and Spalding, *The International Trade in Wastes*, 25–28.

26. Greenpeace USA, "Burnt Offerings," 2nd ed., February 15, 1988, Radio Haiti Papers; Zelko, *Make It a Green Peace*, 4–5.

27. Zelko, *Make It a Green Peace*, 297.

28. Zelko, *Make It a Green Peace*, 313.

29. Interview with Jim Vallette, July 20, 2018.

30. Wills Flowers, "Letter to Denise Voelkers, Rainforest Action Network," May 27, 1987, Jim Vallette private archive; letter from Michael Marshall, Smithsonian Institution, to Greenpeace, May 12, 1987, Jim Vallette private archive.

31. Helvarg, *The War against the Greens*, 253.

32. Pat Costner, "Letter to Ruben Blades," August 21, 1987, Jim Vallette private archive.

33. "The Spidermen of Greenpeace," *Philadelphia Inquirer*, September 9, 1987; "Protesters Climb Tower," *Standard-Speaker* (Hazleton, PA), September 9, 1987.

34. Greenpeace USA, *Burnt Offerings*, 1st ed., September 1987, Radio Haiti Papers; Greenpeace USA, "Ofrendas envenenadas," February 15, 1988, Jim Vallette private archive.

35. Pat Costner and Jim Vallette to Greenpeace headquarters in Amsterdam, "Urgent Proposal for International Contingency Funds for Continuing Campaign against Global Transport of Incinerator Ash from Philadelphia," February 18, 1988, Jim Vallette private archive.

36. Pellow, *Resisting Global Toxics*, 109.

37. Greenpeace USA, *Burnt Offerings*, 2nd ed.

38. Vallette and Spalding, *International Trade in Wastes*.

39. Victor Fiorillo and Liz Spikol, "Ashes to Ashes, Dust to Dust," *Philadelphia Weekly*, January 17, 2001.

40. "Toxic Barge Snubbed (or) Return of Garbage Barge," *Daily Review* (Morgan City, LA), August 31, 1988; David Willey, "Toxic Ship Finds Port in a Storm," *Observer* (London), September 18, 1988.

41. Kate Bouey, "U.K.'s Lax Pollution Standards Spark Outcry," *Ottawa Citizen*, November 28, 1988.

42. Newton, *Environmental Justice*, 90; American Bureau of Shipping, "Shipping Data for Felicia," September 10, 1988, US National Archives, Philadelphia.

43. Borowy, "Hazardous Waste."

44. World Health Organization, *Report of the Scientific Group*, cited in Borowy, "Hazardous Waste," 3.

45. Hamblin, "Environmentalism for the Atlantic Alliance," 55.

46. Borowy, "Hazardous Waste," 3–5.

47. Huismans, "The International Register of Potentially Toxic Chemicals (IRPTC)," 275–76.

48. Kaikati, "Domestically Banned Products," 126–27.

49. United Nations Environment Programme, *The Basel Convention*, 3.

50. Krueger, "Prior Informed Consent," 117; Clapp, *Toxic Exports*, 39; United Nations Environment Programme, *The Basel Convention*, 3.

51. United Nations Environment Programme, *Cairo Guidelines*, 3.

52. McDowall, *Management to Facilitate Compliance*, 11.

53. Rieser, Hörl, and Vilovic, *Incoherent Voices*.

54. Richter, "Giftmüllexporte nach Afrika," 335.

55. Carroll and Kellow, *The OECD*, 213.

56. OECD, *Economic and Ecological Interdependence*, 1.

57. Harjula, "Hazardous Waste," 464; Borowy, "Hazardous Waste," 3.

58. OECD, *Economic and Ecological Interdependence*, 3; Belenky, "Cradle to Border," 124; Harjula, "Hazardous Waste," 465.

59. Harjula, "Hazardous Waste," 464.

60. OECD, *Economic and Ecological Interdependence*, cited in Belenky, "Cradle to Border," 125.

61. Carroll and Kellow, *The OECD*, 226.

62. OECD Environment Committee 1982, cited in Harjula, "Hazardous Waste," 464.

63. Krueger, "Prior Informed Consent," 118; Clapp, *Toxic Exports*, 39; Harjula, "Hazardous Waste," 465.

64. Clapp, *Toxic Exports*, 39.

65. Harjula, "Hazardous Waste," 465.

66. Harjula, "Hazardous Waste," 465.

67. Krueger, "Prior Informed Consent," 118; Clapp, *Toxic Exports*, 39.

68. Harjula, "Hazardous Waste," 467.

69. "The West's Wastebasket," *Africa News*, June 13, 1988.

70. Mehri, "Prior Informed Consent," 366; Clapp, *Toxic Exports*, 39.

71. Knill and Liefferink, *Environmental Politics in the European Union*, 4–5; Delreux and Happaerts, *Environmental Policy and Politics*, 168; J. Davis, *The Global 1980s*, 105–7.

72. J. Davis, *The Global 1980s*, 106.

73. Subcommittee on Human Rights and International Organizations, *Hearing*, 1.

74. Mostafa K. Tolba, cited in "International Treaty on Management on Hazardous Waste," Xinhua English Language News Service, June 10, 1988.

75. United Nations Environment Programme, *The Basel Convention*, 3–4.

76. Clapp, *Toxic Exports*, 39–40.

77. Tolba and Rummel-Bulska, *Global Environmental Diplomacy*, 98, 102, 108.

78. Tolba and Rummel-Bulska, *Global Environmental Diplomacy*, 109–12.

79. Tolba and Rummel-Bulska, *Global Environmental Diplomacy*, 113.

80. Tolba and Rummel-Bulska, *Global Environmental Diplomacy*, 113–14.

81. Greenpeace, "Statement by Greenpeace before UNEP at the third session of the AdHoc Working Group of Legal and Technical Experts with a Mandate to Prepare a Global Convention on the Control of Transboundary Movement of Hazardous Wastes," Geneva, November 7–16, 1988, Jim Vallette Archive.

82. Committee on Foreign Relations, *Basel Convention on the Control of Transboundary Movement of Hazardous Wastes*, 26.

83. Greenpeace, "Statement by Greenpeace before UNEP"; Tolba and Rummel-Bulska, *Global Environmental Diplomacy*, 103.

84. Greenpeace, "There Ought to Be a Law against It: Toxic Trash Trade," *Greenpeace News* 3, 1989.

85. Greenpeace, "Statement by Greenpeace before UNEP."

86. Tolba and Rummel-Bulska, *Global Environmental Diplomacy*, 115.

87. Kevin Stairs, cited in Greenpeace, "There Ought to Be a Law."

88. Testimony of William P. Reilly, January 9, 1990, United States District Court Delaware, Criminal Case Files, Records of District Courts of the United States, US National Archives, Philadelphia, 67; Testimony of Arturo Fuentes Garcia, May 24, 1993, United States District Court Delaware, Criminal Case Files, Records of District Courts of the United States, US National Archives, Philadelphia, 1382.

89. Testimony of William P. Reilly, 71; Testimony of Arturo Fuentes Garcia, 1310, 1388.

90. Testimony of William P. Reilly, 71.

91. Testimony of William P. Reilly, 91.

92. Testimony of William P. Reilly, 91, 85–93.

93. Testimony of Arturo Fuentes Garcia, 1310, 1420.

94. Testimony of William P. Reilly, 95.

95. Testimony of Arturo Fuentes Garcia, 1392.

96. "Asia Dumping Ground for Waste," *Times of India,* February 28, 1994.

SEVEN | Return to Sender

1. Komite Tet Ansanm pou Onè Respè Konstitisyon an, "Retire fatra pwazon an nan Gonayiv," June 10, 1988, Radio Haiti Papers.

2. Komite Tet Ansanm pou Onè Respè Konstitisyon an, "Retire fatra pwazon an nan Gonayiv."

3. George H. W. Bush, "Remarks by the President and Secretary of Health and Human Services Dr. Louis W. Sullivan at Swearing-In Ceremony," Department of Health and Human Services, Washington, DC, cited in Jim Vallette, Testimony before the Subcommittee on Environmental Protection, Committee on Environment and Public Works, US Senate, July 25, 1991, Jim Vallette private archive.

4. Committee on Government Operations, *International Export of US Waste*, 28.

5. Sinclair, "The Offered Hand."

6. Boss and Kilian, *The United Nations Convention*, 283.

7. Sinclair, "The Offered Hand."

8. Statement of William A. Nitze, deputy assistant secretary, Environment, Health and Natural Resources, Bureau of Oceans and International Environmental Scientific Affairs, Department of State, cited in Committee on Foreign Affairs, *Update on Recent International Environment Meetings*, 4.

9. "Bush Endorses International Waste Pact," *Star Press* (Muncie, IN), March 22, 1990; "On Toxic Waste," *St. Louis Dispatch*, March 23, 1990.

10. See, for example, statements of Representatives Mike Synar and Claiborne Pell in Committee on Foreign Relations, *Basel Convention*.

11. Response to questions submitted to William A. Nitze from Representative Ted Weiss following the April 6 meeting, cited in Committee on Foreign Relations, *Update on Recent International Environment Meetings*, appendix 1, 52; see also Committee on Foreign Relations, *Update on Recent International Environment Meetings*, 21.

12. Kirby, "The Basel Convention," 295.

13. Appendix 1, response to questions submitted to William A. Nitze from Representative Ted Weiss following the April 6 Meeting, cited in Committee on Foreign Affairs, *Update on Recent International Environment Meetings*, 52.

14. Department of Environmental Protection Act, H.R. 3847, 101st Cong. (1990).

15. Tolba and Rummel-Bulska, *Global Environmental Diplomacy*, 115.

16. Richard Smith, Department of State, cited in Committee on Foreign Relations, *Basel Convention*, 7, 9.

17. Jim Vallette, cited in Committee on Foreign Relations, *Basel Convention*, 26.

18. Greenpeace USA, "Waste Trade Briefing for Co-sponsors of the Waste Export Campaign," May 30, 1991, Jim Vallette private archive.

19. Waste Export and Import Prohibition Act, H.R. 2580, 102nd Cong. (1991).

20. Mike Synar, cited in Committee on Foreign Relations, *Basel Convention*, 4.

21. Waste Export Control Act, H.R. 2358, 102nd Cong. (1991); Synar, cited in Committee on Foreign Relations, *Basel Convention*, 5.

22. Committee on Foreign Relations, *Basel Convention*, 17.

23. Representative Sonny Callahan, cited in Subcommittee on Transport and Hazardous Materials, *Waste Export Control*, 26.

24. Committee on Foreign Relations, *Basel Convention*, 40–41, 43.

25. United States of America, "Communiqué to UNEP's Secretary General," March 13, 1996, cited in the Basel Convention, www.basel.int/?tabid=4499#US17.

26. Clapp, *Toxic Exports*, 55.

27. Clapp, *Toxic Exports*, 47.

28. Vallette, Testimony before Subcommittee on Environmental Protection.

29. Kirby, "The Basel Convention," 301.

30. Vallette and Spalding, *The International Trade in Wastes*.

31. Clapp, *Toxic Exports*, 47.

32. Jim Vallette, cited in Committee on Foreign Relations, *Basel Convention*, 34.

33. Clapp, *Toxic Exports*, 48.

34. Organisation of African Unity, *Bamako Convention*.

35. Asante-Duah and Nagy, *International Trade in Hazardous Wastes*, 49.

36. Clapp, *Toxic Exports*, 50.

37. Clapp, *Toxic Exports*, 58.

38. Clapp, *Toxic Exports*, 67, 76.

39. DTE Staff, "Basel Ban Amendment Becomes Law," *Down to Earth*, September 10, 2019, www.downtoearth.org.in/news/waste/basel-ban-amendment-becomes-law-6665.

40. Testimony of William P. Reilly, January 9, 1990, United States District Court Delaware, Criminal Case Files, Records of District Courts of the United States, US National Archives, Philadelphia, 2–3.

41. United States of America vs. William P. Reilly, Argued May 2, 1994" United States Court of Appeals for the Third Circuit Collection, Records of the United States Courts of Appeals, US National Archives, Philadelphia, 6–7.

42. Bill Lambrecht, "Odyssey of Waste: Ship Wandered Globe in Search of Port," *St. Louis Post-Dispatch*, November 7, 1989.

43. Testimony of William P. Reilly, 2–3.

44. Testimony of William P. Reilly, 42–44.

45. Testimony of William P. Reilly, 42–44.

46. "Philadelphia Ash Ship Is Still Trying to Unload Cargo," *Asbury Park (NJ) Press*, August 19, 1987.

47. Testimony of William P. Reilly, 49.

48. Testimony of William P. Reilly, 50–51.

49. "After 2 Years, Ship Dumps Toxic Ash," *New York Times*, November 28, 1988.

50. Ruth Youngblood, "Now-Empty Ship Stranded for Having Hauled Toxic Ash," UPI, November 28, 1988.

51. Testimony of William P. Reilly, 95, 97.

52. Sarah Henry, "Poison Trail," *Los Angeles Times Magazine*, September 23, 1990.

53. Henry, "Poison Trail."

54. Henry, "Poison Trail"; Henry Weinstein, "El Toro Man Sentenced in Hazardous Waste Case," *Los Angeles Times*, December 3, 1991.

55. Müller, "Hidden Externalities," 52.

56. United States of America v. William P. Reilly, 5.

57. United States of America v. William P. Reilly, 5.

58. United States of America v. William P. Reilly, 6–7.

59. Lambrecht, "Odyssey of Waste"; Pete Bentley, EPA, internal memo, *Khian Sea/Felicia/Pelicano*, January 25, 1989, Jim Vallette private archive.

60. United States of America v. William P. Reilly, 6–7.

61. United States of America v. William P. Reilly, 8.

62. Mike Synar, cited in Committee on Foreign Relations, *Basel Convention*, 4.

63. International Liaison Office for President Jean-Bertrand Aristide, "US Refuses to Remove Philadelphia's Toxic Ash."

64. Jean Robert Lalane, Asanble Popile Nasyonal, "Not pou la press," March 24, 1988, Radio Haiti Papers.

65. Ramona Smith, "Our Ash Is Back," *Philadelphia Daily News*, February 27, 1988.

66. Mark Jaffe, "Ash Ship Expected in Delaware Bay, Today," *Philadelphia Inquirer*, March 1, 1988.

67. Dan Lovely, Bob Warner, and Joseph P. Blake, "Kicking Up a Dust over Ash," *Philadelphia Daily News*, March 1, 1988.

68. Fitz Longchamp, cited in Lovely, Warner, and Blake, "Kicking Up a Dust over Ash."

69. Danielle Knight, "U.S. Toxic Waste in Haiti May be Returned to Sender," Albion Monitor, February 11, 1998.

70. Pellow, *Resisting Global Toxics*, 109.

71. Jon Sawyer, "Haiti Seeks Removal of US Waste," *Washington Post Dispatch*, May 12, 1991; Paul, cited in Pellow, *Resisting Global Toxics*, 109.

72. Earl Lafontant, cited in Pellow, *Resisting Global Toxics*, 110.

73. Golden, "Human Rights," 2.

74. Buss and Gardner, *Haiti in the Balance*, 72–73.

75. Greenpeace, "Indictment Announced in Philadelphia's Haiti Ash Scandal," July 14, 1992, Radio Haiti Papers.

76. Roland W. Schrecongost, "Philadelphia Incinerator Ash," EPA memorandum, March 4, 1988, Jim Vallette private archive.

77. Radio Haiti, "Gonaives—Déchets Toxiques," November 22, 1988, Radio Haiti Papers, my translation.

78. Greenpeace, "Indictment Announced."

79. Knight, "U.S. Toxic Waste in Haiti."

80. Radio Haiti, "Gonaives—Déchets Toxiques."

81. International Liaison Office for President Jean-Bertrand Aristide, "U.S. Refuses to Remove Philadelphia's Toxic Ash."

82. Knight, "U.S. Toxic Waste in Haiti."

83. Buss and Gardner, *Haiti in the Balance*, 74.

84. Pellow, *Resisting Global Toxics*, 109.

85. International Liaison Office for President Jean-Bertrand Aristide, "U.S. Refuses to Remove Philadelphia's Toxic Ash."

86. Letter from COHPEDA to Madeleine Albright, April 2, 1998, Radio Haiti Papers.

87. Gore, *Earth in the Balance*.

88. Pellow, *Resisting Global Toxics*, 112.

89. Letter from COHPEDA to Madeleine Albright, April 4, 1988, Radio Haiti Papers.

90. Pellow, *Resisting Global Toxics*, 110.

91. Marian Uhlman, "Incinerator Ash May Complete 10-year Odyssey, Returning to U.S. from Haiti," *Greenville News* (SC), January 17, 1998.

92. Pellow, *Resisting Global Toxics*, 110–11.

93. Hope Reeves, "A Trail of Refuse," *New York Times*, February 18, 2001.

94. Knight, "U.S. Toxic Waste in Haiti."

95. Cited in Pellow, *Resisting Global Toxics*, 114.

96. Peter Montague, "Philadelphia Dumps on the Poor," *Rachel's Environment and Health Weekly*, April 23, 1998.

97. Return to Sender Project, 1997, cited in Pellow, *Resisting Global Toxics*, 112.

98. Montague, "Philadelphia Dumps on the Poor."

99. COHPEDA, "Petition to the Parliament and President of the Republic of Haiti," March 29, 1998, Radio Haiti Papers.

100. Radio Haiti, "Sit-In Ambassade Americaine," March 13, 1998, Radio Haiti Papers.

101. Cited in Pellow, *Resisting Global Toxics*, 113.

102. Agence Haitienne de Presse, "Dossier Déchets toxiques," April 6, 1998, Radio Haiti Papers.

103. Montague, "Philadelphia Dumps on the Poor."

104. Pellow, *Resisting Global Toxics*, 114.

105. See, for example, letter from Edward Rendell to Mary H. Jackson, April 17, 1998, cited in Pellow, *Resisting Global Toxics*, 116.

106. Bruce Gledhill, Philadelphia streets commissioner, cited in Committee on Government Operations, *International Export of US Waste*, 38; Mark Jaffe, "City Trash Plan Stresses Recycling," *Philadelphia Inquirer*, October 11, 1990.

107. Pellow, *Resisting Global Toxics*, 116; Sicotte, *From Workshop to Waste Magnet*.

108. Sicotte, *From Workshop to Waste Magnet*, 36.

109. Sicotte, *From Workshop to Waste Magnet*, 52; Michael Janofsky, "Suit Says Racial Bias Led to Clustering of Solid-Waste Sites," *New York Times*, May 29, 1996.

110. Cole and Foster, *From the Ground Up*, 36.

111. Ministère de l'Environnement, "Note de presse," October 7, 1998, Radio Haiti Papers.

112. Agence Haitienne de Presse, "Le bateau doit transporter les déchets toxiques vers les Etats-Unis devrait accoster le Wharf Sedren vendredi," November 9, 1998, Radio Haiti Papers; Radio Haiti, "Déchets Toxiques," November 4, 1998, Radio Haiti Papers.

113. Ministère de l'Environnement, "Note de presse."

114. Agence Haitienne de Presse, "Le bateau."

115. Agence Haitienne de Presse, "Le bateau."

116. Agence Haitienne de Presse, "Le bateau."

117. Radio Haiti, "Blocage du dossier des déchets toxiques," November 24, 1998, Radio Haiti Papers.

118. Radio Haiti, "Commission Justice et Paix," December 12, 1998, Radio Haiti Papers.

119. Agence Haitienne Presse, "Embarquement," November 23, 1998, Radio Haiti Papers.

120. Radio Haiti, "Blocage du dossier des déchets toxiques."

121. Radio Haiti, "Blocage du dossier des déchets toxiques."

122. Radio Haiti, "Ambassade americain," November 25, 1998, Radio Haiti Papers.

123. Essential Action, "University Students Tell Rendell to Get His Ash Home!" news release, Project Return to Sender, April 16, 1999, www.essentialaction.org/return/students.html.

124. Radio Haiti, "Blocage du dossier des déchets toxiques."

125. Cited in Pellow, *Resisting Global Toxics*, 118.

126. Radio Haiti, "Déchets toxiques," May 29, 2000, Radio Haiti Papers.

127. Jaffe, "Hopes for Ash Dashed"; Pellow, *Resisting Global Toxics*, 118.

128. "Waste Management Grows in East," *Miami Herald*, August 18, 1998.

129. "Waste Management Grows in East."

130. Crooks, *Giants of Garbage*, 89–91.

131. Jaffe, "Hopes for Ash Dashed"; Pellow, *Resisting Global Toxics*, 118.

132. Reeves, "A Trail of Refuse."

133. Jaffe, "Hopes for Ash Dashed"; Alex Santoso, "World's Most Unwanted Garbage: Cargo of the *Khian Sea*," Neatorama, August 15, 2007, http://www.neatorama.com /2007/08/15/worlds-most-unwanted-garbage-cargo-of-the-khian-sea.

134. Reeves, "A Trail of Refuse"; Jaffe, "Hopes for Ash Dashed."

135. Pellow, *Resisting Global Toxics*, 119; Santoso, "World's Most Unwanted Garbage."

136. Mark Jaffe, "Garbage Barge (Khian Sea)," in *The Encyclopedia of Greater Philadelphia*, ed. Mid-Atlantic Regional Center for the Humanities (2017), http:// philadelphiaencyclopedia.org/archive/garbage-barge-khian-sea; Jim Hook, "Ash Set to Enter County Today," *Public Opinion* (Chambersburg, PA), June 25, 2002.

137. Jaffe, "Garbage Barge."

CONCLUSION

1. Glenn Henderson, cited in Alex Santoso, "World's Most Unwanted Garbage: Cargo of the Khian Sea," Neatorama, August 15, 2007, www.neatorama.com/2007 /08/15/worlds-most-unwanted-garbage-cargo-of-the-khian-sea.

2. Glenn Henderson, "Healthy Flora Flourishing on Top of Ash Deemed 'Toxic,'" *Palm Beach Post*, April 28, 2002. On the Australian pine in Florida, see Florida Native Plant Society, "Australian Pine: One of Florida's Least Wanted," February 13, 2011, http://fnpsblog.blogspot.com/2011/02/australian-pine-one-of-floridas-least.html.

3. Cited in Henderson, "Healthy Flora Flourishing."

4. Sormunen et al., "Innovative Use of Recovered Municipal Solid Waste."

5. Brown, *Manual for Survival*; Katia Moskvitch, "Chernobyl Plant Life Endures Radioactivity," *BBC News*, September 21, 2010.

6. Dan Elliott, "Wildlife Roams Where U.S. Once Made Nuclear and Chemical Arms," Associated Press News, August 19, 2019.

7. Murphy, "Alterlife and Decolonial Chemical Exposures."

8. Henderson, "Healthy Flora Flourishing."

9. Kersten, *Inwastement*.

10. United Nations Food and Agriculture Organization, *Prevention and Disposal of Obsolete Pesticide Donations*, www.fao.org/agriculture/crops/obsolete-pesticides /why-problem/exces-donat-purch/en, accessed August 5, 2020; Balayannis, "Toxic Sights."

11. Borowy, "Hazardous Waste," 2; Köster, *Hausmüll*, 208.

12. Basel Convention, *National Definitions of Hazardous Wastes*, www.basel.int /Countries/NationalDefinitions/NationalDefinitionsofHazardousWastes/tabid/1480 /Default.aspx, accessed July 21, 2020.

13. Lloyd, "Toxic Trade," 18.

14. Lessenich, *Living Well at Others' Expense*.

15. Clapp, *Toxic Exports*, 3.

16. Lepawsky, *Reassembling Rubbish*; Minter, *Secondhand*, chapter 12.

17. John Reed and Lesli Hook, "The Global Recycling Crisis: Why the World's Recycling System Stopped Working," *Financial Times*, October 25, 2018; Michael Bauchmüller and Thomas Fromm, "Wohin nur mit dem Müll," *Süddeutsche Zeitung*, May 30, 2018, www.sueddeutsche.de/wirtschaft/entsorgung-wohin-nur-mit-all -dem-muell-1.3995420.

18. Delavan, "Economics of Consumption, U.S.," 11.

19. Bruce Gledhill, Philadelphia streets commissioner, cited in Committee on Government Operations, *International Export of US Waste*, 36.

20. IBP USA, *Global Privatization Laws and Regulations Handbook*, 62, 66.

21. Gloria Campisi, "City Trash to Get N.J. Brushoff," *Philadelphia Daily News*, August 16, 1973; Radio Haiti, "Déchet toxiques," March 22, 1988, Radio Haiti Papers; Organisation of African Unity resolution, cited in Philis Williams, "New African Disputes over 'Colonialist Garbage' and 'Toxic Terrorism,'" UPI Spot Weekender, June 6, 1988.

22. Jenny Gitlitz, "Society Must Clean Up Its Act," *Press and Sun Bulletin* (Binghamton, NY), June 20, 1987.

23. Borowy, "Hazardous Waste," 2; Köster, *Hausmüll*, 208; Basel Convention, "National *Definitions* of Hazardous Wastes"; Daven and Klein, *Progress in Waste Management Research*, 95; Richter, "Giftmüllexporte nach Afrika," 334–35.

24. Basel Convention, *Compilation of Country Fact Sheets: Based on Reports from Contracting Parties for the Year 1993*, 7; Basel Convention, *National Definitions of Hazardous Wastes*.

25. Epstein, Brown, and Pope, *Hazardous Waste in America*, 37.

26. Azevedo, "Trade in Hazardous Substances," 145.

27. Jacob Scherr, cited in Committee on Government Operations, *U.S. Export of Banned Products*, 33; see also Azevedo, "Trade in Hazardous Substances," 145.

28. Meyers, cited in Committee on Government Operations, *International Export of US Waste*, 302.

29. Cited in Moyers and Bergman, *Global Dumping Ground*.

30. Armiero, *Wasteocene*, 2021.

31. United Nations, *Stockholm Convention*.

32. UNEP, International Panel on Chemical Pollution (IPCP), *Overview Report II*;

World Health Organization, "Press Release: UN Environment and World Health Organization Agree to Major Collaboration on Environmental Health Risks," 10. January 2018, www.who.int/news-room/detail/10-01-2018-un-environment-and-who-agree-to -major-collaboration-on-environmental-health-risks.

33. Müller, "Toxic Commons."

Bibliography

ARCHIVAL SOURCES

Delaware Valley Toxics Coalition Records, Urban Archives, Temple University, Philadelphia.

Greenpeace International Media Library, Amsterdam.

Jim Vallette private archive, Maine, United States.

Radio Haiti Papers, circa 1934–2003, Bulk 1968–2003, David M. Rubenstein Rare Book and Manuscript Library, Duke University.

United States Court of Appeals for the Third Circuit Collection, Records of the United States Courts of Appeals, US National Archives, Philadelphia.

United States District Court Delaware, Criminal Case Files, Records of District Courts of the United States, US National Archives, Philadelphia.

WPVI News Footage and Logs, 1947–2006 (Inclusive Dates), Urban Archives, Temple University, Philadelphia.

PUBLISHED WORKS

Abd-el Monsef, Hesham, Scot E. Smith, and Kamal Darwish. "Impacts of the Aswan High Dam After 50 Years." *Water Resource Management* 29, no. 6 (2015): 1873–85.

Action Center, "The Basics of a Landfill." March 26, 2003. www.ejnet.org/landfills.

Adam, Barbara. *Timescapes of Modernity: The Environment and Invisible Hazards.* London: Routledge, 1998.

Adas, M. *Dominance by Design: Technological Imperatives and America's Civilizing Mission.* Cambridge, MA: Harvard University Press, 2009.

Akingbade, Tunde. *Nigeria: On the Trail of the Environment.* Bloomington: Author House, 2009.

Alaimo, Stacy. *Bodily Natures: Science, Environment, and the Material Self.* Bloomington: Indiana University Press, 2010.

Alewitz, Sam. "Garbage." In *Encyclopedia of New Jersey*, edited by M. N. Lurie, M. Siegel, and M. Mappen, 299–300. New Brunswick, NJ: Rutgers University Press, 2004.

Allen, R. *Waste Not Want Not: The Production and Dumping of Toxic Waste*. New York: Taylor & Francis, 2013.

Almeida, M. E. W., D. de Mello, N. Rodriguez V., and W. F. Almeida, "Regulatory Toxicology and Tolerances of Pesticide Residues in Latin-America and Caribbean Region." In *Advances in Pesticide Science: Proceedings*, edited by H. Geissbühler and G. T. Brooks, 709–11. Oxford: Pergamon, 1979.

Amsterdam, Daniel, and Domenic Vitiello. "Immigration (1930-Present)." In *The Encyclopedia of Greater Philadelphia*, edited by Mid-Atlantic Regional Center for the Humanities, 2013. https://philadelphiaencyclopedia.org/archive/immigration-1930-present.

Andrews, Alan. "Beyond the Ban: Can the Basel Convention Adequately Safeguard the Interests of the World's Poor in the International Trade of Hazardous Waste?" *Law, Environment, and Development Journal* 5, no. 2 (2009): 167–84.

Andrews, Richard N. L. *Managing the Environment, Managing Ourselves: A History of American Environmental Policy*. New Haven, CT: Yale University Press, 2006.

Ankomah, Baffour. "African Wasteland." *Index on Censorship* 6–7 (1989): 34–37.

Aptheker, B. *The Morning Breaks: The Trial of Angela Davis*. Ithaca, NY: Cornell University Press, 2014.

Armiero, Marco. *Wasteocene: Stories from the Global Dump*. Cambridge: Cambridge University Press, 2021.

Armiero, Marco, and M. de Angelis. "Anthropocene: Victims, Narrators, and Revolutionaries." *South Atlantic Quarterly* 116, 2 (2017): 345–62.

Arnesen, A. P. H. E., and E. Arnesen. *Encyclopedia of US Labor and Working-Class History*. London: Routledge, 2007.

Asante-Duah, D. Kofi, and Imre V. Nagy. *International Trade in Hazardous Wastes*. Abingdon, UK: Taylor & Francis, 1998.

Atkeson, Timothy B., Thomas B. Stoel, Marilyn C. Bracken, Robert E. Herzstein, and Edmund B. Frost. "International Regulation of Toxic Substances." *Proceedings of Annual Meeting (American Society of International Law)* 73 (1979): 76–107.

Azevedo, Mary Patricia. "Trade in Hazardous Substances: An Examination of US Regulation." In *Environment and Trade: The Relation of International Trade and Environmental Policy*, edited by Seymour J. Rubin and Thomas R. Graham, 135–53. Totowa, NJ: Allanheld Osmun, 1982.

Balayannis, A. "Toxic Sights: The Spectacle of Hazardous Waste Removal." *Environment and Planning D: Society and Space* 38, no. 4 (2020): 772–90.

Barakat, Rashida M. R. "Epidemiology of Schistosomiasis in Egypt: Travel through Time." *Journal of Advanced Research* 4, no. 5 (2013): 425–32.

Basel Convention. *Compilation of Country Fact Sheets: Based on Reports from Contracting Parties for the Year 1993.* Geneva: UNEP/SBC, 1996.

Basel Convention. *Compilation of Country Fact Sheets: Based on Reports from Contracting Parties for the Year 2000.* Geneva: UNEP/SBC, 2000.

Beck, Ulrich. *Risk Society: Towards a New Modernity.* London: SAGE Publications, 1992.

Belenky, Lisa T. "Cradle to Border: US Hazardous Waste Export Regulations and International Law." *Berkeley Journal of International Law* 17, no. 1 (1999): 95–137.

Bell, B., and E. Danticat. *Fault Lines: Views across Haiti's Divide.* Ithaca, NY: Cornell University Press, 2013.

Bellegarde-Smith, Patrick. "Dynastic Dictatorship: The Duvalier Years, 1957–1986." In *Haitian History: New Perspectives*, edited by Alyssa G. Sepinwall, 273–84. London: Routledge, 2013.

Bergquist, Ann-Kristin. "Business and Sustainability: New Business History Perspectives." Harvard Business School Working Papers, 18–034 (2017).

Betegon, Anyuri. "An Exploration: Panama Environmental Law History, the General Environmental Law and a Pollution Case in the Villa River Watershed." Senior project, College of the Atlantic, 2015.

Bevington, D. *The Rebirth of Environmentalism: Grassroots Activism from the Spotted Owl to the Polar Bear.* Washington, DC: Island Press, 2012.

Black, Brian, and Michael J. Chiarappa, eds. *Nature's Entrepôt: Philadelphia's Urban Sphere and Its Environmental Thresholds.* Pittsburgh: University of Pittsburgh Press, 2012.

Blaise, Farina. "A Portrait of World Historical Production and World Historical Waste after 1945." *Review (Fernand Braudel Center)* 30, no. 3 (2007): 177–213.

Blum, Elizabeth D. *Love Canal Revisited: Race, Class, and Gender in Environmental Activism.* Lawrence: University Press of Kansas, 2008.

Blumberg, Louis, and Robert Gottlieb. *War on Waste: Can America Win Its Battle with Garbage?* Washington, DC: Island Press, 1989.

Boehm, L. K., and S. H. Corey. *America's Urban History.* New York: Taylor & Francis, 2014.

Bok, D. C. *The State of the Nation: Government and the Quest for a Better Society.* Cambridge, MA: Harvard University Press, 1998.

Borowy, Iris. "Hazardous Waste: The Beginning of International Organizations Addressing a Growing Global Challenge in the 1970s." *Worldwide Waste: Journal of Interdisciplinary Studies* 2, no. 1 (2019).

Boss, A. H., and W. Kilian. *The United Nations Convention on the Use of Electronic Communications in International Contracts: An In-Depth Guide and Sourcebook.* Austin, TX: Wolters Kluwer Law & Business, 2008.

Brañes Ballesteros, R. *El desarrollo del derecho ambiental latinoamericano y su aplicación: Informe sobre los cambios jurídicos después de la Conferencia de las Naciones Unidas sobre el Medio Ambiente y el Desarrollo (Río 1992)*. México: PNUMA, Oficina Regional para América Latina y el Caribe, 2001.

Braveboy-Wagner, J. "Introduction: History and Theory." In *Historical Dictionary of United States-Caribbean Relations*, edited by J. Braveboy-Wagner and C. Griffin, 1–21. Lanham, MD: Rowman & Littlefield Publishers, 2017.

Braveboy-Wagner, J., and C. Griffin, eds. *Historical Dictionary of United States-Caribbean Relations*. Lanham, MD: Rowman & Littlefield Publishers, 2017.

Brown, Kate. *Manual for Survival: A Chernobyl Guide to the Future*. New York: W. W. Norton & Company, 2019.

Brownell, Emily. "Negotiating the New Economic Order of Waste." *Environmental History* 16 (2011): 262–89.

Bulkeley, H., and Walker G. "Environmental Justice: A New Agenda for the UK." *Local Environment* 10, no. 4 (2005): 329–32.

Bullard, Robert D. *Dumping in Dixie: Race, Class, and Environmental Quality*. Boulder, CO: Westview Press, 1994.

Burke, Edmund, and Kenneth Pomeranz, eds. *The Environment and World History*. Berkeley: University of California Press, 2009.

Buttler, Rhett A. "The Rainforest." Mongabay. Accessed June 7, 2020. https://rainforests.mongabay.com/20carib.htm.

Buss, T. F., and A. Gardner. *Haiti in the Balance: Why Foreign Aid Has Failed and What We Can Do about It*. Washington, DC: Brookings Institution Press, 2009.

Carmin, JoAnn, and Julian Agyeman, eds. *Environmental Inequalities beyond Borders: Local Perspectives on Global Injustices*. Cambridge, MA: MIT Press, 2011.

Carroll, P., and A. Kellow. *The OECD: A Study of Organizational Adaptation*. Cheltenham, UK: Edward Elgar Publishing, 2011.

Carson, Rachel. *Silent Spring*. Greenwich, CT: Fawcett, 1964.

Cassá, Roberto. "The Economic Development of the Caribbean from 1880 to 1930." In *General History of the Caribbean: The Caribbean in the Twentieth Century*, edited by P. C. Emmer, B. Brereton, and B. W. Higman. London: Macmillan Caribbean, 2004.

Chung, Chien-Min Chung. "China's Electronic Waste Village." *Time*, 2014. http://content.time.com/time/photogallery/0,29307,1870162_1822148,00.html.

Clammer, P. *Haiti*. Chalfont St Peter, UK: Bradt Travel Guides, 2016.

Clapp, Jennifer. *Toxic Exports: The Transfer of Hazardous Wastes and Technologies from Rich to Poor Countries*. Ithaca, NY: Cornell University Press, 2010.

Colby, J. M. *The Business of Empire: United Fruit, Race, and US Expansion in Central America*. Ithaca, NY: Cornell University Press, 2011.

Cole, L. W., and S. R. Foster. *From the Ground Up: Environmental Racism and the Rise of the Environmental Justice Movement*. New York: NYU Press, 2001.

Collins, C. *Toxic Loopholes: Failures and Future Prospects for Environmental Law*. Cambridge: Cambridge University Press, 2010.

Colten, Craig E., and Peter N. Skinner. *The Road to Love Canal: Managing Industrial Waste before EPA*. Austin: University of Texas Press, 1996.

Committee on Energy and Commerce, US House of Representatives. *Regulation of TRIS-Treated Sleepwear: Hearings before the Subcommittee on Oversight and Investigations 1981*. Washington, DC: US Government Printing Office, 1981.

Committee on Environment and Public Works, US Senate. *Resource Conservation and Recovery Act Oversight. Hearings before the Subcommittee on Hazardous Waste and Toxic Substances, United States Senate, One Hundredth Congress, First Session*. Washington, DC: US Government Printing Office, 1988, 11.

Committee on Foreign Affairs, US House of Representatives. *Export of Hazardous Products: Hearings Before the Subcommittee on International Economic Policy and Trade of the Committee on Foreign Affairs, House of Representatives, Ninety-Sixth Congress, Second Session, June 5, 12, and September 9, 1980*. Washington, DC: US Government Printing Office, 1980.

———. *Hazardous Product Exports: Hearing before the Subcommittee on International Economic Policy and Trade of the Committee on Foreign Affairs, House of Representatives, Ninety-seventh Congress, First Session, March 12, 1981*. Washington, DC: US Government Printing Office, 1983.

———. *Update on Recent International Environment Meetings: Hearing before the Subcommittee on Human Rights and International Organizations, One Hundred First Congress, First Session, April 6, 1989*. Washington, DC: US Government Printing Office, 1989.

Committee on Foreign Relations, US Senate. *Basel Convention on the Control of Transboundary Movement of Hazardous Wastes and Their Disposal: Hearing before the Committee on Foreign Relations, United States Senate, One Hundred Second Congress, Second Session, March 12, 1992*. Washington, DC: US Government Printing Office, 1992.

Committee on Government Operations, US House of Representatives. *International Export of US Waste: Hearing before a Subcommittee of the Committee on Government Operations, House of Representatives*. Washington, DC: US Government Printing Office, 1988.

———. *U.S. Export of Banned Products: Hearings before a Subcommittee of the Committee on Government Operations, Ninety-Fifth Congress, Second Session*. Washington, DC: US Government Printing Office, 1978.

"Congress Tightens Hazardous Waste Controls." *CQ Almanac* 40 (1984): 305–8. http://library.cqpress.com/cqalmanac/cqa184-152936.

Conn, Steven. *Metropolitan Philadelphia: Living with the Presence of the Past*. Philadelphia: University of Pennsylvania Press, 2006.

Conyers, John. "Preface." In *Reagan, Toxics and Minorities: A Policy Report by the Urban Environment Conference, Inc.*, edited by Stephanie Pollack, George Coling and JoAnn Grozuczak, i–iii. Washington, DC: The Conference, 1984.

Cook-Thajudeen, James. "Landfills." In *The Encyclopedia of Greater Philadelphia*, edited by Mid-Atlantic Regional Center for the Humanities, 2016. http://philadelphia encyclopedia.org/archive/landfills.

Corona, Gabriela. "What Is Global Environmental History? Conversation with Piero Bevilacqua, Guillermo Castro, Ranjan Chakrabarti, Kobus du Pisani, John R. McNeill and Donald Worster." *Global Environment* 1, no. 2 (2008): 228–49.

Council on Environmental Quality. *Report of the Council on Environmental Quality on Ocean Dumping: Message from the President of the United States Transmitting a Report of the Council on Environmental Quality on Ocean Dumping*. Washington, DC: US Government Printing Office, 1970.

Craton, Michael, and Gail Saunders. *Islanders in the Stream: A History of the Bahamian People*. Athens: University of Georgia Press, 1998.

Cronon, William. *Nature's Metropolis: Chicago and the Great West*. New York: W. W. Norton, 1992.

Crooks, Harold. *Giants of Garbage: The Rise of the Global Waste Industry and the Politics of Pollution Control*. Toronto: J. Lorimer, 1993.

Crosby, Alfred W. *The Columbian Exchange: Biological and Cultural Consequences of 1492*. Westport, CT: Greenwood, 1972.

Cross, B. L., and M. K. Brohman. *Project Leadership: Creating Value with an Adaptive Project Organization*. New York: Taylor & Francis, 2014.

Cullather, Nick. *The Hungry World: America's Cold War Battle against Poverty in Asia*. Cambridge, MA: Harvard University Press, 2010.

Curlee, T. R. *Waste-to-Energy in the United States: A Social and Economic Assessment*. Westport, CT: Quorum Books, 1994.

Daven, J. I., and R. N. Klein. *Progress in Waste Management Research*. New York: Nova, 2008.

Davis, Charles E., and James P. Lester, "Hazardous Waste Politics and the Policy Process." In *Dimensions of Hazardous Waste Politics and Policy*, edited by Charles E. Davis and James P. Lester, New York: Greenwood, 1988.

Davis, Frederick Rowe. *Banned: A History of Pesticides and the Science of Toxicology*. New Haven, CT: Yale University Press, 2014.

Davis, J. *The Global 1980s: People, Power, and Profit*. New York: Taylor & Francis, 2019.

Delavan, Will. "Economics of Consumption, U.S." In *Encyclopedia of Consumption and Waste*, ed. C. A. Zimring and C. E. William L. Rathje. London: SAGE Publications, 2012.

Delreux, Tom, and Sander Happaerts. *Environmental Policy and Politics in the European Union*. London: Macmillan Education Palgrave, 2016.

Douglas, Mary. *Purity and Danger: An Analysis of the Concept of Pollution and Taboo*. Princeton, NJ: Princeton University Press, 2005.

Dowie, Mark. "The Corporate Crime of the Century." *Mother Jones*, November 1979.

Dubois, L. *Avengers of the New World: The Story of the Haitian Revolution*. Cambridge, MA: Harvard University Press, 2009.

——. *Haiti: The Aftershocks of History*. New York: Henry Holt, 2012.

Dunlap, R. E., and A. G. Mertig. *American Environmentalism: The US Environmental Movement, 1970–1990*. New York: Taylor & Francis, 2014.

Eckes, A. E. *Opening America's Market: US Foreign Trade Policy Since 1776*. Chapel Hill: University of North Carolina Press, 2000.

Eckholm, Erik, and S. Jacob Scherr. "Double Standards and the Pesticide Trade." *New Scientist*, February 16, 1978, 441–43.

Eggert-Crowe, Madison, and Scott Gabriel Knowles. "Bicentennial (1976)." In *The Encyclopedia of Greater Philadelphia*, edited by Mid-Atlantic Regional Center for the Humanities, 2013. https://philadelphiaencyclopedia.org/archive/bicentennial-1976.

Emmer, P. C., B. Brereton, and B. W. Higman. *General History of the Caribbean: The Caribbean in the Twentieth Century*. London: Macmillan Caribbean, 2004.

Encyclopedia Britannica. "Delaware River." www.britannica.com/place/Delaware -River#ref175258.

Engineering and Mining Journal. *E & MJ International Directory of Mining*. New York: Mining Informational Services, 1996.

Environmental Protection Agency. *1972 National Dump Sites Survey Report*. Washington, DC: US Government Printing Office, 1973.

——. *EPA's Program to Control Exports of Hazardous Wastes, Report of Audit*. Washington, DC: US Government Printing Office, 1988.

——. *Federal Register: Hazardous Waste Management System; Notification Concerning the Basel Convention's Potential Implications for Hazardous Waste Exports and Imports*. Washington, DC: Environmental Protection Agency, 1992.

——. "Hazardous Waste Management System: Exports of Hazardous Waste." *Federal Register* 51, no. 49 (1986): 8744–60.

——. *Leptophos Advisory Committee Meeting: Public Session*. Washington, DC: US Government Printing Office, 1976.

——. *National Overview: Facts and Figures on Materials, Wastes and Recycling*. Accessed July 16, 2020. www.epa.gov/facts-and-figures-about-materials-waste-and -recycling/national-overview-facts-and-figures-materials#Trends1960-Today.

———. *Valley of the Drums, Bullitt County, Kentucky*. Washington, DC: US Government Printing Office, 1980.

Epstein, Samuel Stanley, Lester O. Brown, and Carl Pope. *Hazardous Waste in America*. San Francisco: Sierra Club Books, 1982.

Faber, D. *Capitalizing on Environmental Injustice: The Polluter-Industrial Complex in the Age of Globalization*. Lanham, MD: Rowman & Littlefield, 2008.

———. *Environment under Fire*. New York: NYU Press, 1993.

Farmer, Paul. *AIDS and Accusation: Haiti and the Geography of Blame*. Berkeley: University of California Press, 2006.

Feliciano, D. "Bringing about an End to Ocean Dumping." *Water Pollution Control Federation* 53, no. 1 (1981): 276–86.

Ferguson, Niall, ed. *The Shock of the Global: The 1970s in Perspective*. Cambridge, MA: Harvard University Press, 2010.

Flippen, J. Brooks. *Nixon and the Environment*. Albuquerque: University of New Mexico Press, 2000.

Flynn, Kevin. "Bush, Dukakis Target Environment." *Water Pollution Control Federation* 60, no. 8 (1988): 1312–14.

Frenkel, Stephen. "Jungle Stories: North American Representations of Tropical Panama." *Geographical Review* 86, no. 3 (1996): 317–33.

Galanes, Luis. "History of Caribbean Economies." In *Enciclopedia de Puerto Rico*, edited by National Endowment for the Humanities, 2012. https://enciclopediapr.org/en/encyclopedia/history-of-caribbean-economies.

Geffen, Elizabeth. "Industrial Development and Social Crisis, 1841–1854." In *Philadelphia: A 300-Year History*, edited by R. F. Weigley, N. B. Wainwright and E. Wolf, 307–62. New York: W. W. Norton, 1982.

Geissbühler, H., and G. T. Brooks, *Advances in Pesticide Science: Proceedings*. Oxford: Pergamon, 1979.

Gille, Zsuzsa. *From the Cult of Waste to the Trash Heap of History: The Politics of Waste in Socialist and Postsocialist Hungary*. Bloomington: Indiana University Press, 2007.

Girard, P. *Haiti: The Tumultuous History; From Pearl of the Caribbean to Broken Nation*. New York: St. Martin's, 2010.

Gold, M., A. Blum, and B. Ames. "Another Flame Retardant, Tris-(1,3-dichloro-2-propyl)-Phosphate, and Its Expected Metabolites Are Mutagens." *Science* 200, no. 4343 (1978): 785–87.

Golden, Jason A. "Human Rights—Haitian Refugees—Haitian Refugees Housed at Guantanamo Bay Naval Base Held to Have No Valid Constitutional or International Law Claims to Challenge Forced Repatriation by the U.S. Government. Haitian Refugee Center v. Baker, 953 F.2d 1498 (11th Cir. 1992)." *Georgia Journal of International and Comparative Law* 22 (1992): 2.

Goldstein, Joshua. "Waste." In *The Oxford Handbook of the History of Consumption*, edited by F. Trentmann, 326–48. Oxford: Oxford University Press, 2012.

Gore, Albert. *Earth in the Balance: Ecology and the Human Spirit*. New York: Plume, 1992.

Gosine, Andil, and Cheryl Teelucksingh. *Environmental Justice and Racism in Canada: An Introduction*. Toronto: Emond Montgomery, 2008.

Greenpeace USA. *International Trade in Toxic Wastes: Policy and Data Analysis by Greenpeace International*. 2nd ed. Washington, DC: Greenpeace USA, 1988.

Greenwood, Carolyn. "Restrictions on the Exportation of Hazardous Products to the Third World: Regulatory Imperialism or Ethical Responsibility?" *Boston College Third World Law Journal* 5, no. 2 (1985): 129–50.

Grugel, Jean. "The Historical Evolution of the Caribbean Basin." In *Politics and Development in the Caribbean Basin: Central America and the Caribbean in the New World Order*, edited by Jean Grugel, 29–60. London: Macmillan Education UK, 1995.

Guarino, Carmen F., Michael D. Nelson, and Sergio S. Almeida, "Ocean Dispersal as an Ultimate Disposal Method." *Water Pollution Control Federation* 51, no. 4 (1979): 773–74.

Guarino, C. F., M. D. Nelson, and S. Townsend. "Philadelphia Sludge Disposal in Coastal Waters." *Water Pollution Control Federation* 49, no. 5 (1977): 737–44.

Guzman, H. M., P. A. G. Barnes, C. Lovelock, and I. C. Feller, "A Site Description of the CARICOMP Mangrove, Seagrass, and Coral Reef Sites in Bocas del Toro, Panama." *Caribbean Journal of Science* 41, no. 3 (2005): 430–40.

Gwam, Cyril. *Toxic Waste and Human Rights*. Bloomington, IN: Author House, 2010.

Hackworth, J. *The Neoliberal City: Governance, Ideology, and Development in American Urbanism*. Ithaca, NY: Cornell University Press, 2014.

Hall, Bill, Joshua Karliner, and Penelope Whitney. "Garbage Imperialism: An EPOCA Report." *Earth Island Journal* 2, no. 4 (1987): 8–14.

Hamblin, Jacob D. "Environmentalism for the Atlantic Alliance: NATO's Experiment with the 'Challenges of Modern Society.'" *Environmental History* 15, no. 1 (2010): 54–75.

———. *Poison in the Well: Radioactive Waste in the Oceans at the Dawn of the Nuclear Age*. New Brunswick, NJ: Rutgers University Press, 2008.

Hamra, Jackie. "Municipal Incinerator Ash Regulated as Hazardous Waste under RCRA: Costs and Options; City of Chicago v. Environmental Defense Fund." *Journal of Environmental and Sustainability Law* 3, no. 1 (1994): 33–41.

Harjula, Henrik. "Hazardous Waste: Recognition of the Problem and Response." *Annals of the New York Academy of Sciences* 1076, no. 1 (2006): 462–77.

Harris, R. L., and J. Nef. *Capital, Power, and Inequality in Latin America and the Caribbean*. Lanham, MD: Rowman & Littlefield, 2008.

Hawkins, Gay. *The Ethics of Waste: How We Relate to Rubbish*. Lanham, MD: Rowman & Littlefield, 2006.

Hecht, Gabrielle. "Interscalar Vehicles for an African Anthropocene: On Waste, Temporality, and Violence." *Cultural Anthropology* 33, no. 1 (2018): 109–41.

Heid, A. S. "UN Sets Up Global Monitoring Program, Steps Up Other Activities." *Journal Water Pollution Control Federation* 46, no. 8 (1974): 1846–48.

Helvarg, D. *The War against the Greens: The 'Wise-Use' Movement, the New Right, and the Browning of America*. Denver, CO: Johnson Books, 2004.

Hickman, H. Lanier. *American Alchemy: The History of Solid Waste Management in the United States*. Santa Barbara, CA: Forester Press, 2003.

Higman, B. W. *A Concise History of the Caribbean*. Cambridge: Cambridge University Press, 2010.

Hill, M. K. *Understanding Environmental Pollution*. Cambridge: Cambridge University Press, 2010.

Hilz, Christoph. *An Investigation of the International Toxic Waste Trade*. New York: Van Nostrand Reinhold, 1992.

Hird, John A. *Superfund: The Political Economy of Environmental Risk*. Baltimore: Johns Hopkins University Press, 1994.

Hiscox, Michael J. "The Magic Bullet? The RTAA, Institutional Reform, and Trade Liberalization." *International Organization* 53, no. 4 (1999): 669–98.

Huismans, Jan W. "The International Register of Potentially Toxic Chemicals (IRPTC): Its Present State of Development and Future Plans." *Ambio* 7, nos. 5-6 (1978): 275–77.

IBP USA. *Dominican Republic Mineral and Mining Sector Investment and Business Guide, Volume 1: Strategic Information and Regulations*. Washington, DC: International Business Publications, 2013.

———. *Global Privatization Laws and Regulations Handbook—Caribbean Countries: Privatization and Investment Opportunities*. Washington, DC: International Business Publications, 2007.

Ives, Jane H., ed. *The Export of Hazard: Transnational Corporations and Environmental Control Issues*. Boston: Routledge & Kegan Paul, 1985.

Jaffe, Mark. "Garbage Barge (Khian Sea)." In *The Encyclopedia of Greater Philadelphia*, edited by Mid-Atlantic Regional Center for the Humanities, 2016. http://philadelphia encyclopedia.org/archive/garbage-barge-khian-sea.

Jarrige, François, and Thomas Le Roux, *The Contamination of the Earth. A History of Pollutions in the Industrial Age*. Cambridge, MA: MIT Press, 2020.

Jasanoff, Sheila. "Science, Politics, and the Renegotiation of Expertise at EPA." *Osiris* 7 (1992): 194–217.

Jones, Geoffrey. *Profits and Sustainability: A History of Green Entrepreneurship*. Oxford: Oxford University Press, 2017.

Jørgensen, Finn Arne. *Recycling*. Cambridge, MA: MIT Press, 2019.

Kaikati, Jack G. "Domestically Banned Prodcts: For Export Only." *Journal of Public Policy and Marketing* 3 (1984): 125–33.

Kapur, Devesh, J. P. Lewis, and R. C. Webb. *The World Bank: Its First Half Century.* Washington, DC: Brookings Institution Press, 2010.

Karan, P. P., and U. Suganuma. *Local Environmental Movements.* Lexington: University Press of Kentucky, 2010.

Keeley, Martin. *Marvelous Mangroves. Myths and Legends,* Asheville, North Caroline: Pisgah Press, 2014.

Kersten, Jens, ed. *Inwastement: Abfall in Umwelt und Gesellschaft.* Bielefeld: Transcript Verlag, 2016.

Kinkela, David. *DDT and the American Century: Global Health, Environmental Politics, and the Pesticide That Changed the World.* Chapel Hill: University of North Carolina Press, 2013.

Kirby, Rebecca. "The Basel Convention and the Need for US Implementation." *Georgia Journal for International and Comparative Law* 24 (1994): 281–305.

Kirkpatrick, Sale. *The Green Revolution: The American Environmental Movement 1962–1992.* New York: Hill and Wang, 1993.

Knight, Franklin W. "The New Caribbean and the United States." *Annals of the American Academy of Political and Social Science* 533 (1994): 33–47.

Knill, Christoph, and Duncan Liefferink. *Environmental Politics in the European Union: Policy-Making, Implementation and Patterns of Multi-level Governance.* Manchester: Manchester University Press, 2007.

Knowles, S. G. *Imagining Philadelphia: Edmund Bacon and the Future of the City.* Philadelphia: University of Pennsylvania Press, 2011.

Kolltveit, Bard. "Torvald Klaveness." In *Norsk Biografisk Leksikon.* Store Norsk Leksikon, 2009.

Kosmerick, Todd J. "Synar, Michael Lynn." In *Encyclopedia of Oklahoma History and Culture,* edited by Oklahoma Historical Society. www.okhistory.org/publications/enc/entry.php? entry=SY001.

Köster, Roman. *Hausmüll: Abfall und Gesellschaft in Westdeutschland, 1945–1990.* Göttingen: Vandenhoeck & Ruprecht, 2017.

Kraft, Michael E. "U.S. Environmental Policy and Politics: From the 1960s to the 1990s." In *Environmental Politics and Policy: 1960s–1990s,* edited by Graham Otis, 17–42. University Park: Pennsylvania State University Press, 2000.

Kraft, Michael E., and Norman J. Vig. "Environmental Policy in the Reagan Presidency." *Political Science Quarterly* 99, no. 3 (1984): 415–39.

Kramek, Niva, and Lydia Loh. "The History of Philadelphia's Water Supply and Sanitation System." Report for Philadelphia Global Water Initiative for the United Nations Development Programme, Philadelphia, 2007.

Krebs, Stefan, and Heike Weber, eds. *The Persistence of Technology: Histories of Repair, Reuse and Disposal*. Bielefeld: Transcript-Verlag, 2021.

Krenn, M. L. *The Impact of Race on US Foreign Policy: A Reader*. New York: Garland, 1999.

Krueger, Jonathan. *International Trade and the Basel Convention*. London: Earthscan, 1999.

———. "Prior Informed Consent and the Basel Convention: The Hazards of What Isn't Known." *Journal of Environment and Development* 7, no. 2 (1998): 115–37.

Kummer, K. *International Management of Hazardous Wastes: The Basel Convention and Related Legal Rules*. Oxford: Oxford University Press, 1999.

Ladapo, Oluwafemi N. "The Contribution of Cartoonists to Environmental Debates in Nigeria: The Koko Waste-Dumping Incident." *RCC Perspectives*, no. 1 (2013).

Langston, Nancy. "New Chemical Bodies: Synthetic Chemicals, Regulation, and Human Health." In *The Oxford Handbook of Environmental History*, edited by Andrew C. Isenberg, 259–81. Oxford: Oxford University Press, 2014.

Lanoue, David. "Retrospective and Schematic Assessments of Presidential Candidates: The Environment and the 1988 Election." *Polity* 25, no. 4 (1993): 547–63.

———. *Toxic Bodies*. New Haven, CT: Yale University Press, 2011.

Laurian, Lucie. "Environmental Injustice in France." *Journal of Environmental Planning and Management* 51, no. 1 (2008): 55–79.

Lepawsky, J. *Reassembling Rubbish: Worlding Electronic Waste*. Cambridge, MA: MIT Press, 2018.

Lessenich, Stephan. *Living Well at Others' Expense: The Hidden Costs of Western Prosperity*. Cambridge: Polity, 2019.

Liboiron, Max. *Pollution Is Colonialism*. Durham, NC: Duke University Press, 2021.

Liboiron, Max, Maneul Tironi, and Nerea Calvillo. "Toxic Politics: Acting in a Permanently Polluted World." *Social Studies of Science* 43, no. 3 (2018): 331–49.

Lindsay-Poland, J., G. M. Joseph, G. Castro, and E. S. Rosenberg. *Emperors in the Jungle: The Hidden History of the US in Panama*. Durham, NC: Duke University Press, 2003.

Linowes, Richard, and Mollie Brown Hupert. "The Tropical Waste Dilemma: Waste Management in Panama." *Cases for Management Education* 1, no. 3 (2006): 101–12.

Lloyd, Jason. "Toxic Trade: International Knowledge Networks and the Development of the Basel Convention." *International Public Policy Review* 3, no. 2 (2008): 17–27.

Loomis, E. *Out of Sight: The Long and Disturbing Story of Corporations Outsourcing Catastrophe*. New York: New Press, 2015.

Louis, Garrik E. "A Historical Context of Municipal Solid Waste Management in the United States." *Waste Management and Research* 22, no. 4 (2004): 306–22.

Lurie, M. N., M. Siegel, and M. Mappen. *Encyclopedia of New Jersey*. New Brunswick, NJ: Rutgers University Press, 2004.

Macekura, S. *Of Limits and Growth: The Rise of Global Sustainable Development in the Twentieth Century*. Cambridge: Cambridge University Press, 2015.

Mart, Michelle. *Pesticides, a Love Story: America's Enduring Embrace of Dangerous Chemicals*. Lawrence: University Press of Kansas, 2015.

Martini, E. A. *Agent Orange: History, Science, and the Politics of Uncertainty*. Amherst: University of Massachusetts Press, 2012.

Martyn, John. *Report on the Evaluation of INFOTERRA for the United Nations Environmental Programme*. Paris: UNESCO, 1982.

Mason, Robert J. "Metropolitan Philadelphia: Sprawl, Shrinkage, and Sustainability." In *Nature's Entrepôt: Philadelphia's Urban Sphere and Its Environmental Thresholds*, edited by Brian Black and Michael J. Chiarappa, 187–203. Pittsburgh: University of Pittsburgh Press, 2012.

McCarthy, James, and Mark E. Reisch. *Hazardous Waste Fact Book*. Washington, DC: US Government Printing Office, 1987.

McCarthy, T. *Auto Mania: Cars, Consumers, and the Environment*. New Haven, CT: Yale University Press, 2007.

McCrory, Kenda Jo M. "The International Exportation of Waste: The Battle against the Path of Least Resistance." *Penn State International Law Review* 9, no. 2 (1991): 339–58.

McDaniel, Marie Basile. "Immigration and Migration (Colonial Era)." In *The Encyclopedia of Greater Philadelphia*, edited by Mid-Atlantic Regional Center for the Humanities, 2014. https://philadelphiaencyclopedia.org/archive/immigration-and-migration-colonial-era.

McDowall, R. L. *Management to Facilitate Compliance with Global Conventions During Hazardous and Toxic Waste Cleanup Projects in Asia*. Irvine, CA: Universal Publishers, 2006.

McGurty, Eileen. "Solid Waste Management in 'The Garbage State': New Jersey's Transformation from Landfilling to Incineration." In *New Jersey's Environments: Past, Present, and Future*, edited by Neil M. Maher, 28–47. New Brunswick, NJ: Rutgers University Press, 2006.

———. *Transforming Environmentalism: Warren County, PCBs, and the Origins of Environmental Justice*. New Brunswick, NJ: Rutgers University Press, 2009.

McHarg, Ian L. *Design with Nature*. New York: John Wiley & Sons, 1992.

McKee, Guian A. *The Problem of Jobs: Liberalism, Race, and Deindustrialization in Philadelphia*. Chicago: University of Chicago Press, 2010.

McNeill, John Robert. "The Environment, Environmentalism, and International Society in the Long 1970s." In *The Shock of the Global: The 1970s in Perspective*, edited by Niall Ferguson, 263–80. Cambridge, MA: Harvard University Press, 2010.

———. *Something New under the Sun: An Environmental History of the World in the 20th Century*. London: Penguin, 2001.

Meade, T. A. *A History of Modern Latin America: 1800 to the Present.* Hoboken, NJ: Wiley, 2009.

Meditz, Sandra W., and Dennis M. Hanratty, eds. *Caribbean Islands: A Country Study.* Washington, DC: US Government Printing Office, 1987.

Mehri, Cyrus. "Prior Informed Consent: An Emerging Compromise for Hazardous Exports." *Cornell International Law Journal* 21, no. 2 (1988): 365–89.

Melosi, M. "Down in the Dumps: Is There a Garbage Crisis in America?" In *Urban Public Policy: Historical Modes and Methods,* edited by M. A. Melosi and M. V. Melosi, 100–127. College Park: Pennsylvania State University Press, 2010.

———. *Fresh Kills: A History of Consuming and Discarding in New York City.* New York: Columbia University Press, 2020.

———. *Garbage in the Cities: Refuse, Reform and the Environment.* Pittsburgh: University of Pittsburgh Press, 2005.

———. *The Sanitary City: Environmental Services in Urban America from Colonial Times to the Present.* Pittsburgh: University of Pittsburgh Press, 2008.

———, ed. *Urban Public Policy: Historical Modes and Methods.* College Park: Pennsylvania State University Press, 2010.

Merchant, Carolyn. *American Environmental History: An Introduction.* New York: Columbia University Press, 2007.

Merskin, D. L. *The SAGE International Encyclopedia of Mass Media and Society.* London: SAGE Publications, 2019.

Meyer, Robinson. "How the U.S. Protects the Environment, from Nixon to Trump." *The Atlantic,* March 29, 2017.

Middlebrook, K. J., and C. Rico. *The United States and Latin America in the 1980s.* Pittsburgh: University of Pittsburgh Press, 1986.

Milanović, Branko. *Global Inequality: A New Approach for the Age of Globalization.* Cambridge, MA: Harvard University Press, 2018.

Milroy, Elizabeth, "Pro Bono Publico: Ecology, History and the Creation of Philadelphia's Fairmount Park System." In *Nature's Entrepôt,* edited by Brian Black and Michael J. Chiarappa, 35-57 Pittsburgh: University of Pittsburgh Press, 2012.

Minter, Adam. *Secondhand: Travels in the New Global Garage Sale.* New York: Bloomsbury, 2019.

Mintz, J. A. *Enforcement at the EPA: High Stakes and Hard Choices.* Austin: University of Texas Press, 1995.

Mires, Charlene, and John Hepp. "Railroad Suburbs." In *The Encyclopedia of Greater Philadelphia,* edited by Mid-Atlantic Regional Center for the Humanities. Accessed August 8, 2020. https://philadelphiaencyclopedia.org/archive/chemical-industry.

Mongillo, J. F., and L. Zierdt-Warshaw. *Encyclopedia of Environmental Science.* Phoenix, AZ: Oryx Press, 2000.

Montague, Peter. "Philadelphia Dumps on the Poor." *Rachel's Environment and Health Weekly*, April 23, 1998.

Montrie, Chad. *The Myth of Silent Spring: Rethinking the Origins of American Environmentalism*. Oakland: University of California Press, 2018.

Moore, Jason W. *Capitalism in the Web of Life: Ecology and the Accumulation of Capital*. London: Verso, 2015.

Moore, Steven J. "Troubles in the High Seas: A New Era in the Regulation of US Ocean Dumping." *Environmental Law* 22, no. 3 (1992): 913–51.

Moyers, Bill D., and Lowell Bergman. *Global Dumping Ground*. TV Documentary. PBS and Center for Investigative Reporting. October 2, 1990.

Mukherjee, A., B. Debnath, and Sadhan Kumar Ghosh. "A Review on Technologies of Removal of Dioxins and Furans from Incinerator Flue Gas." *Procedia Environmental Sciences* 35 (2016): 528–40.

Müller, Simone M. "Corporate Behaviour and Ecological Disaster: Dow Chemical and the Great Lakes Mercury Crisis, 1970–1972." *Business History* 60, no. 3 (2018): 399–422.

———. "'Cut Holes and Sink 'Em': Chemical Weapons Disposal and Cold War History as a History of Risk." *Historical Social Research* 41, no. 1 (2016): 263–84.

———. "Hidden Externalities: The Globalization of Hazardous Waste." *Business History Review* 93, no. 1 (2019): 51–74.

———. "The Life of Waste." Environment and Society Portal, *Virtual Exhibitions*, 2018, no. 3. Rachel Carson Center for Environment and Society.

———. "Rettet die Erde vor den Ökonomen." In *Archiv für Sozialgeschichte: Sozialgeschichte des Kapitalismus*, edited by Friedrich-Ebert-Stiftung, 353–71. Bonn: Dietz, 2016.

———. "Toxic Commons: Toxic Global Inequality in the Age of the Anthropocene." Contribution for Roundtable on Toxins in Environmental History. In *Environmental History* 26, no. 3 (2021): 444–50.

———. "Umwelt- und Klimapolitik in den USA: Lokale Interessen und globale Verantwortung." In *Handbuch Politik in den USA*, edited by Christian Lammert, Markus Siewert and Boris Vormann, 479–98. Frankfurt: Springer-Verlag, 2014.

Müller, Simone M., and May-Brith Ohman Nielsen, eds. *Toxic Timescapes: Examining Toxicity across Time and Space*. Athens: Ohio University Press, 2023.

Müller, Simone M., and David Stradling. "Water as the Ultimate Sink: Linking Fresh- and Saltwater History." *International Review of Environmental History* 5, no. 1 (2019).

Murphy, Michelle. "Alterlife and Decolonial Chemical Exposures." *Cultural Anthropology* 32, no. 4 (November 2017): 494–503.

———. *Sick Building Syndrome and the Problem of Uncertainty: Environmental Politics, Technoscience, and Women Workers*. Durham, NC: Duke University Press, 2006.

Nading, Alex M. "Central America." In *Encyclopedia of Consumption and Waste,* edited by C. A. Zimring and C. E. William L. Rathje. London: SAGE Publications, 2012.

Nelson, Michael, and Barbara Perry, eds. *41: Inside the Presidency of George H. W. Bush.* Ithaca, NY: Cornell University Press, 2014.

Nevins, D., R. Barlas, and J. L. Yong. *Bahamas.* London: Cavendish Square, 2019.

Newman, Richard S. *Love Canal: A Toxic History from Colonial Times to the Present.* New York: Oxford University Press, 2015.

Newsday Inc., ed. *Rush to Burn: Solving America's Garbage Crisis?* Washington, DC: Island Press, 1989.

Newton, D. E. *Environmental Justice: A Reference Handbook.* Santa Barbara, CA: ABC-CLIO, 2009.

Nixon, Richard. "Message to the Congress: Transmitting a Study on Ocean Pollution by the Council on Environmental Quality," Washington, DC, October 7, 1970.

Norris, Ruth, A. Karim Ahmed, S. Jacob Scherr, and Robert Richter, eds. *Pills, Pesticides and Profits.* Croton-on-Hudson, NY: North River Press, 1982.

Nützenadel, Alexander, and Daniel Speich Chassé. "Editorial: Global Inequality and Development after 1945." *Journal of Global History* 6, no. 1 (2011): 1–2.

Oberholtzer, E. P. *Philadelphia A History of the City and its People.* Altenmünster: Jazzybee, 1912.

O'Brien, T. F., and L. L. Johnson. *Making the Americas: The United States and Latin America from the Age of Revolutions to the Era of Globalization.* Albuquerque: University of New Mexico Press, 2007.

OECD. *Economic and Ecological Interdependence: A Report on Selected Environment and Resource Issues.* Paris: OECD, 1982.

O'Neill, Kate. *Waste.* Cambridge: Polity, 2019.

Onstenk, Lori. "Mixed News on Dumping." *Mother Jones.* January 1981.

Oppelt, Timothy, E., and E. T. Oppelt. "Incineration of Hazardous Waste: A Critical Review." *Journal of the Air and Waste Management Association* 37, no. 5 (1987): 558–86.

Organisation of African Unity. *Bamako Convention on the Ban on the Import into Africa and the Control of Transboundary Movement and Management of Hazardous Wastes within Africa,* Bamako: OAU, 1998.

Organization of American States. *Bahamas National Report: Integrating Management of Watersheds and Coastal Areas in Small Island and Developing States (SIDS) of the Caribbean*2000. www.oas.org/reia/iwcam.pdf/bahamas/bahamasreport.

Organization of Eastern Caribbean States. *Biodiversity of the Caribbean,* A Learning Resource prepared by Ekos Communications Inc, Victoria BC, February 2009.

Pearson, Charles S., ed. *Multinational Corporations, Environment, and the Third World.* Durham, NC: Duke University Press, 1987.

Pellow, David N. *Resisting Global Toxics: Transnational Movements for Environmental Justice.* Cambridge, MA: MIT Press, 2007.

———. *Garbage Wars: The Struggle for Environmental Justice in Chicago.* Cambridge, MA: MIT Press, 2002.

Philadelphia Bureau of Surveys. *Report on the Collection and Treatment of the Sewage of the City of Philadelphia.* Philadelphia, n.p., 1914.

Plummer, Brenda Gayle. *Haiti and the United States: The Psychological Moment.* Athens: University of Georgia Press, 1992.

Pollack, Stephanie, George Coling, and JoAnn Grozuczak, eds. *Reagan, Toxics and Minorities: A Policy Report by the Urban Environment Conference, Inc.* Washington, DC: The Conference, 1984.

Pomeranz, Kenneth. *The Great Divergence: China, Europe, and the Making of the Modern World Economy.* Princeton, NJ: Princeton University Press, 2000.

Pomper, David. "Recycling Philadelphia v. New Jersey: The Dormant Commerce Clause, Postindustrial 'Natural' Resources, and the Solid Waste Crisis." *University of Pennsylvania Law Review* 137, no. 4 (1989).

Public Interest Law Center. "50 Years of Fighting for Environmental Justice." 2019. www.pubintlaw.org/50-years-fighting-for-environmental-justice.

Randel, Lucy Ann. "Hazardous Waste in Philadelphia." Honors thesis, University of Pennsylvania, 1984.

Reith, Reinhold. *Umweltgeschichte der Frühen Neuzeit.* Berlin: De Gruyter, 2011.

Richter, Roland. "Giftmüllexporte nach Afrika: Bestandsaufnahme eines Beispiels der Zusammenhänge zwischen Öko-system, Ökonomie und Politik im Rahmen der Nord-Süd Beziehungen." *Africa Spectrum* 23, no. 3 (1988): 315–50.

Rieser, Anja, Sophia Hörl, and Ivan Vilovic, *Incoherent Voices: The Basel Convention, Its Members and the International Legislation of Hazardous Waste.* Munich: DFG-Emmy Noether Research Group, April 2017.

Robert Futrell. "Politics of Space and the Political Economy of Toxic Waste." *International Journal of Politics, Culture, and Society* 13, no. 3 (2000): 447–76.

Roett, Riordan. "The Debt Crisis and Development in Latin America." In *The United States and Latin America in the 1990s: Beyond the Cold War,* edited by J. Hartlyn, L. Schoultz and A. Varas, 131–50. Chapel Hill: University of North Carolina Press, 2014.

Roland Richter. "Giftmüllexporte nach Afrika: Bestandsaufnahme eines Beispiels der Zusammenhänge zwischen Ökosystem, Ökonomie und Politik im Rahmen der Nord-Süd Beziehungen." *Africa Spectrum* 23, no. 3 (1988): 315–50.

Rome, Adam Ward. *The Bulldozer in the Countryside: Suburban Sprawl and the Rise of American Environmentalism.* Cambridge: Cambridge University Press, 2001.

———. *The Genius of Earth Day: How a 1970 Teach-in Unexpectedly Made the First Green Generation.* New York: Hill and Wang, 2013.

————. "'Give Earth a Chance': The Environmental Movement and the Sixties." *Journal of American History* 90, no. 2 (2003): 525–54.

Rome, Adam Ward, and Hartmut Berghoff, eds. *Green Capitalism? Business and the Environment in the Twentieth Century*. Philadelphia: University of Pennsylvania Press, 2017.

Rosenfeld, Paul E., and Feng, Lydia G. H. *Risks of Hazardous Wastes*. Oxford: William Andrew, 2011.

Ross, Benjamin, and Steven Amter. *The Polluters: The Making of Our Chemically Altered Environment*. Oxford: Oxford University Press, 2010.

Rubin, Seymour J. "A Predominantly Commercial Policy Perspective." In *Environment and Trade: The Relation of International Trade and Environmental Policy*, edited by Seymour J. Rubin and Thomas R. Graham, 3–21. Totowa, NJ: Allanheld Osmun, 1982.

Rubin, Seymour J., and Thomas R. Graham, eds. *Environment and Trade: The Relation of International Trade and Environmental Policy*. Totowa, NJ: Allanheld Osmun, 1982.

Rupert, Clark D. "The Delaware River Basin Commission: A Unique Partnership." *Water Resources Impact* 16, no. 5 (2014): 3–6.

Santoso, Alex. "World's Most Unwanted Garbage: Cargo of the Khian Sea." Neatorama, August 15, 2007. www.neatorama.com/2007/08/15/worlds-most-unwanted-garbage -cargo-of-the-khian-sea.

Satz, Debra. *Why Some Things Should Not Be for Sale: The Moral Limits of Markets*. New York: Oxford University Press, 2010.

Scherr, Jacob S. "Hazardous Exports: US and International Policy Developments." In *Multinational Corporations, Environment, and the Third World*, edited by Charles S. Pearson. 129–48. Durham, NC: Duke University Press, 1987.

Schiller, Reuel. "Courts, Deregulation, and Conservatives, 1980–94." In *Making Legal History: Essays in Honor of William E. Nelson*, edited by Daniel Hulsebosch and R. B. Bernstein. New York: NYU Press, 2013.

Schuck, P. H. *Agent Orange on Trial: Mass Toxic Disasters in the Courts*. Cambridge, MA: Harvard University Press, 1987.

Science Newsbrief. "Ocean Dumping." *Science News* 98, no. 15 (1970): 302.

Selcer, Perrin. *The Postwar Origins of the Global Environment: How the United Nations Built Spaceship Earth*. New York: Columbia University Press, 2018.

Shabecoff, Philip. *A Fierce Green Fire: The American Environmental Movement*. Washington, DC: Island Press, 2012.

Shimizu, H. *Japanese Firms in Contemporary Singapore*. Singapore: NUS Press, 2008.

Shipnostalgia, "Khian Sea." Accessed June 4, 2020. www.shipsnostalgia.com/gallery /showphoto.php/photo/237515/title/khian-sea/cat/510.

Ship Spotting. "Khian Sea—IMO 6930180." Accessed June 4, 2020. www.shipspotting
.com/gallery/photo.php? lid=2979699.

Shiva, Vandana. *The Violence of the Green Revolution: Third World Agriculture, Ecology, and Politics.* Mapusa: Other India Press, 1991.

Sicotte, Diane. *From Workshop to Waste Magnet: Environmental Inequality in the Philadelphia Region.* New Brunswick, NJ: Rutgers University Press, 2016.

———. "Saving Ourselves by Acting Locally: The Historical Progression of Grassroots Environmental Justice Activism in the Philadelphia Area, 1981–2001." In *Nature's Entrepôt: Philadelphia's Urban Sphere and Its Environmental Thresholds,* edited by Brian Black and Michael J. Chiarappa, 231–49. Pittsburgh: University of Pittsburgh Press, 2012.

Sierra Club, ed. *Putting a Lid on Waste: Towards a Recycling Economy.* Washington, DC: Sierra Club Books, 1991.

"Sierra Leone." *Facts on File World News Digest.* "February 29, 1980."

Simon, Roger. *Philadelphia: A Brief History.* Mansfield: Pennsylvania Historical Association, 2017.

Sinclair, Barbara. "The Offered Hand and the Veto Fist: George Bush, Congress, and Domestic Policy Making." In *41: Inside the Presidency of George H. W. Bush,* edited by Michael Nelson and Barbara Perry, 143–65. Ithaca, NY: Cornell University Press, 2014.

Smarth, Luc. "Popular Organizations in the Transition to Democracy in Haiti." In *Community Power and Grassroots Democracy: The Transformation of Social Life,* edited by Michael Kaufman and Haroldo Dilla Alfonso, 102–25. Ottawa: Zed Books, 2010.

Smith, John Kenly. "Chemical Industry." In *The Encyclopedia of Greater Philadelphia,* edited by Mid-Atlantic Regional Center for the Humanities, 2016. https:// philadelphiaencyclopedia.org/archive/chemical-industry.

Soderlund, J. R. *Lenape Country: Delaware Valley Society before William Penn.* Philadelphia: University of Pennsylvania Press, 2015.

Soluri, J. *Banana Cultures: Agriculture, Consumption, and Environmental Change in Honduras and the United States.* Austin: University of Texas Press, 2009.

Sormunen, Annika, Kanniainen Teo, Salo Tapio, and Rantsi Riina. "Innovative Use of Recovered Municipal Solid Waste Incineration Bottom Ash as a Component in Growing Media." *Waste Management and Research* 34, no. 7 (2016): 595–604.

Statistica, "Largest Countries and Territories in the Caribbean, by Total Area." April 2019. www.statista.com/statistics/992416/largest-countries-territories-area -caribbean.

Stokes, Raymond G., Roman Köster, and Stephen C. Sambrook. *Business of Waste.* Cambridge: Cambridge University Press, 2014.

Strasser, Susan. *Waste and Want: A Social History of Trash.* New York: Henry Holt, 2013.

Street, Lairold M. "US Exports Banned for Domestic Use, but Exported to Third World Countries." *Maryland Journal of International Law* 6, no. 1 (1980): 95–105.

Subcommittee on Human Rights and International Organizations, US House of Representatives. *US Waste Exports: Hearing before the Subcommittee on Human Rights and International Organizations and the Subcommittee on International Economic Policy and Trade of the Committee on Foreign Affairs, House of Representatives, One Hundred First Congress, First Session, July 12, 1989.* Washington, DC: US Government Printing Office, 1989.

Subcommittee on the Environment and the Atmosphere, US House of Representatives. *The Environmental Effects of Dumping in the Oceans and the Great Lakes: Hearings before the Subcommittee on the Environment and Atmosphere of the Committee on Science and Technology, US House of Representatives, Ninety-Fourth Congress, First Session.* Washington, DC: US Government Printing Office, 1976.

Subcommittee on Transport and Hazardous Materials, US House of Representatives. *Waste Export Control: Hearing before the Subcommittee on Transportation and Hazardous Materials of the Committee on Energy and Commerce House of Representatives, One Hundred First Congress, First Session on H.R.2525, July 27, 1989.* Washington, DC: US Government Printing Office, 1989.

Sutter, Paul S. "Nature's Agents or Agents of Empire? Entomological Workers and Environmental Change during the Construction of the Panama Canal." *Isis* 98, no. 4 (2007): 724–54.

———. "What Can US Environmental Historians Learn from Non-US Environmental Historiography?" *Environmental History* 8 (2003): 109–29.

Sykes, James Enoch. *Past and Present Delaware River Shad Fishery and Considerations for Its Future.* Washington, DC: US Government Printing Office, 1957.

De Sylva, Donald P., Frederik A Kalber, and Carl N. Shuster. *Fishes and Ecological Conditions in the Shore Zone of the Delaware River Estuary: With Notes on Other Species Collected in Deeper Water.* Newark: University of Delaware Marine Laboratories, 1962.

Sze, Julie. *Environmental Justice in a Moment of Danger.* Berkeley: University of California Press, 2020.

———. *Noxious New York: The Racial Politics of Urban Health and Environmental Justice.* Cambridge, MA: MIT Press, 2010.

Thampi, Gayatri. "Indigenous Contestations of Shifting Property Regimes: Land Conflicts and the Ngobe in Bocas del Tore, Panama." PhD diss., Ohio State University, 2013.

Theoharis, J. *The Rebellious Life of Mrs. Rosa Parks.* Boston: Beacon Press, 2015.

Tolba, Mostafa Kamal, and Iwona Rummel-Bulska. *Global Environmental Diplomacy:*

Negotiating Environment Agreements for the World, 1973–1992. Cambridge, MA: MIT Press, 1998.

Trentmann, F. ed. *The Oxford Handbook of the History of Consumption.* Oxford: Oxford University Press, 2012.

Tripp, James T. B., and Daniel J. Dudek. "The Swampbuster Provisions of the Food Security Act of 1985. Stronger Wetland Conservation if Properly Implemented and Enforced." *Environmental Law Reporter* (1986): 10120–23.

Trouillot, Michel-Rolph. "The Odd and the Ordinary: Haiti, the Caribbean, and the World." *Cimarrón* 2, no. 3 (1990).

Trzyna, T. C., E. Margold, J. K. Osborn, *World Directory of Environmental Organizations: A Handbook of National and International Organizations and Programs.* London: Routledge, 1996.

Tucker, Richard P. *Insatiable Appetite: The United States and the Ecological Degradation of the Tropical World.* Berkeley: University of California Press, 2000.

Turner, James Morton, and Andrew C. Isenberg. *The Republican Reversal: Conservatives and the Environment from Nixon to Trump.* Cambridge, MA: Harvard University Press, 2018.

UNESCO. *Convention on Wetlands of International Importance especially as Waterfowl Habitat, Ramsar, Iran, 2.2.1971, as amended by the Protocol of 3.12.1982 and the Amendments of 28.5.1987.* Paris: UNESCO, 1994. https://www.ramsar.org/sites /default/files/documents/library/scan_certified_e.pdf.

UNESCO Institute for Statistics, "Haiti." 2020. http://uis.unesco.org/en/country/ht.

UNEP, International Panel on Chemical Pollution (IPCP), *Overview Report II: An Overview of Current Scientific Knowledge on the Life Cycles, Environmental Exposures, and Environmental Effects of Select Endocrine Disrupting Chemicals (EDCs) and Potential EDCs,* Nairobi: UNEP, 2017.

United Nations. *Draft Report to the General Assembly at Its 36th Session Concerning Exchange of Information on Banned Hazardous Chemicals and Unsafe Pharmaceutical Products in Response to Resolution 34/173 of 17 December 1979, January 5, 1980,* Geneva: United Nations, 1980.

———. *Report of the United Nations Conference on the Human Environment, Stockholm, 5–16 June 1972.* Geneva: United Nations, 1972.

———. *Stockholm Convention on Persistent Organic Pollutants.* New York: United Nations, 2004.

United Nations Environment Programme. *The Basel Convention: A Global Solution for Controlling Hazardous Wastes.* New York: United Nations, 1997.

———. *Cairo Guidelines and Principles for the Environmentally Sound Management of Hazardous Waste: Decision 14/30 of the Governing Council of UNEP, of 17 June 1987.* Nairobi: UNEP, 1987.

United Nations Food and Agriculture Organization. *The World's Mangroves, 1980–2005*. FAO Forestry Paper 153. 2007.

United States Congressional Research Service. *Waste Exports: US and International Efforts to Control Transboundary Movement*. Washington, DC: US Government Printing Office, 1989.

———. *Natural Resources Defense Council v. Export-Import Bank*. Civ. No. 77-0080, filed January 14, 1977.

United States General Accounting Office. *Better Regulation of Pesticide Exports and Pesticide Residues in Imported Foods Is Essential*. Washington, DC: US Government Printing Office, 1979.

United States Office of Technology Assessment. *Facing America's Trash: What Next for Municipal Solid Waste*? Washington, DC: US Government Printing Office, 1989.

Vallette, Jim, and Heather Spalding. *The International Trade in Wastes: A Greenpeace Inventory*. Washington, DC: Greenpeace USA, 1990.

Vera-Morales, Luis R. "Dumping in the International Backyard: Exportation of Hazardous Wastes to Mexico." *Tulane Environmental Law Journal* 7, no. 4 (1994): 353–89.

Vig, Norman and Michael E. Kraft. *Environmental Policy. New Directions for the Twenty-First Century*. 9th ed. London: SAGE Publications, 2017.

Voyles, T. B. *Wastelanding: Legacies of Uranium Mining in Navajo Country*. Minneapolis: University of Minnesota Press, 2015.

Waldo, Andrew. "A Review of US and International Restrictions on Exports of Hazardous Substances." In *The Export of Hazard: Transnational Corporations and Environmental Control Issues*, ed. Jane H. Ives, 3754. Boston: Routledge, 1985.

Walker, J. Samuel. *The Road to Yucca Mountain: The Development of Radioactive Waste Policy in the United States*. Berkeley: University of California Press, 2009.

Walsh, Edward Joseph, Rex H. Warland, and D. Clayton Smith. *Don't Burn It Here: Grassroots Challenges to Trash Incinerators*. University Park: Pennsylvania State University Press, 1997.

Walter, Ingo. "Economic Repercussion of Environmental Policy." In *Environment and Trade: The Relation of International Trade and Environmental Policy*, edited by Seymour J. Rubin and Thomas R. Graham, 22–45. Totowa, NJ: Allanheld Osmun, 1982.

Warde, Paul, Libby Robin, and Sverker Sörlin. *The Environment: A History of the Idea*. Baltimore: Johns Hopkins University Press, 2018.

Warner, Sam B. "If All the World Were Philadelphia: A Scaffolding for Urban History, 1774–1930." *American Historical Review* 74, no. 1 (1968): 26–43.

———. *The Private City: Philadelphia in Three Periods of Its Growth*. Philadelphia: University of Pennsylvania Press, 1987.

Weiler, Conrad. *Philadelphia: Neighborhood, Authority, and the Urban Crisis*. New York: Praeger, 1974.

Weinstein-Bacal, Stuart. "The Ocean Dumping Dilemma." *Lawyer of the Americas* 10, no. 3 (1978): 868–920.

Weir, David, and Mark Schapiro. *Circle of Poison: Pesticides and People in a Hungry World.* Oakland: Institute for Food and Development Policy, 1981.

Wittich, R. M. *Biodegradation of Dioxins and Furans.* Berlin: Springer, 1998.

Wolfinger, James. "African American Migration." In *The Encyclopedia of Greater Philadelphia*, edited by Mid-Atlantic Regional Center for the Humanities, 2013. https:// philadelphiaencyclopedia.org/archive/african-american-migration.

World Health Organization. *Occupational Health Programme: Report by the Director General.* Geneva: WHO, 1978.

———. "Press Release: UN Environment and World Health Organization Agree to Major Collaboration on Environmental Health Risks." January 10, 2018, www.who .int/news-room/detail/10-01-2018-un-environment-and-who-agree-to-major -collaboration-on-environmental-health-risks.

———. *Report of the Scientific Group on the Treatment and Disposal of Wastes.* Geneva: WHO, 1967.

———. *Safe Use of Pesticides*: *Twentieth Report of the WHO Expert Committee on Insecticides* [*Meeting held in Geneva from 10 to 16 October 1972*]. Geneva: WHO, 1973.

Yost, Nicholas. "American Governmental Responsibility for the Environmental Effects of Actions Abroad." *Albany Law Review*, no. 43 (1979): 528–37.

Zachmann, Karin, and Sarah Ehlers, eds. *Wissen und Begründen: Evidenz als umkämpfte Ressource in der Wissensgesellschaft.* Baden-Baden: Nomos, 2019.

Zelko, Frank S. *Make It a Green Peace! The Rise of Countercultural Environmentalism.* New York: Oxford University Press, 2013.

Zierler, David. *The Invention of Ecocide: Agent Orange, Vietnam, and the Scientists Who Changed the Way We Think about the Environment.* Athens: University of Georgia Press, 2011.

Zimbalist, A. S., and J. Weeks. *Panama at the Crossroads: Economic Development and Political Change in the Twentieth Century.* Berkeley: University of California Press, 1991.

Zimring, C. A. *Cash for Your Trash: Scrap Recycling in America.* New Brunswick, NJ: Rutgers University Press, 2009.

Zimring, C. A., and C. E. William L. Rathje. *Encyclopedia of Consumption and Waste.* London: SAGE Publications, 2012.

Index

Page numbers in *italics* refer to illustrations

Bamako Convention on the Ban of
the Import into Africa and the
Control of Transboundary Movement
and Management of Hazardous
Wastes within Africa (1991), xii, 3,
139, 161

Banja, 87, 88, 92. *See also* A/S
Bulkhandling

Bark, 8–9, 50, 52, 55, 56, 57, 69, 72, 139;
and Philadelphia, 84, 85, *87*. *See also*
A/S Bulkhandling

Basel Convention on the Control of
Transboundary Movements of Hazardous Wastes and Their Disposal
(UN, 1989), xii, 3, 4, 7, 10, 124–29, *129*,
133; and African nations, 125–27, 139;
and Cairo Guidelines, 120–21, 124;
and United States, 133, 134–37, 138, 143,
144, 156. *See also* Greenpeace; United
Nations

Bernstorff, Andreas, 111, 112

Bulkhandling. *See* A/S Bulkhandling

Bush, George H. W., 93, 105, 135, 145, 147, 148

Canada: and international waste trade,
39, 103, 108, 121, 126, 132

Caribbean, greater (region): activists
in, 162; and American waste traders,
81, 112; and colonization, 40–41; and
deforestation, 43, 46; economic situation of, 40–42, 46; environment of,
40, 41, 42–43, 44, 45, 46; and garbage
imperialism, 34; and hazardous waste,
165; and the *Khian Sea*, 109, 118, 119;
and latifundistas' plantations, 43; and
markets for US waste, 39–40, 45, 47;
resources of, 40, 41, 42–43, 46; science
infrastructure in, 79; and slavery, 40,
41; and United States, 40–43, 106. *See*

also Bahamas; Cayman Islands; Costa
Rica; Cuba; Dominican Republic;
Guadaloupe; Guatemala; Haiti; Marti-
nique; Panama

Caribbean Sea, 43, 44, 64

Carson, Rachel, 79, 94, 159

Carter, Jimmy, 28, 98, 100, 101, 160, 164

caveat emptor, notion of, 96, 97

Cayman Islands, 46, 61, 64

Central American countries, 40–44, 81,
139; and United States, 40–43, 106

chemicals: banned, 94–95, 144, 164;
endocrine-disrupting, 6, 73, 104; synthetic, 6, 159. *See also* "right-to-know"
legislation

Chernobyl nuclear disaster, 124, 158

Chile, 47, 54, 64, 102

Clinton, Bill, 148–149, 152; administration
of, 137

Coastal Carriers Shipping Corporation:
and ash disposal, 49, 52, 53; bankruptcy filing by, 89; John Patrick Dowd
as president of, 2, 10, 82–83, 131; and
Arturo Fuentes Garcia, 2; in Haiti, 60,
82; and the *Khian Sea*, 92, 129, 131; and
William P. Reilly, 2, 9, 10, 38, 45, 46–47,
61, 89, 132, 144; as US representative of
Amalgamated, 2, 38, 45, 141, 144; and
waste disposal, 52–53, 92

Colbert, Charles, 110, 113, 143, 145, 164

Colbert, Jack, 110, 113, 143, 145, 164

Collectif Haïtien pour la Protection de
l'Environnement et un Développement
Alternatif (COHPEDA), 9, 66. *See also*
environmental activism; Haiti

Commoner, Barry, 74

Connett, Paul, 74, 75

Conyers, John, 91, 92, 105–6, 107, 108, 109,
110, 135

113; and the *Banja*, 88; and the *Bark*, 84–88, *87*, 113; and capital Conakry, 84, 85; and incinerator ash, 84–88, 92; and Kassa Island, 85, 86, 87, 112–14, 156; and the *Khian Sea*, 112; and Norwegian consul, 115

Guinea-Bissau, 107, 108, 112, 123

Haiti: activists in, 106, 149, 154; and ban on waste imports, 63, 67, 138; and democracy, 69, 70, 147; dictatorship in, 62–63, 66, 69, 106; elections in, 63, 67, 68, 147, 149; environmental injustice in, 8, 147–48; and incinerator ash, 118, 146–48, 150–54, 157; and the *Khian Sea*, 3, 21, 52, 61, 65, 66, 70, 81, 82, 112, 117; military of, 62–63, 68–69; and Ministry of Commerce, 67, 81–82; and neighborhood committees, 66, 68–70; 1987 constitution of, 54, 63, 67–70, 82; poverty in, 61–63, 66, 68; protests in, 9, 62–63, 65–67, 69, 81–82; removal of ash from, 153–56; and United States, 61–63, 66–67, 102, 104, 146–52; and US hazardous waste exportation, 4, 102, 108; and US imports, 67, 68, 111; and waste imports, 63, 66–68, 70, 82, 104, 156. *See also* Gonaïves, Haiti; Radio Haiti-Inter; Radio Lumière

Hazardous and Solid Waste Amendments (HSWA), 74, 104

hazardous waste, 39, 43, 73–81, 83–84, 85, 88–89, 90, 92–93, 114–15, 119–24, 132, 140, 148, 155, 159, 160; trade in, x–xii, 3–5, 8, 9; in United States, 6–7, 10, 24–28, 29, 74, 101–10, 121, 134–37, 139, 143–44, 145, 161–63, 165. *See also under* Philadelphia; Sierra Leone; US Environmental Protection Agency

health: and environmental concerns, 43, 73, 76–78, 83, 85–86, 89, 109, 113–14, 121, 147–48, 152, 159–61; and safety regulations, 4, 26, 73–77

heavy metals, 24, 83–85; contamination, 14, 24, 76, 85, 157; dumped in oceans, 14; in incinerator ash, 58, 68, 76–77, 86, 88, 155, 158; tests for, 79, 86, 92

Honduras: and the *Khian Sea*, xi, 3, 64, 79, 119, 131; and Puerto Castilla, 47–48; and William P. Reilly, 61, 80

household waste, 73, 74, 107, 135

human rights, 18, 60, 65, 94, 146, 154

illegal dumping, 27–28, 30, 145

incineration: Greenpeace campaign against, 58; and Philadelphia, xi, 14–16, 32–33, 36, *37*, 38, 49, 55, 60, 71–77, 80–81, 151; ocean, 25, 117, 139; and waste-to-energy (WTE), 36, 73, 74–75, 76. *See also* Commoner, Barry; Connett, Paul; US Environmental Protection Agency

incinerator ash, 72–74, 76–79, 82–83, 84, 89–90; alternative destinations for, 46–49, 52–53; contract with A/S Bulkhandling, 52–55; contract with Paolino, 35; and *déchete toxique*, 9–10, 65, 67–70; disposal in Bahamas, 39, 55, 112, 144; disposal in New Jersey, 32–33; and Kassa Island, 84–86, 112–13; and land reclamation, 45; and ocean dumping, 132–33, 141, 144–45; piling up of, in Philadelphia, 11, 36, 38, 49–50, 60, 84; return to sender of, 145, 146, 149, 153–56; as topsoil fertilizer, xi, 2, 63, 81–82, 146, 157; and toxicity, 26, 37, 71–82, 87–90, 92, 126, 135 industrial waste, 8, 24, 27, 28, 29–31, 114, 116, 160

International Atomic Energy Agency, 7

International Monetary Fund (IMF), 42

Italy, 3, 8, 112, 114–15, 118–19, 124, 138

Jaffe, Mark, 8, 56, 117, 133

Jamaica, 45, 46, 61, 64

Johnson, Lyndon B., 22, 25

Joseph Paolino & Sons: contract with Amalgamated, 39, 45, 79–80; contract with Philadelphia, 2, 35, 36–38, 45, 53, 63, 141, 146; and export of ash to Bahamas, 38–39, 45; and the *Khian Sea*, 149; lawsuit, 141; and payment to Amalgamated, 89, 142; and torching of pier, 1, 142, 144; and waste disposal, 35–39, 49, 52–53, 63, 72, 92

Kasten, Robert, 93, 108

Khian Sea: and Amalgamated Shipping Corporation, 39, 45, 63, 81, 89, 92, 129, 130–31, 141; and ash to Virginia, 152–53; and Caribbean region, xi, 2, 9, 16, 44–47, 52, 63–64, 81–83, 132; and Central America, 132; crew of, 2, 68, 142–43, 145; and deal with the Bahamas, 60–61; and Delaware Bay, 92, 130; and Delaware River, 18, 33, 119, 129, 142; and J. Patrick Dowd, 143, 145, 156; as the *Felicia*, xii, 3, 119, 129, 132, 141; and garbage imperialism, xi, xii, 113; and Haiti, 10, 63–68, 70, 81–84, 112, 117, 133, *134*, 145; and Indian Ocean, 145; and international waste trade, 8, 10, 57, 108, 111, 112, 132, 161; and liability in US courts, 141–43; and Liberian flag, 1, 2, 129; and ocean dumping, 132, 141–45, 156; owner of, 38, 129, 132, 142;

as the *Pelicano*, xii, 3, 119, 130, 132; and Philadelphia, 34–35, 36, 44, 52, 71–72, 119, 158; and Romo Shipping Company, 129–30, 132, 144; sale of, 130–31, 144; as the *San Antonio*, 3, 141, xii; and Suez Canal, 3, 130–32, 142, xi; and testing of cargo, 8, 9–10, 79; and Yugoslavia, 131–32, 142, 144–45. *See also* Greenpeace; incinerator ash

landfills, 26–32, *37*, 133, 158, 163; and EPA, 74, 78–79; exports to, 39; and incinerator ash, 37–38, 46–47, 56, 86, 90, 149, 155–56; and Love Canal, 101; in Philadelphia, 14–16, 27, 36, 73, 76

land reclamation, 39, 44–46, 53, 58, 72, 78, 162. *See also* wetlands

Latin America, 39, 42, 44, 54, 104, 138. *See also* Chile; Honduras; Panama

leachates, 78–79

lead, 76, 77, 78

Le Collectif Haïtien pour la Protection de l'Environnement, 9, 66. *See also* environmental activism

Liberia, 2, 102, 114

Lily Navigation, 2, 34, 38, 39, 129, 131, 144

Love Canal, 28, 101, 105

Manigat, Leslie, 63, 68, 69, 70. *See also* Haiti

Marine Protection, Research, and Sanctuaries Act (Ocean Dumping Act), 24, 164

Maryland, 24, 36, *37*

Martinique, 79

medical waste, ix, 6, 119

Mexico: and international waste trade, 39, 104, 126, 137; and *Mobro 4000*, 58; and waste disposal, x, 39

Torrijos, Omar, 53–54

Toxic Substances Control Act, 96

toxic waste, 7, 30, 100, 104–7, 114, 120,
    158–59; categorizing, 26; determining
    toxicity, xi–xii, 24, 72, 76; dumping, 14,
    28; and Greenpeace actions, 58, 83–84,
    93, 111, 116, 132–33; in Philadelphia, 16,
    28–31, 33, 38, 73–78; recategorized, 81–
    83; regulations, 27. *See also* Gonaïves,
    Haiti; Guinea; Haiti; incinerator ash;
    Philadelphia

tris-treated sleepwear, 97, 101, 164

United Nations: Basel Convention,
    3–4, 124–29, 137–38, 140, 160–61;
    and environmental conference in
    Stockholm, 54, 163; Environmental
    Programme, xii, 43, 86, 99, 114, 120–24,
    126, 137, 163, 165; and hazardous waste
    dangers, 159–60; and hazardous waste
    regulation, 110, 114, 124–29, 137–38, 163

United States: and cities' waste
    management, 9, 13–16, 20, 25–26,
    55, 73, 74; and classification and
    regulation of waste, 7, 25–26;
    determining toxicity, xi–xii, 7, 73–74;
    environmental injustice in, 8, 106;
    and export of hazardous substances,
    94–110, 134, 135–37; and foreign
    relations, 103, 137; garbage crisis in,
    ix–xi; and international chemical
    trade, 94–96, 110; and international
    waste trade, 136–37, 139, 143, 147, 161;
    and pesticides, 94–97; and private
    waste haulers, 16, 27, 29–30; and safety
    of products for export, 94–98; and
    unequal waste trade, 38–40, 43, 46. *See
    also* environmental governance; *and
    specific locations and agencies*

United States Agency for International
    Development (USAID), 42, 77–78, 95,
    96–97

United States Export-Import Bank, 95, 97

US Coast Guard, 2, 105

US Council on Environmental Quality, 98

US Environmental Protection Agency
    (EPA): and air pollution standards, 32;
    creation of, 23, 32, 54, 75; criticisms of,
    7, 72, 77, 88; and determining toxicity,
    89–90; and export of hazardous
    substances, 104–5, 108, 109–10; *Flash
    Report*, 78; and hazardous waste, 75,
    77–78, 88–89, 94–96, 104–5, 109, 146;
    and health threats from waste, 6,
    77–79; and household waste, 73–74;
    and incinerator ash, xiii, 9–10, 72–74,
    76–81, 85, 88–90; inspector general of,
    78, 80, 85, 90, 92; and permits about
    waste, 26, 29–30; and pesticides, 94,
    107; and polychlorinated biphenyls
    (PCBs), 40, 107; and products banned
    in the United States, 97, 107; regulatory
    and scientific duties of, 75–77, 96, 103;
    and testing of incinerator ash, 76,
    80, 88, 155; and waste incineration,
    72–74, 76, 80; and waste-to-energy
    (WTE) incinerators, 72–73, 76. *See also*
    environmental governance

US Food and Drug Administration
    (FDA), 96, 97

US House Committee on Government
    Operations, 92

US Resource Conservation and Recovery
    Act (RCRA), 25–28, 73–74, 101, 103,
    105, 143, 160, 162

Valette, Jim, 111–12, 117, 119

vermin, 14, 76

waste: burying of, 25, 26, 28; chemical, 24, 26, 28, 43, 73, 79, 113, 143–44; classification of, 25–26, 73, 81, 123–24, 135, 159, 160, 163; as a commodity, 33, 38, 47, 159; concepts of, 5, 124; and construction material, 85, 87; and consumer products, 101, 104; cost of, disposal, 27, 32–33, 74, 155–56, 162; cost of, removal, 150–52; data on, 7–8, 36, 76, 78, 86, 140; determining toxicity of, 79–81, 86, 88; disposal of, ix–xi, 2–10, 20–21, 44, 46, 64, 70, 74, 84, 90, 93, 104, 113–15, 120–23, 135–38, 140, 142–43, 160–63, 165; exports of, 89, 91, 93–95, 102–5, 108–16; generation of, 5, 6, 13, 16, 26, 27, 55, 161, 163; and industrialization, 5–6, 14, 17, 18, 26, 28; international regulation of, xii, 102–4, 114, 119–24, 134–40; and international waste trade, 7–10, 33, 38–40, 47–48, 72, 88–90, 92–93, 102–4, 107–12, 119–24, 132, 134, 139–40, 160–61; management of, 54–55, 60, 88, 101, 107, 109, 117, 120–24, 135, 154–56; permits about, 30, 37, 45, 61, 63, 82, 103, 149, 153, 154; and prior informed consent, 123–24, 127, 128, 134–36, 138; regulation of, 7, 10, 54, 77, 93, 107–10, 160–61; reuse of, 38, 55, 107, 113, 161; rising levels of, 10, 12, 13, 16, 24, 25, 38, 49, 52–53, 119; storage of, 26, 27, 30, 60, 93, 103, 108; and synthetic products, 14, 26; testing of, 26, 37, 68, 72–74, 76–81, 83–84, 86, 88, 146, 155; transport of, 26, 36–40, 55, 58, 63, 69, 71, 84, 93, 103, 111, 121, 139, 140; and unequal trade, 116, 119–24, 138, 145, 158–59. *See also* environmental governance; incineration; incinerator ash

Waste Export Control Act, 93

waste export policies, 10, 38–40, 57, 93, 102–5, 107–10, 132

Waste Export Prohibition Act, 93, 107–8

waste haulers, 16, 27, 29–30, 72, 92, 149

Waste Management, Inc., 92, 154, 155

waste trade, international, 3, 4, 121, 161; exports to Africa, 87, 107, 110; exports to Asia, 132, 161; and markets for US, 39, 84, 102; regulations, 10, 39, 119, 138

water: contamination, 29, 43, 148; pollution, 114, 117

Water Pollution Control Act, 18

West Africa, xi, 3, 84, 87, 92, 102, 107, 132, 165

West Germany, 82–84, 108, 114, 121, 132

wetlands, 44, 48–49, 58, 76–79, 162; and countries in Ramsar Convention, 48–49; as waste dumps, 32, 33, 39

World Bank, 42, 44, 108

World Health Organization (WHO), 96, 120, 165

World War II, 6, 13–15, 18, 34, 40, 41

Yugoslavia, 129, 131, 132

Zimbabwe, 113, 144

Weyerhaeuser Environmental Books

Defending Giants: The Redwood Wars and the Transformation of American Environmental Politics, by Darren Frederick Speece

The City Is More Than Human: An Animal History of Seattle, by Frederick L. Brown

Wilderburbs: Communities on Nature's Edge, by Lincoln Bramwell

How to Read the American West: A Field Guide, by William Wyckoff

Behind the Curve: Science and the Politics of Global Warming, by Joshua P. Howe

Whales and Nations: Environmental Diplomacy on the High Seas, by Kurkpatrick Dorsey

Loving Nature, Fearing the State: Environmentalism and Antigovernment Politics before Reagan, by Brian Allen Drake

Pests in the City: Flies, Bedbugs, Cockroaches, and Rats, by Dawn Day Biehler

Tangled Roots: The Appalachian Trail and American Environmental Politics, by Sarah Mittlefehldt

Vacationland: Tourism and Environment in the Colorado High Country, by William Philpott

Car Country: An Environmental History, by Christopher W. Wells

Nature Next Door: Cities and Trees in the American Northeast, by Ellen Stroud

Pumpkin: The Curious History of an American Icon, by Cindy Ott

The Promise of Wilderness: American Environmental Politics since 1964, by James Morton Turner

The Republic of Nature: An Environmental History of the United States, by Mark Fiege

A Storied Wilderness: Rewilding the Apostle Islands, by James W. Feldman

Iceland Imagined: Nature, Culture, and Storytelling in the North Atlantic, by Karen Oslund

Quagmire: Nation-Building and Nature in the Mekong Delta, by David Biggs

Seeking Refuge: Birds and Landscapes of the Pacific Flyway, by Robert M. Wilson

Toxic Archipelago: A History of Industrial Disease in Japan, by Brett L. Walker

Dreaming of Sheep in Navajo Country, by Marsha L. Weisiger

Shaping the Shoreline: Fisheries and Tourism on the Monterey Coast, by Connie Y. Chiang

The Fishermen's Frontier: People and Salmon in Southeast Alaska, by David F. Arnold

Printed in the USA
CPSIA information can be obtained
at www.ICGtesting.com
CBHW020153290224
4723CB00008BA/16